Universities

Universities

AMERICAN, ENGLISH, GERMAN

Abraham
FLEXNER

With a new introduction by
CLARK KERR

Transaction Publishers
New Brunswick (U.S.A.) and London (U.K.)

Library of Congress Catalog Number: 94-2280
ISBN: 1-56000-737-0
Printed in the United States of America

Library of Congress Cataloging-in-Publication Data

Flexner, Abraham, 1866–1959
    Universities : American, English, German / Abraham Flexner ; with a new introduction by Clark Kerr.
        p. cm. — (Foundations of higher education)
    Originally published: New York : Oxford University Press, 1930.
    Includes bibliographical references and index.
    ISBN 1-56000-737-0
    1. Universities and colleges. I. Title. II. Series.
LA184.F54 1994
378—dc20   94-2280
                                                               CIP

THIS VOLUME IS GRATEFULLY INSCRIBED TO

MY WIFE

ANNE CRAWFORD FLEXNER

AND MY ELDEST BROTHER

DR. J. A. FLEXNER

CONTENTS

INTRODUCTION TO THE TRANSACTION EDITION

REMEMBERING FLEXNER

FLEXNER'S *Universities* was the big book on higher education when it was first published in 1930 and continued to be such until the appearance of Robert Maynard Hutchins' *The Higher Learning in America* in 1936. *Universities* continues to be one of the great books in the field more than sixty years later—but for quite different reasons now than then.

Universities in 1930 drew attention because Abraham Flexner was already a public figure in American higher education, perhaps the greatest of his time along with A. Lawrence Lowell at Harvard (1909–33) and Hutchins at Chicago (1930–51). Most of the many reviews of his book started out by talking about who Flexner was and what he had done. His respected name drew expectations about the impact of his new book (expectations that he shared) based on his accomplishment in prior years. "The book may mark a real turning-point in American education" (*The Bookman*, May 1931). "It is a tremendously substantial, forward-looking contribution, demanding prayerful, penitent attention" (*The Survey*, March 1931). It "will take a prominent place as a historic milestone in the evolution of higher institutions of learning in America and possibly to a lesser extent in other countries" (Snedden, *Journal of Higher Education*, October 1931). "Certainly good will come from the publica-

[ix]

tion of this book" (*The Library Quarterly*, April 1931).
This expectation of "good" consequences was, in the
longer run, to be disappointed. It was disappointed
because Flexner was so wrong about the German
universities he so revered, so wrong about how good
they really were—they had collapsed by 1933 and partly
of their own doing; and so wrong about the American universities that he so scorned—they were on their
way to becoming the best in the world. I will return
to these points later.

Yet *Universities* in the 1990s is still a great book,
even though the name of Flexner has faded into history and even though he was wrong not only about
German and American universities but also about the
English (although much less so) which increasingly
now follow the scorned American model, rather than
the other way around as Flexner thought should
happen.

How could this be—that *Universities* is still a great book?

1. Flexner set up an historic model of the university—he called it "the idea of the modern university" as a pure center of pure research, as
Cardinal Newman had advanced another model
as the training ground for gentlemen with a liberal education ("at home in any society"), as
Ortega y Gasset was doing a little later (late
1930s) with his model of a place where the great
ideas and great issues of the age were developed
and discussed, as Hutchins did as a source of
continuing contributions to the great philosophical discourse started by the Greeks. The Flexner
model took its place as one of the alternative
models on the short list.

2. Flexner developed some themes of criticism of the American university, as had never been done so well before, that have echoed down the decades—of the university as prolongation of secondary education, as a "service station" for the crasser and to him almost unmentionable functions of society, and as a series of "vocational schools." Abraham Flexner, it was said, "seeks an honest-to-goodness university; and in America he finds not one. The Johns Hopkins began right, but could not stay on the straight and narrow path" (*School and Society*, May 7, 1932). Flexner thought that even Johns Hopkins had "deteriorated through dilution and adulteration."[1] In Flexner, "we have almost all the earmarks of the old cultural and aristocratic outlook with many of the old terms: the learned versus the unlearned (no hint of gradual merging), culture (versus use), idealism (trade is sordid), intelligence versus hands (dualism of mind and body, excellence belonging only to mind), caste (limited to the few, excellence is a matter of status)" (Kilpatrick, *The Journal of Higher Education*, October 1931).

Contrasting with his highly negative evaluation of 1930, however, for more than a half-century Abraham Flexner devoted his prodigious talents and energies to the cause of higher education in America in a most positive way. As participant and contributor, as chronicler and critic, and as innovator, he helped shape the course of American education—and particularly medical education—during a great period of modernization and growth; and always for the better.

3. Flexner wrote the first comparative study of modern systems of higher education to be followed by such additional classics as Eric Ashby (*Universities: British, Indian, African*, 1966), Joseph Ben-David (*Centers of Learning*, 1977), and Burton R. Clark, (*The Higher Education System: Academic Organization in Cross-National Perspective*, 1983).

4. The experience of Flexner with this book holds out two warnings to later explorers in the field. One is to look at the current reality and not at a glamorized perception of an earlier reality. A second is that history can take sharp turns and it can be risky to see the future as simply reflected in a rear-view mirror. The German universities of the 1920s were not identical with those of the 1880s; nor those of the middle 1930s with those of the middle 1920s.

This is a book that appears quite differently to current readers than it did to the early reviewers; a book that remains the same in content but that has been perceived in quite changing ways; a book that has undergone a metamorphosis as the context within which it is read has evolved; in fact, it might be said, it is two books as seen then and now.

It might be noted, in passing, that Flexner also wrote about the undergraduate college in the United States (*The American College*, 1908). Here he was equally critical about what was wrong but not equally assured about what should be done. He rejected both the older classical curriculum as not appropriate in modern

[xii]

times and the then newer system of electives as too helter-skelter. He wanted what he identified as "coherence." He believed that "some things are more important than others" but there was no agreement on what they were nor did he say what he thought they were—this is a problem with which we are still trying to find an answer with no more success than Flexner. Flexner thought that first there must be an agreed-upon curriculum for the high school (a "common substratum"), and none existed. This must have been the only time in his life when Flexner did not know exactly what he thought should be done. *The American College* was, consequently and uncharacteristically, half a book.

Flexner's first encounter with American higher education was singularly propitious, and its influence was to last a lifetime. Through the financial sacrifice of an older brother, Flexner, then seventeen, was sent to Johns Hopkins University in 1884. The university was less than ten years old, but, under the dynamic presidency of Daniel Coit Gilman, it was well launched on the course of advanced study, research, and high academic standards that earned its position as the first fully modern university in America. An aura of intellectual excellence, excitement, and challenge pervaded the institution. "My attitude toward the university, toward President Gilman, toward the members of the faculty . . . was one of reverence," Flexner later wrote. And, again, "Those who know something of my work long after Gilman's day . . . will recognize Gilman's influence in all I have done or tried to do."[2]

Flexner had just enough funds to spend two years at Johns Hopkins. With the characteristic energy and determination that marked his whole career, he made do. Electing the rigorous classics course, he taught himself sufficient Greek in six weeks to catch up with the regular classics students. He was excused from physics classes after passing an oral examination, and from English composition after he showed faculty members the communications that he had already had printed in *The Nation*. For the rest, he simply doubled up on classes. When the first year-end examinations came, he found that several test times conflicted. He took his problem to Gilman, and the astonished president, after investigation, authorized rescheduling of the conflicting examinations. In the two years at his disposal, Flexner earned his degree.

Returning to Louisville and a teaching position in the local high school, Flexner immediately put to the test his commitment to academic excellence. He was nineteen, and teaching Greek to many of his fellow students of two years earlier. At the end of the first year, he failed an entire class of eleven students. This unprecedented action became a local *cause celebre*, reached the newspapers, and culminated in a school board hearing at which Flexner was sustained.

But Flexner was anxious to have a freer hand with curriculum and class organization. At the age of twenty-three he left the high school to form his own school, preparing boys for entry into the Eastern universities. Nine years after "Mr. Flexner's School" opened its door, Flexner received a letter from President Eliot of Harvard, whom he had never met. Eliot stated that boys from Flexner's school were entering Harvard younger and graduating more quickly than students from any other school. "What are you doing?" he asked. Flexner outlined his approach and, at Eliot's suggestion, wrote an article about it for *The Educational Record*, the first of his many writings in the educational field. He closed the school in 1905 to do graduate study at Harvard and in Germany, but his interest in secondary school matters continued. When, subsequently, both he and President Eliot were members of the Rockefeller-endowed General Education Board, Eliot revived the topic of "Mr. Flexner's School" and the Board asked Flexner to write about the school and his ideas in the secondary field. The resulting pamphlet, "A Modern School," published in 1916, led to the endowment of the experimental Lincoln School of Columbia Teachers' College, which pioneered in secondary education for three decades.

After a year at Harvard, Flexner spent two years in Europe, studying at the great German universities whose programs of advanced study and research had guided Gilman in the design of Johns Hopkins. This was followed by his being asked by The Carnegie Foundation for the Advancement of Teaching to undertake a study of medical education in America. When Flexner pointed out that he had never set foot in a medical school before, Foundation officials replied that what they wanted was not a practitioner but an observant educator.

They got precisely that. In the next eighteen months Flexner set foot in every one of the 155 medical schools then existing in the United States and Canada. He found medical education in a sorry state, with rare exceptions such as Johns Hopkins Medical School. Students were often admitted with less than two years of high school education. Laboratories were nonexistent or pitifully under-equipped. Hospitals were not generally under the control of the medical schools, and there was almost complete separation of the scientific and the clinical instruction. Flexner minced no words when he wrote *Medical Education in the United States and Canada* in 1910. His scathing report aroused broad concern and inspired a revolution in the teaching of medicine in America. He recommended that 120 of the then existing medical schools be closed as inadequate, and he identified them by name. As a matter of fact, nearly all of them did disappear, and, in substantial part, because of his report. It had the cutting edge of a surgical knife.

From 1913 to 1928 Flexner worked for the General Education Board, which had been established by Rockefeller in 1902 as the first strictly educational foundation to operate on a nationwide basis in the United States. As a member of the Board and its secretary, Flexner was at first involved in projects for assisting Negro educational institutions and for helping Southern states to develop statewide systems of secondary education. But his interest returned repeatedly to medical education, and he was instrumental in encouraging Rockefeller to provide a total of $50 million for the modernization of American medical schools, and in helping to allocate the then huge sum. Flexner was particularly instrumental in the establishment or renovation of the medical schools at Washington University in St. Louis, Rochester, Cornell, Vanderbilt, and Iowa—schools that remain among the greatest to this day. He could write with truth that "the revolution this accomplished brought American medicine from the bottom of the pile to the very top."[3]

In 1928 Flexner retired from the General Education Board, only to plunge into his preparation for the Rhodes Lectures at Oxford and the writing of the present volume. As an immediate consequence of its publication, he was approached by two people who wished his advice about the educational use to which "a considerable sum of money" might be put. The sum was, in fact, five million dollars; the donors, a prominent New Jersey merchant, Louis Bamberger, and his sister, Mrs. Felix Fuld. The use proposed by Flexner was the establishment in the United States of a center for advanced scholarship and science resembling the Rockefeller Institute in the field of medicine; and, undoubtedly also, All Souls College where he had stayed during his Rhodes Lectures, and the Kaiser Wilhelm Gesellschaft (now the Max Planck Institute) which he so greatly admired. The donors accepted Flexner's proposal on the condition that he should head the new center, and thus was created the Institute for Advanced Study at Princeton. At the age of sixty-four, Flexner entered yet another career in education, this time as director of the institute, a post he held until his retirement in 1939. Under his directorship the institute took form and assembled distinguished scholars, including Albert Einstein, from throughout the world, some of them by then refugees from the once-great German institutions Flexner had so profoundly admired. The institute continues today to play a distinguished part in the intellectual life of the United States.

Nearly all of Flexner's contributions to education— whether writings, proposals, negotiations, or administrative actions—were addressed to immediate problems, and they had an immediate impact. He thought of himself not as a philosopher but as "something of a practical idealist" with "enthusiasm for the feasible."[4] Of all his many contributions, this present volume (along with *The American College*), however, had the least direct impact on the course of American education. Yet it seems destined to stand for a long time to come as a milestone in the philosophical discussions of the university and its place in society. Why?

The American historian Daniel J. Boorstin has pointed out that certain writings may acquire an "afterlife" that makes them significant far beyond the times in which they were created, and sometimes for far different reasons than the author envisioned.[5] Thus it was with Flexner's *Universities*. Flexner thought he was describing the ideal modern university—an institution whose outlines he had glimpsed at Johns Hopkins and Berlin and whose realization throughout America, England, and Germany awaited only certain reforms which he enumerated. Instead, as the passage of history has revealed, he was writing a valedictory to a university form which was already passing—already evolving to a new stage. In so doing, he preserved for us, in perhaps its purest and most completely reasoned form, the "idea of a modern university" at a crucial stage of its development, just as Cardinal Newman, seventy-five years before, had so eloquently preserved the "idea of a University" at an earlier, equally important, and equally passing stage. By the time Flexner wrote in 1930, Johns Hopkins, he sadly noted, had become a "local institution",[6] and the German universities were on the brink of their greatest catastrophe.

The expression of such ideal types, however, is immensely valuable both to the understanding and the evaluation of our contemporary institutions. They contain the roots of the past, "the soil out of which we grow," to use Flexner's own words, "accumulated treasures of truth, beauty, and knowledge, experience, social, political, and other, which only a wastrel would ignore."[7] They stand as a yardstick against which to measure the accomplishments of the present. They provide reference points for trends from past to present, and so help us to speculate about the future course of our institutions. Thus the student of present-day universities may read Newman and Flexner with greater benefit than he will receive from most of the more contemporary analyses.

The university of Cardinal Newman focused upon one essential function—the conservation of knowledge and ideas and manners and their transmission to an elite body of largely undergraduate students. Newman believed that research should be performed outside the university. "If its object were scientific and philosophical discovery," he wrote "I do not see why a University should have any students."[8]

The "modern university" of Flexner, taken from the German model, united for the first time the functions of advanced teaching and research—particularly research in science. The university became, as Flexner pointed out, "an institution consciously devoted to the pursuit of knowledge, the solution of problems, the critical appreciation of achievement, and the training of men at a really high level."[9] Thus the university broadened its mission—but there were strict limits. Flexner rejected—or urged rejecting—much undergraduate teaching which he thought was really on the secondary level and ought to be done elsewhere. He believed that most professional training, except for the traditional university training in medicine and law, ought also to be done elsewhere. Similarly with most adult education, consulting, "business" research, and a host of other activities that we now regard as the service function of today's university.

Flexner did not disapprove of these activities per se. He simply thought they had no place in a university, as Newman before him had thought research had no place in a university. Flexner's fear was that these activities would dilute the university's commitments to advanced teaching and research. He warned: "A university . . . may thus readily find itself complicating its task and dissipating energy and funds by doing a host of inconsequential things."[10]

Time has proved Flexner's fear largely groundless. The service function and undergraduate instruction have been interwoven with the advanced teaching and research functions in many of America's great institutions of learning. The university is performing a far broader mission in today's society, and certainly few would argue that graduate teaching and research have been thereby weakened or endangered. Rather, graduate teaching and research have weakened undergraduate instruction, and have become dominant over service activities; they are not the subservient elements.

Flexner saw the university as "an organism, characterized by highness and definiteness of aim, unity of spirit and purpose."[11] Had the university retained an organic structure, its efforts might well have been diluted and dissipated by the addition of numerous professional schools, the multiplication of undergraduate students, the performance of a broad array of service activities. But the contemporary university is not an integrated organism. It is a pluralistic organization with many component parts, each of them capable of "highness and definiteness of aim, unity of spirit and purpose," each of them (in the best of all university worlds) possessing the energy and the funds to accomplish its specific task.

Today's university, then, is not Flexner's. But it owes a debt to that earlier university, and retains its finest elements: the high regard for academic excellence, the firm alliance of advanced teaching and research, the partnership of graduate student and professor, the commitment to intellectual discovery. For his eloquent espousal of that university model, scholars everywhere are in Abraham Flexner's debt. His strictures against an overemphasis on intercollegiate athletics (paying the coach more than the president), against "absurd topics for the Ph.D.," against the "shameless humbuggery" in some curricula,[12] against "wild, uncontrolled, and uncritical expansion"[13] echo down the decades in the hallways and faculty clubs and committee rooms of academe.

Francis Bacon is said to have written (although I could never find it) that "truth is more likely to emerge out of error than out of confusion"—Flexner was never confused. Acknowledging how often Flexner had been right in the past and was in the future with the Institute of Advanced Studies, we can still acknowledge that he made errors in *Universities*; and we can try to learn from them. I find his errors in three parts of his presentation.

AMERICAN UNIVERSITIES

Flexner's strictures on American universities echo down the decades, but Flexner, in the essential viewpoint he expressed in *Universities*, was, I think, quite wrong.

"Neither Columbia, nor Harvard, nor Johns Hopkins, nor Chicago, nor Wisconsin is really a university, for none of them possesses unity of purpose or homogeneity of constitution."[14] However, without either unity or homogeneity, the greatest of American universities, including several on his list, have taken their places among the outstanding universities of the world—surpassed by none, equaled by few.

"Fifty years ago, the degree of Ph.D. had a meaning in the United States; today it has practically no significance. The same is true of research."[15] However, only five percent of the Nobel Prizes were held by Americans before World War I; and forty percent after World War II. And, it is to the United States, not to Germany, that many of the most promising potential Ph.D.s from around the world now flock in the hundreds of thousands.

"The American professoriate is a proletariat."[16] However, today it is quite obviously part of the affluent society, and not the least part.

Many American universities, "more especially in the South and West—though the East is not free—are hotbeds of reaction in politics, industry, and religion, ambitious in pretension, meagre in performance, doubtful contributors, when they are not actual obstacles, to the culture of the nation."[17] However, hotbeds they indeed may be today, but not of reaction; and the cultural awakening in America finds much of its impetus on the campus. The "hotbeds of reaction" turned out to have been not in the United States but in Germany—and fifteen million people died.

The really Golden Age was not behind the American university in 1930, but ahead. And the path was not the one laid out by Flexner. The Harvard Graduate School of Business, "pretentious" and "dangerous,"[18] did not become the "Boston School of Business," separated from Harvard. Teachers' College at Columbia did not disappear from the face of the earth. Nor did the undergraduate colleges at Columbia or at Chicago. The "most incomprehensible"[19] Institute of Human Relations at Yale survived. There was no "ruthless abolition of trivial courses, trivial chairs, trivial publications, and ridiculous 'research.'"[20] "The make-believe professions" and "majors, minors, units, credits"[21] were not driven out of the temple. The universities that "thoughtlessly and excessively catered to fleeting, transient, and immediate demands"[22] kept on doing so, and prospered—even in advanced teaching and research. American universities became, even more, "administrative aggregations"[23] instead of "organisms"; and they also became more productive in scholarship. The universities did all the wrong things—undergraduate instruction, professional schools (other than law and medicine), service activities, vocational courses, extension work. They did all the wrong things—and they entered their most Golden Age. In any current list of the top universities in the world, rated as Flexner would have rated them on the quality of their research and Ph.D. training, at least twenty of the leading thirty would be American. The most golden of all "Golden Ages" for universities was ahead in the United States.

Flexner saw too little in America, and too little in overall social forces. America was moving forward to world leadership, and so were its universities. Germany was facing upheaval, and so were its universities. England was coming to share leadership with others, and so were its universities. The university system cannot be separated from the performance of the society that supports it; it is not a thing apart. The German and English universities of today look more to American universities than the other way around.

Flexner correctly saw the university as "an expression of the age,"[24] but he did not understand the age in America—the populist drive for more education for more people as against the elitist traditions of the older aristocracy, the desire of a technological society for knowledge made more available through service, the rise of new professions to stand alongside the old.

Flexner saw too much in criticism as a driving force. It had worked with the medical schools, which in 1910 were too often schools for butchers. It worked less well for the universities as a whole in 1930, which were both much better and moving more favorably than the medical schools of 1910. Shock treatment was less justified and less effective. Flexner was too addicted to all-out criticism as a mechanism of change. This led him to look mostly for items to criticize in

American universities. This led him to unbalanced views. This led him to unbalanced judgments about needed reforms—too drastic.

GERMAN UNIVERSITIES

Flexner was at least as wrong about German universities as he was about American: He was too respectful of the German university. In 1930 he could write that "the political upheavals which occur in American universities are beyond imagining in Germany"; the "most serious" problem then in Germany was merely the "lack of money."[25] However, in 1930, German universities were class institutions in a class society, centers of reaction in a nation well on its way to fascism. They were dominated by the few full professors and excessively dependent on the will of public officials. There was less of merit in the German university of 1930 and more in the University of London (which he thought had the faults of an American university) than Flexner thought.

Flexner either did not know about or ignored the warnings of Germany's greatest social scientist of the early twentieth century—Max Weber. Weber had earlier written that "If I compare Italian, French, and, at the moment, even Russian conditions with this condition of ours, I have to consider it a shame of a civilized nation."[26] He was particularly upset at the difficulty of getting faculty appointments for highly qualified Social Democratic and Jewish scholars. Edward Shils has noted that "the capitulation of so many German academic figures to the Nazi regime may be plausibly interpreted as evidence of the correctness of Max Weber's diagnosis regarding the complaisance of the German academic profession in its eager subservience to the authority of the state and the erosion of its moral rectitude."[27] Weber's views were well known in Germany, but they may never have come to the attention of Flexner. Other observers, however, were well acquainted with the "Althoff system" of governmental control of professorial appointments on political and religious grounds in German universities.

He did not recognize how much the German model had changed—how nationalistic and politicized it had become, strengthening one line of development that led to Hitler. It was in the 1920s both anti-Social Democratic and anti-Semitic. By 1930, "the tactics of the storm troopers were applied to the universities."[28] The Mandarins "helped to destroy the Republic"[29] and, in doing so, also some of the ideals they held dear like academic autonomy and academic freedom. But all that Flexner found wrong with the German universities was that they were overcrowded with students even though they had no students from working-class backgrounds, and that they had too few Social Democrats on the faculty—but these were rather minor faults as against their great virtues. And nothing about the Herr Professor as an academic authoritarian.

Flexner knew that universities were greatly affected by what happened to their societies, that "they have changed profoundly—and commonly in the direction of the social evolution of which they are part."[30] The university "is not outside, but inside the general social fabric of a given era. It is not something apart."[31] Yet, no word of what was happening within Germany—

the great wartime defeat, the Draconian peace, the destructive inflation, the rising unemployment. Societies do not always develop along straight lines, and Germany was at a climacteric in its history, turning in some new directions. Universities cannot escape history and the German universities most certainly did not.

Flexner ignored, if he knew, some basic truths about higher education in a more democratic and industrialized world: that it is not wise to be tied to a single class (the aristocracy or the technocracy), a single political orientation (rabidly nationalistic), or to a single level of the labor force (the professions); and that new knowledge grows out of contact with practical problems as well as out of ivory tower reflections (as the agricultural sciences in the United States have well demonstrated).

Yet, even in his *I Remember* (1940) and after drawing Einstein and other German refugees to his Institute, he did not retreat on his views in *Universities*. Why was this? Remembering much else, did he not remember what he had written about German universities in 1930? Under date of 1940, he wrote that "despite the ravages of the war," the German universities are "still the best in the world."[32] Sad. Was he too Hegelian? Was he too convinced of the advance in the role of the mind alone in guiding civilization in general and of the supremacy of the German mind in particular?

THE EVOLUTION OF HIGHER EDUCATION

Flexner was also wrong about the model of the "modern university" as the one and only true model

[xxvii]

for the future. Flexner thought *Universities* had laid out the one correct road to Mecca: "It made a great stir among academic folk and in the newspapers, for once more I had told the truth."[33] "How much effect the Rhodes Lectures have had, I have no way of knowing, but time will work in their favor."[34] But the road to Mecca went the other way; and time worked in a contrary fashion.

Flexner did not realize how many functions can be combined within a single university—even apparently inconsistent functions. Particularly, he did not see how service functions might draw support and money to a university, so that it could perform better also in advanced teaching and research. American universities did not "break beneath the incongruous load placed upon them."[35] He saw too much in unity and cohesion, and too little in pluralism and diversity.

Flexner drew a clearer line of distinction between law and medicine, with their "intellectual and altruistic purposes" and their "code of honour," on the one hand, and the "make-believe professions" of business and religion and library science, on the other, than the facts would warrant. Law and medicine were more distinguished by traditional acceptance than by the special virtues that Flexner thought they alone upheld.

Flexner did not understand that quality and quantity could be combined. Hopkins did not lose out comparatively because it came to have too many students. And Berkeley, despite its size, came to be rated both as the highest-quality graduate center in the United States (by the American Council on Education in 1964 and 1969 and by the Conference Board of Associated Research Councils in 1982), and also as the most productive source of doctoral degrees (by the National Center for Education Statistics in 1966–67 and still in 1989–90).

Flexner saw too much in Gilman, and too little in all the forces that drive an institution ahead; too much in the role of the president in an actual "modern university." The university president can be a key figure, particularly in a new institution, a fast-growing institution, a period of fundamental change in higher education; but there may be other key figures too— among trustees and faculty members and government leaders. In particular, Flexner underrated "faculty government" as "confusion worse confounded."[37] And yet he greatly admired Oxford and Cambridge which gloried in the most faculty-oriented government of all. He also saw the German universities which "were more highly developed, more nearly autonomous, far more highly respected and exerted a wider influence"[38] than any others—and they had no presidents; instead they had state ministers of education and rectors who were more "impotence" than "magnificence" as their titles stated. And he worked with Eastman and Brookings—the successful businessmen—in bringing modern medical schools to Rochester and Washington University. There were a few Gilmans in American universities, but there were also many other constructive forces at work.

Thus Flexner saw too much in a decaying model and too little in the new buds of growth, too much abroad and too little at home, too much in criticism and too little in the existing reality, too much in research and too little in service, too much in purity and too little in the creative tensions of divergent forces, too much in the old professions and too little in the new, too much in small size and too little in the possibilities inherent in growth, too much in presidential leadership and too little in the other animating forces, too much within the institution and too little in the environment that sustains it, too much in the forces of the past and too little in the urgings of the present. The "truth" he sought too often lay on the other side of the argument.

Flexner was also right. He was right in developing a clear-cut model of the university against which other models and reality could both be tested. He was right in being among the first to recognize the importance of the university in society and to study it carefully. He was right in wishing to reform the university, in trying to make it better, for then as now it can be made better. He was right, in particular, in his desire to eliminate the "rubbish." He was right in fighting for a better university, as he had so effectively fought for better medical education. He was right in fighting for it on the actual battle lines: "Utopia, in so far as humanly possible, can be realized only by 'trench warfare.'"[39] But, in the end, he was fighting in the wrong trenches.

Flexner had a great career. He wrote a great book—despite its great central errors. Under the testing of time, however, the Wisconsin Idea of America proved to be better fitted to the emerging world than the Humboldt Idea of Germany—with opportunity as well as merit, with practice as well as theory, with body as well as mind, with the community college as well as the research university. The actual modern university and actual systems of higher education around the world owe more to Wisconsin than to Berlin. But this is 1994 and not 1930—it was not so clear then.

Clark Kerr

NOTES

[1] Abraham Flexner, *Universities: American, English, German* (New York: Oxford University Press, 1968 [1930]), p. 192.

[2] Abraham Flexner, *I Remember* (New York: Simon and Schuster, 1940), pp. 52, 59.

[3] *Ibid.*, p. 308.

[4] *Ibid.*, p. 399.

[5] Daniel J. Boorstin, ed., *An American Primer* (Chicago and London: The University of Chicago Press, 1966), p. xvii.

[6] Flexner, *Universities*, p. 192.

[7] *Ibid.*, p. 4.

[8] John Henry Cardinal Newman, *The Idea of a University* (New York: Longmans Green and Co., 1947), p. xxvii.

[9] Flexner, *Universities*, p. 42.

[10] *Ibid.*, p. 25.

[11] *Ibid.*, pp. 178-79.

[12] Flexner, *I Remember*, p. 355.

[13] Flexner, *Universities*, p. 222.

[14] *Ibid.*, p. 179.

[15] *Ibid.*, p. 124.

[16] *Ibid.*, p. 208.

[17] *Ibid.*, p. 45.

[18] *Ibid.*, p. 162.

[19] *Ibid.*, p. 112.

[20] *Ibid.*, p. 204.

[21] *Ibid.*, p. 215.

[22] *Ibid.*, p. 44.

[23] *Ibid.*, p. 179.

[24] *Ibid.*, p. 3.

[25] *Ibid.*, pp. 348 and 360.

[26] Max Weber, *From Max Weber: Essays in Sociology* (New York: Oxford University Press, 1946), p. 19.

[27] Edward Shils, introductory note in *Max Weber on Universities: The Power of the State and the Dignity of the Academic Calling in Imperial Germany*, trans. and ed. by Edward Shils (Chicago: University of Chicago Press, 1974), p. 2. [Originally published in *Minerva* 11 (October 1973): 572.]

28 Fritz Ringer, *The Decline of the German Mandarins: The German Academic Community, 1890–1933* (Cambridge, Mass.: Harvard University Press, 1969), p. 437.

29 *Ibid.*, p. 446.

30 Flexner, *Universities*, p. 4.

31 *Ibid.*, p. 3.

32 Flexner, *I Remember*, p. 347.

33 *Ibid.*, p. 355.

34 *Ibid.*, p. 356.

35 *Ibid.*, p. 222.

36 *Ibid.*, p. 30.

37 Flexner, *I Remember*, p. 335.

38 Flexner, *Universities*, p. 345.

39 Flexner, *I Remember*, p. 399.

PREFACE

THIS volume is an expansion of three lectures on *Universities* given at Oxford in May 1928 on the invitation of the Rhodes Trust. The invitation stipulates that the lecturer reside at Oxford during the entire term in which the lectures are given — a provision that may be unreservedly commended, first, because the lecturer is thus enabled to feel something of Oxford's charm, secondly, because quite unconsciously he gains rather more than he is likely to impart. This is true of one Rhodes lecturer, at least.

From the autumn of 1928 to the summer of 1929, I visited the universities of Germany and England for the purpose of obtaining a fresh view of their situation, problems, and efforts. The whole of the next year, 1929–1930, was devoted to gathering additional data and to rewriting. In May 1930 the Oxford University Press printed and bound the original proof sheets in page form, and I was thus enabled to submit the text to about thirty men, professors and administrators in America and Europe, who read it with care and commented on it freely and helpfully. During the summer of 1930 I revised the book. I state these facts in order that the reader may know that, though the ultimate responsibility is wholly mine, I have spared no effort to obtain the facts and to submit my views in advance to competent criticism. I am quite sure that the result will completely satisfy no one: but I shall have achieved my purpose if I have opened for discussion a few fundamental questions respecting the function of the university in modern life.

The reader will observe that my discussion of existing universities is unsymmetrical. I have not tried to pour universities into one mould, to view them from a single point of view, or to ask the same questions about all of them. Rather, having in mind the " idea of a modern university," I have approached the universities of America, England, and Germany from the standpoint of their individual characteristics. I have asked myself: where, with this ideal before us, do they now satisfy? Where do they now fall short? Of their history I have mentioned only the salient points essential to an understanding of the answers to these questions. And I have given rather more space to the latter question than to the former, because I feel sure that, if errors and abuses are once corrected, the ideal will almost of its own force assert itself — differently, in different countries, of course, but to the same ultimate purpose. At first sight it may seem that I have devoted a disproportionately large amount of space to American universities. Such is, I think, not the case. American universities require more space because they do so many more things; and I could not possibly expect my readers — foreign or American — to understand them, if I did not quote and discuss a sufficient number of concrete instances.

I am under so many obligations that it is impossible for me to specify any one in particular. I should have indeed to go back more than forty years, for the present volume represents not merely the work of the last few years but the net result of an experience with universities in this country and abroad that began when my eldest brother sent me to the Johns Hopkins in 1884. From that day to this, I have been fortunate enough to have been enabled in one way or another to keep in almost constant contact with university life. Quite obviously, a book of this kind is not original; but just as obviously the author himself cannot know whom to thank, or, if he has erred, whom — beside himself — to blame.

I may not, however, omit to thank by name the Rhodes Trustees, Philip Kerr, Esq., now the Marquess of Lothian, Secretary of the Rhodes Trust, Sir Francis J. Wylie, the Oxford Secretary of the Trust, and the Warden and Fellows of All Souls College, of which I was made a member during my residence in Oxford, for courtesy, kindness, and hospitality which I cannot adequately describe. I am also once more bound to express appreciation of the untiring efforts of my Secretary, Mrs. Esther S. Bailey, who has assisted me in the collection of illustrative data, has checked statements of fact, and practically put the volume through the press.

ABRAHAM FLEXNER

NEW YORK, Oct. 1, 1930.

PART I

THE IDEA OF A MODERN UNIVERSITY

I

SEVENTY-FIVE years ago, an eminent Oxonian, Cardinal Newman, published a book entitled *The Idea of a University*. I have adopted in a modified form the title of that volume. I am undertaking in this chapter to discuss the idea of a *modern* university. In inserting the word " modern " I am endeavouring to indicate in the most explicit fashion that a university, like all other human institutions — like the church, like governments, like philanthropic organizations — is not outside, but inside the general social fabric of a given era. It is not something apart, something historic, something that yields as little as possible to forces and influences that are more or less new. It is, on the contrary — so I shall assume — an expression of the age, as well as an influence operating upon both present and future. I propose to elaborate this point of view and, as I proceed, to ask myself to what extent and in what ways universities in America, in England, and in Germany have made themselves part of the modern world, where they have failed to do so, where they have made hurtful concessions, and where they are wholesome and creative influences in shaping society towards rational ends.

Quite obviously I am assuming that to some extent, however slight, we are masters of our fate. The modern world is developing under the pressure of forces that reason cannot readily control. Pitted against

[3]

these forces, our abilities may for the moment seem feeble and ineffectual. But the existence of universities implies there is something, perhaps much, in the past for which it is worth while to fight, to which it is worth while to cling; and that there is something — no one knows how much — which we may ourselves do to mould to our liking the civilization of the future. Man, as Professor Woodbridge has admirably said, "is not content to take nature as he finds her. He insists on making her over."[1] But the modern world — no matter how new we think it to be — is rooted in a past, which is the soil out of which we grow, a past during which poets and scientists and thinkers and peoples have accumulated treasures of truth, beauty, and knowledge, experience, social, political, and other, which only a wastrel would ignore. On the other hand, science, democracy, and other forces steadily increasing in intensity are creating a different world of which universities must take account.

II

Universities differ in different countries; if, as Lord Haldane says, "it is in universities that . . . the soul of a people mirrors itself,"[2] then it would be absurd to expect them to conform to a single pattern. Moreover, as a matter of history, they have changed profoundly — and commonly in the direction of the social evolution of which they are part. The Paris of 1900 has little in common with the Paris of 1700; the Oxford of the twentieth century, externally so largely the same, is nevertheless a very different thing

[1] Frederick J. E. Woodbridge, *Contrasts in Education* (New York, 1929), p. 17.
[2] Viscount Haldane, *Universities and National Life* (London, 1912), p. 29.

from the Oxford of the eighteenth century; Althoff's
Berlin is not Wilhelm von Humboldt's, though they
are separated by hardly a hundred years; very different indeed is the Harvard, of which Mr. Eliot became president in 1869, from the Harvard which he
left on his retirement in 1909. Historians have traced
certain aspects of this evolution in detail; and nothing in their stories is more striking than the adjustments — sometimes slow and unconscious, sometimes
deliberate and violent — made in the course of centuries by institutions usually regarded as conservative, frequently even as the stronghold of reaction. I
say then that universities have in most countries
changed; but have they latterly changed profoundly
enough, or have they been so intelligently modified
as to be the effective and formative agencies which are
needed in a society that is driven it knows not whither
by forces of unprecedented strength and violence? An
American sociologist has invented the term " social
lag." Institutions as such tend for quite obvious reasons to lag behind the life which they express and further. To what extent are the universities of America,
England, and Germany hampered by " social lag "?

III

There is danger at precisely the opposite end of the
line. I have spoken of the intelligent modification of
universities — of their modification in the light of
needs, facts, and ideals. But a university should not
be a weather vane, responsive to every variation of
popular whim. Universities must at times give society,
not what society wants, but what it needs. Inertia and
resistance have their uses, provided they be based on
reasonable analysis, on a sense of values, not on mere

habit. In response to the criticism that universities lag, instances in plenty can — and will — be given by way of showing that universities are up to date or even ahead of the times. But the two characteristics are not mutually exclusive. Universities are complex and organic institutions: their arms may be sound, while both legs may be broken. They may lag fundamentally, even while superficially catering to whim or fashion; they may lag fundamentally at the very moment when at this or that point they are as expert as newspapers and politicians in catching the current breeze. A proper amount of critical resistance, based on a sense of values, would — as we shall see — save them from absurd, almost disastrous blunders.

IV

Of all this, more hereafter. In the present chapter, I shall not discuss universities, but merely the idea of a university, and I am going to procure a free field for speculation by assuming the impossible and, indeed, the undesirable; suppose we could smash our existing universities to bits, suppose we could remake them to conform to our heart's desire, what sort of institution should we set up? We should not form them all alike — English, French, American, German. But, whatever allowances we might make for national tradition or temperament, we should see to it somehow that in appropriate ways scholars and scientists would be conscious of four major concerns: the conservation of knowledge and ideas; the interpretation of knowledge and ideas; the search for truth; the training of students who will practise and " carry on." I say, to repeat, " the major concerns " of scholar and scientist. Of course, education has other and im-

[6]

portant concerns. But I wish to make it plain at the outset that the university is only one of many educational enterprises. It has, in the general educational scheme, certain specific functions. Other agencies discharge or should discharge other functions. We shall see whether universities now discern and discharge their special functions or whether they meddle with functions which do not constitute their proper business.

The conservation of knowledge and ideas is and has always been recognized as the business of universities, sometimes, perhaps, as almost their only business, occasionally, even today, as too largely their business. In any event, universities have always taken this to be one of their functions; and however universities may change, no reconstruction will or should deprive them of it. But one should add this: conservation and interpretation are one thing in institutions that are concerned with merely or chiefly that; they are a different thing in a university where fresh streams of thought are constantly playing upon the preserved treasures of mankind.

Original thinkers and investigators do not therefore represent the only type of university professor. They will always be the distinguished figures; theirs will usually be the most profound and far-reaching influence. But even universities, modern universities, need and use men of different stamp — teachers whose own contributions to learning are of less importance than their influence in stimulating students or their resourcefulness in bringing together the researches of others. Michael Foster was not the less a great university professor, though he was not himself a great original thinker: in subtle ways that defy expression, he created the great Cambridge school of physiology. So,

too, Paulsen was not the less a great university professor, though he was not himself a great original thinker,
but rather a broad and profound scholar of sound
judgment and beautiful spirit who helped hundreds,
struggling with the perplexities of life and thought,
to find themselves. But, be it noted, both did this not
for boys, but for mature students, under conditions
that threw upon them responsibility for efforts and results. And this is a university criterion of first-rate importance. The university professor has an entirely objective responsibility — a responsibility to learning, to
his subject, and not a psychological or parental responsibility for his students. No fear that he will in
consequence be dehumanized. What could be more
charming, more intimate, more personal, more coöperative than the relations between the great continental masters and their disciples during the best part
of the nineteenth century?

It is, however, creative activity, productive and
critical inquiry — all in a sense without practical responsibility — that must bulk ever larger and larger
in the modern university. Conservation continues to
be not only important, but essential alike to education
and to research; but, as other educational agencies
improve and as our difficulties thicken, it is destined,
I think, to become incidental to the extension of
knowledge, to training at a high level, and to a critical
attempt to set a value upon the doings of men.

Of the overwhelming and increasing importance
of the study and solution of problems or the advancement of knowledge — they are interchangeable
phrases — one can readily convince one's self, no
matter where one looks. Let us consider for a moment
the social and political situation within which we live,
and I take this realm first, because it is the realm in

which universities are doing least, the realm which is most difficult and dangerous to approach, the realm which is for these reasons perhaps the most important to master. Democracy has dragged in its wake social, economic, educational, and political problems infinitely more perplexing than the relatively simple problems which its credulous crusaders undertook to solve. Society cannot retreat; whatever may happen sporadically or temporarily in Italy or Spain, we shall in the end probably fare better, if the adaptations and inventions requisite to making a success of democracy are facilitated. But adaptations in what ways? Statesmen must invent — not statesmen, fumbling in the dark or living on phrases, but statesmen equipped by disinterested students of society with the knowledge needed for courageous and intelligent action. Now the postulates, ideas, terminology, phraseology, which started the modern world on new paths, have become more or less obsolete, partly through their own success, partly through changes due to science and the industrial revolution. To be sure, men have always acted blindly, ignorantly; but for the time being at least, the chasm between action, on the one hand, and knowledge, on the other, is widening rather than contracting. Practice cannot be slowed down or halted; intelligence must, however, be accelerated.

This contention could be equally well illustrated by Germany, France, England, or the United States. What has happened in the United States? There was between 1776 and 1790 a revolution based upon a simple philosophy. Time, even a brief century, brought changes; but the philosophy had meanwhile crystallized. A thin rural population living on the seaboard had increased beyond a hundred millions spread over an empire; steam and electricity had transferred

[9]

importance from agriculture to industry; huge cities had grown up; enormous discrepancies of wealth had been created. But the documentary basis of government and society remains essentially the same. We find ourselves therefore now enmeshed in a phraseology that is discordant with the facts. The phraseology tends to hold things fixed; but readjustments have somehow to be effected. Publicists and jurists have therefore been forced to make inherited formulae mean something that they do not mean and could not have meant. The easy and effective reconceiving and rewording of theory and ideas are thus gravely hampered. Somewhere, away from the hurly-burly of practical responsibility and action, the social and political problems involved in these discords must be exposed. The "great society" must and wants to understand itself — partly as a matter of sheer curiosity, partly because human beings are in a muddle and cannot get out unless they know more than they now know. Towards fundamental knowing the newspaper cannot help much; men of action — politicians and business men — help but slightly. They themselves know too little; they are not disinterestedly concerned with finding out; they have usually their own axes to grind. Almost the only available agency is the university. The university must shelter and develop thinkers, experimenters, inventors, teachers, and students, who, without responsibility for action, will explore the phenomena of social life and endeavour to understand them.

I do not mean to say that this is altogether a novelty. Great scholars have in all countries in fragments of time snatched from routine duties made important contributions to political and economic thought: "in fragments of time snatched from routine duties" —

from administrative burdens, from secondary instruction, from distracting tasks undertaken to piece out a livelihood. But though individuals differ in their requirements, no university in any country has made really adequate provision or offered really adequate opportunity and encouragement. I have not in mind the training of practical men, who, faced with responsibility for action, will do the best they can. That is not the task of the university. Between the student of political and social problems and the journalist, industrialist, merchant, viceroy, member of Parliament or Congress, there is a gap which the university cannot fill, which society must fill in some other way. Perhaps no outright educational institution should be expected to fill it; educated men can be allowed to do some things for themselves — though, at the moment, we appear to be under a different impression.

One may go further: a study of mediaeval charters, of the financing of the Napoleonic Wars, of the rise of Prussia, of the origins of local government in the American Colonies, of the ideas of Plato, Aristotle, or Hobbes — these topics — just slightly musty — would be generally regarded as appropriately academic, for they may be investigated in a library. But is it equally good form — academically speaking — to study Mr. Keynes rather than Ricardo, the war debts with which successive commissions have wrestled rather than the repudiated state debts which most Americans quite wrongly prefer to regard as possessing merely historic interests, the present-day consequences of the industrial revolution rather than its early evolution? A field expedition to unearth an Assyrian palace is admittedly a proper undertaking for university professors; but should coal strikes, Indian unrest, rubber, oil, and American lynchings be for the present mainly left to journalists, travellers, and politicians? Do they become proper subjects of academic interest only when they approach the post-mortem stage? Quite the contrary: with all the difficulties arising from contemporaneousness, the task of the scientist, dealing with present social phenomena, is probably easier than that of the Hellenist or mediaevalist, intent upon reconstructing the past. "Think of the happiness of the scholar if he could see a Greek republic or a Roman colony actually living under his own eyes — granted that he recover from the havoc of some of his best established delusions!" [3]

I have said that data of one kind or another are not so difficult to obtain. But generalization is another matter. The social scientist may resent the premature generalizations of his predecessors. He will himself not get very far unless he himself tentatively generalizes; unless, in a word, he has ideas as well as data. Essays and investigations may be piled mountain high; they will never by themselves constitute a science or a philosophy of economics, psychology, or society. The two processes — the making of hypotheses and the gathering of data — must go on together, reacting upon each other. For in the social sciences as elsewhere generalization is at once a test of and a stimulus to minute and realistic research. The generalizations will not endure; why should they? They have not endured in mathematics, physics, and chemistry. But, then, neither have the data. Science, social or other, is a structure: "a series of judgments, revised without ceasing, goes to make up the incontestable progress of science. We must believe

[3] Salvador de Madariaga, *Aims and Methods of a Chair of Spanish Studies* (Clarendon Press, Oxford, 1928), p. 12.

in this progress, but we must never accord more than a limited amount of confidence to the forms in which it is successively vested." [4]

The task, then, of finding a basis and providing a methodology for the social sciences, is today more pressing than it has ever been because of the accelerated rate of social change and the relatively more rapid progress in the physical and biological sciences: "The events of 1914–1918, to quote a single example, showed that the statesmen, the social scientists, the moral and religious teachers of Europe, to whom belonged, as their main duty, the preservation of peace, failed utterly; the directors and inventors of the physical sciences had assigned to them as their main duty the killing of as many of the national enemies as possible, and they succeeded magnificently. Twenty years hence the same situation may recur; and unless the two disciplines concerned can meanwhile come to an understanding, half the population and all the accumulated wealth of Europe may be destroyed with even more complete efficiency." [5]

As long as evolution proceeded slowly over centuries, men could feel their way and make adjustments imperceptibly on an empirical basis. But the restraints which for centuries slowed down or limited adjustments have been largely removed. Societies have to act — intelligently, if possible — if not, then unintelligently, blindly, selfishly, impulsively. The weight and prestige of the university must be thrown on the side of intelligence. If the university does not accept this challenge, what other institution can or will? In this present-day world, compounded of tradition,

[4] Duclaux, *Pasteur — The History of a Mind* (translated by Smith and Hedges, Philadelphia and London, 1920), p. 111.

[5] Graham Wallas, *Physical and Social Science* (Huxley Memorial Lecture 1930, London), p. 1. The quotation is slightly paraphrased.

good and bad, racial mixtures, nationalistic and internationalistic strivings, business interests, physical forces of incredible power for good or ill, emancipated workers and peasants, restless Orientals, noisy cities, conflicting philosophies — in this world rocking beneath and around us, where is theory to be worked out, where are social and economic problems to be analysed, where are theory and facts to be brought face to face, where is the truth, welcome or unwelcome, to be told, where are men to be trained to ascertain and to tell it, where, in whatever measure it is possible, is conscious, deliberate, and irresponsible thought to be given to the task of reshaping this world of ours to our own liking, unless, first and foremost, in the university? The wit of man has thus far contrived no other comparable agency.

The urgency of the need is not, as I have said, without its dangers. The history of the more manageable sciences contains a warning which the social scientist will do well to heed. Chemistry made no progress as long as men were concerned immediately to convert base metal into gold; it advanced when, for the time being, it ignored use and practice. Today chemical theory and chemical practice are continuously fertilizing each other. So, again, medicine stood almost still until the pre-clinical sciences were differentiated and set free — free to develop without regard to use and practice. The same situation has more recently developed on the clinical side; disease is most likely to be understood — and ultimately combatted — if it is approached as a phenomenon, and patients and problems must be selected on the basis of the clinician's interest, in so far as he is engaged in investigation. The social sciences have not yet developed far enough to win assured scientific status. A sympathetic onlooker is fearful lest the frail theoretic or scientific structure is being subjected to a practical strain that it is not competent to bear. To be sure, the social scientist must find his material in the thick of events; but quâ scientist, he must select and approach and frame his problems, from the viewpoint of science, without incurring responsibility for policies. In the social as in the physical sciences, the university is, in so far as scientific effort to understand phenomena is concerned, indifferent to the effect and use of truth. Perhaps, in due course, use and theory may in the social sciences also prove mutually helpful; perhaps social experimentation, involving application, may prove the only laboratory. But even so, it is one thing to incur responsibility for policies, and quite another to set up an experiment primarily in the interest of ascertaining truth or testing theory. The modern university must neither fear the world nor make itself responsible for its conduct.

I have been urging that universities maintain contacts with the actual world and at the same time continue to be irresponsible. Are the two attitudes incompatible? Can they really take an objective position in reference to social, political, and economic phenomena? Can they study phenomena without wanting to tell legislatures, communities, municipal authorities, and chambers of commerce what they ought to do at any particular moment about some particular thing? I think they must and can. It is a question of ideals and organization.[6] For experimental purposes they may, without sacrifice of intellectual integrity, make suggestions and watch results;

[6] The present British Government has set up an Economic Advisory Council, an academic group which discusses, from the academic or theoretic point of view, economic and political questions; the Council does not decide policies: that is left to the Government.

but this is different from running a city government or a political party, involving, as such responsibilities do, compromises of principle that are fatal to
fearless thinking. The analogy of the medical clinic,
already mentioned, is not complete, but it is suggestive. The professor of medicine needs patients, just
as the social scientist needs his environment. The
professor of medicine ought to be thoroughly humane,
realizing fully that he is dealing with, and in that
sense responsible for, human life. But the professor of
medicine is primarily a student of problems and a
trainer of men. He has not the slightest obligation to
look after as many sick people as he can; on the contrary, the moment he regards his task as that of caring
for more and more of the sick, he will cease to discharge his duty to the university — his duty to study
problems, to keep abreast of literature, to make his
own contributions to science, to train men who can
" carry on." The greatest and most productive of
American surgical thinkers lived his entire scientific
life in this fashion: he was considerate and humane
in the care of his patients; he trained a group of re-
markably competent surgeons; but his central thought
and activity never swerved from the study of problems; one problem after another yielded its mystery
to him; but having solved a problem, he ceased to
occupy himself actively with it; other persons could
do that, while he pushed on to something new, important, unknown. "We are still, as you know, groping more or less in the dark," he once wrote, " and
always shall be, I trust; for otherwise there would be
no game in medicine. There are, however, light spots
back of us, where before there was darkness." [7] In

[7] Extract from a letter written by Dr. William S. Halsted, Professor
of Surgery, Johns Hopkins Medical School, 1889–1922.

those words the university professor spoke — the professor of surgery, of medicine, of law, of economics,
of all subjects whatsoever.

Industry has found ways of utilizing the sheerest
scientific research — it does not require that of the
university; medicine is groping about for a similar
connecting link — the medical faculty would be
ruined if it served in both capacities. The social
sciences must be detached from the conduct of business, the conduct of politics, the reform of this, that,
and the other, if they are to develop as sciences,
even though they continuously need contact with
the phenomena of business, the phenomena of politics,
the phenomena of social experimentation.

V

The situation is not essentially different in respect
to the so-called " exact sciences," though universities
have in the more vigorous western countries become
more hospitable to their cultivation for their own sake.
These sciences — mathematics, physics, chemistry,
and biology — have made greater progress in the last
century than in many preceding centuries. Even so,
they are still in their infancy. In what is usually called
their " pure " form — I mean their cultivation without reference to application — they have now so se-
curely established themselves, theoretically at least,
that I need not emphasize their importance. It is,
however, not so generally realized that science, pure
or applied, creates more problems than it solves.
First, on the theoretic or philosophic side : we have become increasingly and painfully aware of our abysmal
ignorance. No scientist, fifty years ago, could have
realized that he was as ignorant as all first-rate

scientists now know themselves to be. It was but recently that we believed that Newton had arrived at rock-bottom! It is a disquieting change from that complacent state of mind to the attitude of Charles Peirce, who described the laws of nature as habits or customs; or to the attitude of Gilbert Lewis who asks: "Can we not see that exact laws, like all the other ultimates and absolutes, are as fabulous as the crock of gold at the rainbow's end?"[8] The theoretic consequences of scientific discovery may thus be very disconcerting; for the scientist, bent perhaps merely upon the gratification of his own curiosity, periodically and episodically destroys the foundations upon which both science and society have just become used to reclining comfortably. We listen nowadays not to one Copernicus — a voice crying in the wilderness — but to many, and their voices are magnified and transmitted through the entire social and intellectual structure. Physics and chemistry, viewed as merely intellectual passions, will not stay "put"; they have an elusive way of slipping through the fingers of the investigator.

I have spoken of the theoretic consequences of scientific progress and of the need of a place in which calm, philosophic reflection can be brought to bear upon them. Consider now the practical consequences of scientific advance, the problems thus created, and the need of opportunities for their consideration and solution. Medicine offers an obvious example. Whether out of humanitarian or sheer scientific interest, men study the phenomena of disease. What happens? A problem is solved — the problem of this or that infection or contagion. Quite unexpected consequences ensue. One problem is solved; other prob-

[8] G. N. Lewis, *The Anatomy of Science* (Yale University Press, 1926), p. 154.

lems are created. Life is lengthened. Thereupon we are confronted by a new crop of diseases, almost negligible as long as the infancy death rate was high and the expectation of life limited to the thirties; thus has medical science increased, not diminished, its own burden. But this is not all: men live longer and more safely; they live more healthily and contentedly in huge cities than in small villages or in the open country. At once, serious social problems, involving education, government, law, custom, morality, arise from the congestion of population following improved sanitation. Nor is this all. There are more people — many more. They must be fed and clothed. Raw materials are needed; the excess of manufactured products must be marketed. Competition becomes more and more intense — for raw materials, for colonies, for markets. War is no longer a solution — it merely creates additional problems. Thus science, in the very act of solving problems, creates more of them. Such are the consequences of progress in a portion of the physical and biological sciences in a small corner of the western world. Inevitably, the sciences will be more thoroughly and more widely cultivated. What new problems will be thereby created, we are powerless to conceive. But so much at least is clear: while pure science is revolutionizing human thought, applied science is destined to revolutionize human life. We are at the beginning, not at the end, of an epoch. Problems therefore abound and press upon us — problems due to ignorance, problems created by knowledge. They must be studied before intelligent action can be taken. Hand-to-mouth contrivance does not suffice. Who is going to study them? Who and where? There will be, of course, from time to time a lonely Mendel or a lonely Darwin, who may do epoch-making things. But more and more the worker needs co-workers and facilities such as the individual is not likely to possess; he needs, also, soil in which to grow. However deeply the flash of genius may penetrate, the bulk of the world's work in research and teaching will be done in universities — if universities are what they ought to be.

VI

Our world is not, however, merely a matter of democracy and science. Indeed, if some sort of cultural equilibrium is to be attained, the humanistic disciplines, in which philosophy is included, necessarily become of greater rather than less importance; and by humanistic disciplines I refer not only to the humanities as such, but to the human values inherent in a deep knowledge of science itself. With the quick march of science, philosophy and humanism have gone under a cloud; when they assert themselves, they are prone to do so apologetically, on the ground that they too are, or can be, scientific. To be sure, they are and can; I shall in a moment have a word to say on that point. But quite aside from their pursuit in a scientific spirit, the world has not lost, and, unless it is to lose its savour, will never lose the pure, appreciative, humanistic spirit — the love of beauty, the concern for ends established by ideals that dare to command rather than to obey. Now science, while widening our vision, increasing our satisfactions, and solving our problems, brings with it dangers peculiarly its own. We can become so infatuated with progress in knowledge and control — both of which I have unstintedly emphasized — that we lose our perspective, lose our historic sense, lose a philosophic outlook, lose sight of relative cultural values. Something like this has happened to many, perhaps to most, of the enthusiastic, clear-headed, forward-looking, perhaps too exclusively forward-looking, and highly specialized young votaries of science. They are, culturally, too often thin and metallic; their training appears technological rather than broadly and deeply scientific. I have urged that science, quâ science, is indifferent to use and effect. Taste and reason do not intervene to stop the scientist prosecuting his search for truth; they do sit in judgment on the uses to which society puts the forces which the scientist has set free. I say, our younger scientists not infrequently appear to have been dehumanized; so also do some humanists. In the modern university, therefore, the more vigorously science is prosecuted, the more acute the need that society be held accountable for the purposes to which larger knowledge and experience are turned. Philosophers and critics, therefore, gain in importance as science makes life more complex — more rational in some ways, more irrational in others.

But there are other senses in which humanism must be promoted by modern universities. For humanism is not merely a thing of values — it has, like science, consequences. At first sight, what can be more innocent than the resurrection of a dead language? But every time a dead language is exhumed, a new nationality may be created. The humanists, not merely the Turks or the politicians or the newspapers, are at least partly responsible for the Balkanization of Eastern Europe and for the recrudescence of Celtic feeling. Like the scientist, the humanist creates as well as solves problems; he helps to free the Serbs and the Greeks from Turkish rule; he helps both to create and to solve the Home Rule problem in Great Britain — irresponsibly in either instance; he assists powerfully in stimulating self-consciousness in India, in Egypt, in China, and among the American Negroes; he finds himself one of the causes of an exacerbation of nationalism and racialism which no one has yet learned to mollify or cure. He has, I repeat, no practical responsibility for the trouble he makes; it is his business and duty to preserve his independence and irresponsibility. But he must go on thinking; in that realm his responsibility is of the gravest. And, perhaps, in the fullness of time, the very licence of his thought may, without intention or forethought on his part, suggest inventions or profoundly influence solutions, as it has done heretofore.

I cannot presume, even if I had space, to enumerate all the reasons for desiring a vigorous renascence of humanistic studies. But I must touch on one more point. During the last century, palaeontologist and historian have shown us how little we know of the story and import of man's career on this planet. A tremendous gap remains to be filled by archaeologists, philologists, and palaeographers — by Greek and Latin scholars working in libraries and in the field, by Orientalists, digging at Megiddo, in the Nile Valley, at Dura, and elsewhere. The story of the Athenian Empire will have to be rewritten in the light of recent readings of the pieced-together fragments of a few Greek tablets; who knows what will happen when the Agora discloses its secrets? And were the Hittite, Sumerian, and Malay languages and remains properly cultivated, we might arrive at very different conceptions than are now accepted as to the origin, development, and spread of culture. I need not labour the point by dwelling on the importance of a humanistic development covering mediaeval and modern times. Suffice it to say that further study of mediaeval and modern art, literature, music, and history will inevitably revise notions formed on the basis of the defective data which have hitherto controlled our thinking.

Intensive study of phenomena under the most favourable possible conditions — the phenomena of the physical world, of the social world, of the aesthetic world, and the ceaseless struggle to see things in relation — these I conceive to be the most important functions of the modern university. We shall get further with the physical world than with the social world or the aesthetic world; but the difference is only one of degree — all are important, all are worth while — worth while in themselves, worth while because they have bearings, implications, uses. But the university will not exhaust its function when it piles up its heaps of knowledge. Within the same institution that is busy in ascertaining facts, intelligence will be at work piecing facts together, inferring, speculating. There will be a Rutherford, breaking up the atom, and a Whitehead or Eddington, trying to make out what it all means; a Virchow demonstrating cellular pathology, and a Banting bringing from the four corners of the earth the various bits that, fitted together, produce insulin. When the late Jacques Loeb was asked whether he was a chemist or physiologist, he is reported to have replied, "I am a student of problems." It is fashionable to rail at specialization; but the truth is that specialization has brought us to the point we have reached, and more highly specialized intelligence will alone carry us further. But, of course, specialization alone does not suffice; there must somehow be drawn into the university also minds that can both specialize and generalize. The philosophic intelligence must be at work, trying new patterns, trying, however vainly, to see things in the large, as new material is accumulated. And this process should go on in the university more effectively than anywhere else, just because the university is the active centre of investigation and reflection and because it brings together within its framework every type of fundamental intelligence.

VII

A modern university would then address itself whole-heartedly and unreservedly to the advancement of knowledge, the study of problems, from whatever source they come, and the training of men — all at the highest level of possible effort. The constitution of the stars, the constitution of the atom, the constitutions of Oklahoma, Danzig, or Kenya, what is happening in the stars, in the atom, in Oklahoma, what social and political consequences flow from the fact that the politician is becoming more and more obsolescent while the business man and the idealist are playing a larger part in determining the development of society — all these are important objects to know about. It is not the business of the university to *do* anything about any of them. The university cannot regulate the weather in Mars, it cannot run business, it cannot directly influence what happens at Westminster or Washington. But neither can it hold itself aloof.

There are dangers to be encountered in modernizing universities, in the sense in which I have used the term. Quite obviously, such a modern university has more things to think about than a mediaeval institution given to expounding Aristotle, the Fathers, and the classic philosophers. But precisely because modern universities have many interests, they must be ex-

tremely critical of every claimant. Now, men — especially mediocre men — do not always distinguish
the serious from the trivial, the significant from the
insignificant. A university, seeking to be modern, seeking to evolve theory, seeking to solve problems, may
thus readily find itself complicating its task and dissipating energy and funds by doing a host of inconsequential things.

There is a second danger. The moment a real idea
has been let loose, the moment technique has been
developed, mediocrity is jubilant; the manufacture of
make-believe science flourishes. Learning has never
been free from pedantry or from superficiality. But
the modern world, what with its abundant facilities for publication and its ridiculous fondness for
"learned" degrees, groans under a tropical growth
of make-believe. Now, as against this tendency,
against the tendency towards specialization of a mechanical or technological kind, we need to remember
that universities depend on ideas, on great men. One
Virchow, one Pasteur, one Willard Gibbs can change
the entire intellectual order in his respective sphere.
But great men are individuals; and individuals and
organizations are in everlasting conflict. The university is an institution. It cannot, on the one hand,
be amorphous or chaotic. Neither, on the other, can
it flourish unless it is elastic enough to supply the different conditions that different productive individuals
find congenial. It may well turn out that these conditions are just as favourable to somnolence as to productivity. It does not much matter that some persons
go to sleep, provided only enough others are wide
awake and fertile at the maximum of their powers.
The important thing is not that a few persons doze
or loaf or are ineffectual; the important thing is that a

Hertz, a Maxwell, a Mommsen, and a Gildersleeve find within the university the conditions that suit them as individuals — conditions favourable to their own development and to the development of a varied group of co-workers.

VIII

I do not wish now to anticipate what I shall have to say of American, English, and German universities. But it must be obvious already that my criticism will cover two points, viz., what universities do not now touch, what they have no business to touch. The program which I have sketched is surely not lacking in extent or difficulty; its successful execution would call for more talent and more money than any university now possesses. Moreover, the kind of work that such universities should do requires proper conditions — books, laboratories, of course, but also quiet, dignity, freedom from petty cares, intercourse at a high social and intellectual level, a full and varied life, nicely adjusted to individual idiosyncrasies. We shall have occasion in subsequent chapters to consider with how much intelligence universities nowadays draw the line in these matters. Let me concede, for the purpose of argument (and for that only), that all the things that universities do are in themselves worth doing — a very large concesssion. Does it follow that universities *should* do them? Does it follow that universities *can* do them? I answer both questions in the negative. If universities are charged with the high functions that I have enumerated, they will do well to discharge them effectively — do well to assemble the men, to gather the money, to provide the facilities that are requisite to their performance. I think it can be shown that universities do not yet discharge these functions well; that they assume obligations that are irrelevant and unworthy. If the functions, against which I should draw the line, are really worth discharging, society must find other ways of discharging them. Of course there is nothing sacrosanct about the three or four traditional faculties or the traditional subjects. As the world has changed, new faculties have been needed; new subjects have from time to time been created. But even in the most modern university a clear case must be made out, if for no better reason than the fact that expansion means increase of professors and students — the former difficult to obtain, the latter likely through sheer size to destroy the organic character of the institution. And the case, as I see it, must rest on the inherent and intellectual value of the proposed faculty or the proposed subject. Practical importance is not a sufficient title to academic recognition: if that is the best that can be said, it is an excellent reason for exclusion. A university is therefore not a dumping ground. Universities that are held to their appropriate tasks will be unfit to do other tasks. A far-reaching educational reconstruction may thus become necessary. In no two countries is it going to be brought about in identical fashion. Indeed, it need not be uniformly accomplished in any one country. But, however this may be, the reorganization of universities, in order that they may do supremely well what they almost alone can do, may accomplish much by forcing the reorganization of the rest of the educational system.

IX

On the basis which I have discussed, the pursuit of science and scholarship belongs to the university. What else belongs there? Assuredly neither secondary,

[27]

technical, vocational, nor popular education. Of course, these are important; of course, society must create appropriate agencies to deal with them; but they must not be permitted to distract the university.

With merely technical, merely vocational, or merely popular education we shall encounter no difficulty in dealing; but the term " secondary education " is so vague and so variously used that I must explain the sense in which I shall use it throughout these pages. To my mind, the difference between secondary and university education is the difference between immaturity and maturity. Secondary education involves responsibility of an intimate kind for the student, for the subject-matter that he studies, even for the way in which he works, lives, and conducts himself — for his manners, his morals, and his mind. The university has no such complicated concern. At the university the student must take chances — with himself, with his studies, with the way in which he works. The freedom of the university does not mean either that the professor is indifferent or that at the very outset the student should attack a piece of research independently: on the contrary, he has, while free, to work through a difficult apprenticeship before he attains independence. In the same way, the entire texture of secondary education need not be uniform. Freedom and responsibility may be increased, as adolescence advances; in one way or another, the peculiar character of the secondary school may taper off, as the university approaches. But in any event, there will be a break, a jolt, a crisis, precisely as there is a break when a grown boy or girl leaves home. It is not the business of education to avoid every break, every jolt, every crisis. On the contrary, the boy having become a man, a jolt tests his mettle; unless he survives and gains in moral and intellectual strength, the university is no place for him, for the university should not be even partly a secondary school.[9]

Of the professional faculties, a clear case can, I think, be made out for law and medicine;[10] not for denominational religion, which involves a bias, hardly perhaps for education, certainly not at all for business, journalism, domestic " science," or library " science," to which I shall return in detail later.[11] It is true that most physicians and most lawyers are mere craftsmen; it is even true that their training largely occupies itself with teaching them how to do things. I should go further: I should add that an unproductive faculty of law or medicine is no whit the better for being attached to a university; it has no business there; it would do as well by society and by its students if it were an independent vocational school.

How are we to distinguish professions that belong to universities from vocations that do not belong to them? The criteria are not difficult to discern. Professions are, as a matter of history — and very rightly — " learned professions "; there are no unlearned professions. Unlearned professions — a contradiction in terms — would be vocations, callings, or occupations. Professions are learned, because they have their roots deep in cultural and idealistic soil. Moreover, professions derive their essential character from intelligence. Of course, the surgeon uses his hands; the

[9] It is clear, for example, that, as I employ the term, the American high school is not co-extensive with secondary education: on the contrary, in the United States, " secondary education " would swallow not only the high school, but much, perhaps most of the college. See p. 53.

[10] I do not in this volume discuss schools of law or schools of technology, for the simple reason that I have never studied them. The omission implies no opinion of any kind.

[11] See pp. 158–9, 172.

physician uses a stethoscope; the lawyer uses a clerk and an accountant. But these are the accidents of activity. The essence of the two professions resides in the application of free, resourceful, unhampered intelligence to the comprehension of problems — the problems of disease, the problems of social life, bequeathed to us by history and complicated by evolution. Unless legal and medical faculties live in the atmosphere of ideals and research, they are simply not university faculties at all.

Professions may be further distinguished by their attitude towards results. The scientist or the scholar who takes shape in the physician or the jurist has objects to accomplish. The achievement of these objects incidentally brings in a livelihood; but the livelihood is, theoretically at least (and for many centuries practically too), of secondary or incidental, even though to the individual, of essential, importance. Professions have primarily objective, intellectual, and altruistic purposes. A profession is therefore an order, a caste, not always in fact free from selfish aims, but in its ideals at least devoted to the promotion of larger and nobler ends than the satisfaction of individual ambitions. It has a code of honour — sometimes, like the Hippocratic oath, historically impressive.

It will become clear, as we go on, that, compared with present theory and practice, the conception of the university which I have outlined is severe. Have I lost sight of the importance of " training " — training college teachers or educational administrators or candidates for governmental posts? I think not. I have merely assumed that persons who have had a genuine university education will emerge with disciplined minds, well stored with knowledge, possessing a critical, not a pedantic edge, and that such persons may thereafter for the most part be safely left to their own devices. I suspect, if I must tell the whole truth, that persons who sacrifice broad and deep university experience in order to learn administrative tricks will in the long run find themselves intellectually and vocationally disadvantaged. From the standpoint of practical need, society requires of its leaders not so much specifically trained competency at the moment as the mastery of experience, an interest in problems, dexterity in finding one's way, disciplined capacity to put forth effort. Lower or special schools or experience itself will furnish technique, if that is what students desire.

X

The emphasis which I have placed upon thinking and research may create the impression that I am really discussing institutes of research rather than universities. Such is not the case. Institutes of research, as we know them, differ in certain respects from universities as I am trying to conceive them. In the first place, the research institute stands or falls by its success in research, whereas, in projecting the modern university, I have been careful to associate training with research. The history of research institutes throws light upon this point. The modern research institute was first set up in Paris for Pasteur, because within the French university of Pasteur's time one could not procure the conditions requisite to scientific research. The movement broadened in Germany under the influence of Friedrich Althoff, the forceful and fertile administrator who from 1882 to 1907 was the guiding spirit of the Prussian *Cultus Ministerium*. A jurist and a bureaucrat, Althoff was especially interested in medicine; and to some extent at least, his general program was governed by his ideals of medical education and research. He strove with tireless energy and splendid success to equip all the faculties of the Prussian universities, so that they might, under modern conditions, realize and develop the conception of training and research which had been embodied in the University of Berlin at its origin. Althoff perceived, however, that even under ideal university conditions a small number of rare geniuses might squander in teaching or administration rare abilities that ought to be concentrated upon research. He was thus led to plan a series of institutes in which the most fertile minds might be devoted to research in fields in which fundamental progress had already been made — fields, in which the basic sciences had already attained definiteness and solidity, in which problems, theoretic as well as substantive, could be clearly formulated, in which personnel of high quality had already been trained. The feasibility of the research institute was thus pretty narrowly circumscribed. It does not follow that, because the research institute is feasible and timely in physics, chemistry, or medicine, it is either feasible or timely in less well developed fields of interest, however urgent the need.

The points just mentioned suggest at once the strength and the weakness of the research institute. The research institute is a sort of flying column, that can be directed hither or yon, wherever results seem attainable, wherever personnel of exceptional character is available. But so specific is the research institute that its particular activities depend on an individual or a small group. Whatever the institute be called, its energies centre about a person. The important things are not subjects, but persons; when the person goes, the subject goes. If a university chair is vacated, it must usually be filled — with a productive scholar and teacher if possible, with a scholar, at any rate, if a productive scholar is not obtainable. Not so, the research institute. In 1911, an institute of experimental therapeutics was set up at Dahlem for Wassermann; when Wassermann died in 1920, there was no successor, or the situation had changed. His institute was turned over to Professor Neuberg as an institute of bio-chemistry. What happened was not that one institute was abolished and another created; what really happened was that Wassermann died, and that Neuberg was enabled to carry on his own work. The research institute does not have to include all subjects within a definite field; it can demobilize as readily as mobilize. The university may have to employ makeshifts temporarily; the research institute, never.

From the standpoint of progress under favourable conditions, these are great advantages. But there are disadvantages. Forecasting in *The New Atlantis* a foundation aiming to obtain "the knowledge of causes," Bacon conceived an institution equipped with the paraphernalia of what we term research, including fellows and "novices and apprentices that the succession do not fail." The university has at hand a student body from which "novices and apprentices" may be drawn by professors who have had opportunity to ascertain their merits. The research institute, lacking a student body of its own, must seek out young men, possessed of ability and training. If financially strong, it can take the risk; but its "novices and apprentices" are rarely known at first hand, as they may easily be within the university.

Again, in the complexity of modern science, there is no telling from what source the magic fact or the magic conception will come. The very breadth of the university increases greatly its potential fertility. The research institute may therefore be hampered by limitations consequent upon intense concentration. Too highly specialized institutes, especially if somewhat practically minded, are likely to be fruitless. Althoff foresaw this danger. " If," says his recent biographer,[12] " the research institute is detached from the university and made directly accountable to the ministry, this idea must not be too narrowly interpreted. All these institutions serve the purposes of the university, namely, teaching and investigation. Indeed, the Prussian educational authorities are so strongly convinced of the soundness of the universities that all the most recent organizations are in some way or other more or less intimately connected with the universities." Thus a research institute, set up within or in connection with a modern university, might escape some of the limitations to which the isolated institute is exposed.

There is a further point on which I must touch. The research institute enjoys, I have said, the advantages of concentration and mobility. Yet Althoff was right in opposing a narrow conception. Too definite a conception or formulation may eliminate the element of surprise — important to both teaching and research. Both research institute and university laboratory are engaged in solving problems; both are engaged in training men. Is the head of a research division only seeking knowledge? By no means. He has about him a group of assistants — younger men whom he sifts and trains, precisely as does the university professor. His students are simply more advanced, more highly

[12] Arnold Sachse, *Friedrich Althoff und Sein Werk* (Berlin, 1928), p. 294.

selected. Thus the research institute might be described as a specialized and advanced university laboratory, enjoying certain marked advantages and not free from possible disadvantages. Successful research institutes are no substitute for universities. Indeed, they cannot succeed, unless universities furnish them a highly trained personnel — a debt, I hasten to add, which they repay as they give further training to men and women, many of whom become university teachers. Far more hopeful, in my opinion, than the rapid multiplication of research institutes at this moment would be the freeing of existing universities from inhibitions and encumbrances, and their development into instruments competent to perform well their proper functions.

XI

So much in general. I began by saying that in this chapter I should discuss the idea of a university that would answer the intellectual needs of this modern age. It is the idea, not the organization that I have been speaking of. To organization excessive importance is likely to be attributed. Nevertheless, organization or lack of organization is not entirely immaterial. We shall see in subsequent chapters how in one country excessive organization and in another poor organization obstruct the realization of the idea of a university. In all countries university reform is now the subject of earnest discussion. In all countries, history, traditions, vested interests hamper reconstruction. Obstacles are not always bad: a rich and beautiful past may interfere with reconstruction, while at the same time offering considerable compensation. When therefore the moment for action arises, one needs to view existing realities against the background of a clearly defined general principle. We shall find both conditions and possibilities highly varied — absurdities that may easily be eliminated, sharp corners that need to be cautiously turned, preconceptions that need to be vigorously combatted, historic values that must not be sacrificed, practical commitments that can only be gradually shifted to other agencies. In the end, when reconstruction has been achieved, we shall find ourselves not with a standardized, but with a very varied result — in no two countries alike, and total uniformity in not even one. Our chances of meeting the needs of modern life will be better, if we are content to accept anomalies and irregularities, though there are also anomalies and irregularities which are intolerable. The line is not easy to draw; different countries, different individuals may draw it in different places; but the precise point at which it is drawn is of relatively little importance, as long as the main function of the modernized university stands out with sufficient prominence.

PART II

AMERICAN UNIVERSITIES

I

STRUGGLE and instability are at this moment the striking characteristics of American life. Tradition — good and bad — is a stabilizing influence; America, for better as for worse, has practically no traditions either to retard progress or to uphold cultural ideals. Over the flat plains of the new world, breezes blow unchecked; no windbreak stops them or lessens their force. The mere fact that within a brief period millions of people mostly of humble origin, uprooted from their homes and released from repression of one sort or another, have occupied a vast and rich continent would to a considerable degree explain these phenomena. But when other facts are considered — the naïve notions of democracy, political, social, and intellectual, that were rapidly disseminated, the sudden and unprecedented flood of wealth, the dissolution of ethical and religious concepts, the complications created by the applications of modern science, and latterly the partial paralysis of Europe through war and consequent poverty — one cannot be surprised that America is a seething chaos, in which things get the better of ideas. It is idle to predict the future, even the near future, of America. No one can possibly tell whether America is going to make to civilization a contribution commensurate with its resources and opportunities. Undoubtedly, it is much to give comfort and opportunity of one kind or another to millions who otherwise would have enjoyed little of either.

But comfort, opportunity, numbers, and size are not synonymous with civilization — not even essential to it; if they were, New York and Chicago would be more civilized than Florence, Paris, Berlin, London, or Oxford — which is assuredly not the case. " Size," writes an acute English critic, " is an uninteresting kind of variation, to which, if the spirit is not actually insensible, it does not care to respond." [1] Not a few Europeans, visiting America, fail to grasp this point. They are suddenly aware of unfamiliar and general hope and well-being; here and there they perceive noble buildings, innumerable conveniences, a few institutes of research, a few galleries, and call America "wonderful." And most Americans take the same view. A minority, however, increasingly vocal and ironic, weary of kaleidoscopic change, exhausted by the pulsations of restless, bounding, and over-confident energy, and missing the solid cultural foundations of European society, are less disposed to identify civilization with continuous bustle, momentary prosperity, and increasing numbers.

Differences of opinion about America are thus not unknown in America. The huge scale upon which operations are conducted — in business, in education, and otherwise — and the rapid development of the " science " of advertising make for standardization and uniformity at a relatively low spiritual level. On the other hand, there is comfort to be derived from noting that no social bar blocks ability in any direction, and that protest is louder, individuality more fearless and assertive, precisely because of the closer

---

[1] J. Middleton Murry, *The Evolution of an Intellectual* (London, 1927), p. 184. Mr. Murry proceeds, " Forty miles of calico is not really a more worthy object of enthusiasm than half a yard; and if the calico happens to be infamously printed — *occidit miseros*. It is the variations of quality that matter."

organization of material interests, precisely because of the disheartening prominence and tiresomeness of Wall Street, Main Street, Middletown, porcelain tubs, central heating, motor cars, efficiency, and Mr. Babbitt. However the battle seems for the moment to be going, thoughtful Americans more and more vigorously insist that reason shall be heard in determining the direction in which America shall develop. Their task is both easier and harder than that of progressive leaders in other countries: easier, enormously easier, because tradition, caste, and lack of funds do not combine to oppose them; harder, enormously harder, because in the absence of any possibility of centralized and intelligently directed authority and the lack of institutions which possess and may be counted on to maintain ideals, America must flounder in, and perhaps ultimately out of, chaos.

Thoughtful America, I say, assumes consciously or unconsciously that knowledge and reason may be factors in determining the direction of our evolution. In the increase of knowledge, in bringing reason into play, in setting up and maintaining genuine distinctions, the university is or ought to be the most important of all agencies. The status and character of American universities are therefore a fairer index of the status and prospects of American civilization at the moment than are population, battleships, skyscrapers, aeroplanes, or the annual production of pig-iron.

II

I shall have much to say in criticism of American universities. For that very reason, I begin on an appreciative note. Scholars we have always had — usually stranded in the old-fashioned college, the ministry, or the law. But a university in the sense in which I use the term — an institution consciously devoted to the pursuit of knowledge, the solution of problems, the critical appreciation of achievement, and the training of men at a really high level — a university in this sense we did not possess until the Johns Hopkins University modestly opened its portals in 1876. That is slightly more than fifty years ago. A half century ago, therefore, the opportunities for advanced or critical training in America were very scarce and very limited. The change, since that day, has been amazing, immensely to the credit of a people that within a few generations has had to subdue a continent, create a social and political order, maintain its unity, and invent educational, philanthropic, sanitary, and other agencies capable of functioning at all. Higher opportunities have within this brief period become abundant — less abundant, I think, than external appearances frequently indicate, yet abundant in almost every direction — in the older disciplines, in the newer, in the professions and in state-supported as well as in endowed institutions. Sums of which no one could then have dreamed have been assembled; buildings, apparatus, books have been provided. The country cannot, of course, dispense with Europe; but in the realm of higher education America has become in certain fields a country with which Europe cannot any longer dispense, either. I shall go into details as I proceed. But this categorical statement I make now at the outset, in order that the reader may know that, however severely I reprobate many of the doings of our universities, I do full justice to their solid achievements. Perhaps candid criticism may help them to regain the main road.

I have already emphasized strongly the importance of adjustment. Every age, every country, has its unique concrete needs and purposes. For that reason, there can be no uniform university type, persisting through the ages, transferable from one country to another. Every age does its own creating and re-shaping; so does every country. But we are not therefore left to meaningless flux. There are intellectual standards by which *quality* may be judged. Subjects change; problems change; activities change. But ideas and quality abide. The difference between froth and depth, between material and immaterial, between significant and insignificant — that difference persists. In general, as I pointed out, universities have, in fact, over long periods of time, adjusted themselves to the genuine needs and pressure of life; occasionally they have taken the lead, and society has had to quicken its pace in order to adjust itself to them; this, as we shall see, was conspicuously true of Germany in the nineteenth century. Within a given university, one finds inevitably at a given moment both adjustment and maladjustment, both leading and lagging. The American university, closely in contact with the phenomena and personalities of the moment, and situated in the midst of a materialistic society, has been in a singularly exposed position. It was, on the whole, bound to respond to pressure and need — even though the survival of individuals in important posts retarded adaptation here and there. The danger was not that in the long run the American university would be an obstacle, that it would not respond. The danger was that a sound sense of values would not or could not be preserved. I may say at once that there lies the gist of my criticism: a sound sense of values has not been preserved within American universities. That I might not be misunderstood, I began by saying that they offer today facilities and opportunities for scholarly and scientific work of the highest quality, such as not even the most sanguine could have predicted a generation ago. They have responded, as was right and sound, to the call and pressure of the age. But this is not all they have done. They have thoughtlessly and excessively catered to fleeting, transient, and immediate demands; they have mistaken the relative importance to civilization of things and ideas; they have failed, and they are, in my opinion, more and more failing to distinguish between ripples and waves. " The gods approve the depth and not the tumult of the soul." The American university is becoming more and more tumultuous. Our universities have then, I say, increased their genuine facilities and opportunities; they have simultaneously and needlessly cheapened, vulgarized, and mechanized themselves. Perhaps the phenomena I have in mind are transient — mere symptoms developed on the way to something better. Suppose they are; for our generation at least they are serious and disquieting. Are we to follow the line of least resistance, or are we to take a hand in determining, as far as we can, the character and quality of American civilization? Feeble as our abilities may be, when pitted against the powerful current of events, I am all for the latter course — for endeavouring by deliberate effort to modify to our liking the character and quality of our civilization. Indeed, universities exist, partly at least, in order that they may influence the direction in which thinking and living move. I do not wish to minimize the extent to which American scholars are doing this very thing. But often in the same universities men are doing precisely the opposite — encouraging forces that should be restrained, making infinitely harder the task of those who cherish humane and civilized ideals, making much more doubtful the ultimate outcome. " And for this," as Socrates said, " I may gently chide them."

IV

The term " university" is very loosely used in America; I shall not pause to characterize the absurdities covered by the name. I propose, rather, to concentrate attention on the most highly developed and prominent of American institutions, to ask what they do, how they are constituted, how they fare from the standpoint of the ideal which I have set up. As for the others — and they run into the hundreds — it is impossible in this volume to take them into account; fine minds and souls will be found here and there in them; many of them, more especially in the South and West — though the East is not free — are hotbeds of reaction in politics, industry, and religion, ambitious in pretension, meagre in performance, doubtful contributors, when they are not actual obstacles, to the culture of the nation.

The great American universities which I shall discuss are composed of three parts: they are secondary schools and colleges for boys and girls; graduate and professional schools for advanced students; " service " stations for the general public. The three parts are not distinct: the college is confused with the " service " station and overlaps the graduate school; the graduate school is partly a college, partly a vocational school, and partly an institution of university grade. For the sake of simplicity, however, I shall ex-

[45]

amine each part separately; later we can observe the strange ways in which they mingle and the effect of this intermingling.

V

The American college reproduced the English college as it existed " at a time when the university in England was eclipsed by its constituent colleges." [2] It was, and has to this day remained, a *teaching* institution, largely at the secondary level. We cannot, however, understand the secondary school work of the American college or university, unless we understand the American high school. And this is no easy task, for the American high school is greatly lacking in uniformity, varying in size, for example, from a staff of three or four teachers — and most American high schools belong to this category — to a staff of a hundred teachers or more. Amazing to relate, also, the staff of three will offer courses of study that on paper bear much resemblance in respect of substance and extent to the courses offered by the staff numbering a hundred. At one time viewed as the people's college, the high school is apparently coming to be a place where an increasingly large segment of American youth can get a little knowledge of almost every imaginable subject, practical, often in the most trivial sense, or cultural, sometimes in the best sense. Subject-matter, like Latin, mathematics, or history, and skills, like typewriting or cooking, are ingeniously combined on an utterly fallacious theory into " units," " points," and " counts "; [3] and when by a

[2] C. H. Haskins, *The Rise of Universities* (New York, 1923), p. 30.

[3] " Count " and " credit " are Americanisms: the words mean that a given subject has been studied in class so many hours a week for so many weeks or months; at the end of the period, a written examination is held. Students who pass have finished with the subject — usually for good and

simple arithmetical process enough "points" have been accumulated and enough hours and years been consumed in the process, the pupil has received "a four-year high school education." Calculation by means of arithmetically added "points" serves, unintentionally, greatly to reduce intellectual effort. The four-year course is first broken up into bits; it is easier to master bits than to master a whole; the credits accumulate from year to year. "*Divide et impera.*" The prevailing philosophy of education tends to discredit hard work. Individuality must be respected. Undoubtedly. The child's creative possibilities must be allowed to unfold. Certainly. But by the time several such considerations have come into play, discipline through effort has been relegated to a very subordinate position.

The high school used to be a sieve of a certain kind. But American democracy objects to sieves. Would not selection and distribution of students on the basis of industry, ability, and capacity to go forward on intellectual lines be democratic? Most certainly, yes. Yet the high school cannot be democratic in this sense. It is, on the contrary, a kind of bargain-counter on which a generous public and an overworked and underpaid teaching staff display every variety of merchandise — Latin, Greek, science, agriculture, busi-

---

all. They are hardly likely to hear of it again and are free to forget all about it. Most American high schools and colleges determine achievement and fitness for the degree on this basis, though a reaction is taking place.

When a college catalogue states that fifteen units of high school work are required for matriculation, a unit, as defined by the College Entrance Examination Board, represents one year's study in any one subject in a high school, constituting approximately a quarter of a full year's work. A four years' high school course yields sixteen units. Fifteen units are required for entrance to most colleges. What relation is there between the arithmetical accumulation of fifteen more or less disjoined units and "education"?

ness, stenography, domestic arts — leaving the student, with such advice and direction as he may get from teachers, parents, and college matriculation requirements, free to piece together, under restrictions that sometimes amount to much and sometimes to little, a course of study that by the end of four years will yield "counts" or "units of credit" enough to win a diploma or to enable him to satisfy the entrance requirements of the college of his choice. In this little matter, the university is not above helping him; as if the university did not have enough to do anyway, institutions like Wisconsin and Chicago offer extension or home study courses of high school grade which prepare for regular matriculation, though no particular standard is set up for the extension or home study students.[4]

Undoubtedly the free American high school has its good points. Sir Michael Sadler has recently declared that it is the most important single contribution to modern social life. It represents a laudable ambition — the ambition to keep children from drifting into blind alleys, industrially or economically. It is part of the great American melting pot; it is socially and physically wholesome. And the social development of American youth represents a solid contribution to educational philosophy and practice, for if American youth can be kept sane and wholesome, we may

[4] Written permission from the Director of Admissions must be procured at Columbia. The Home Study Department of Columbia advertises as follows: "Our Home Study Department offers complete high school and college preparatory training through courses covering the equivalent of four years of high school study." New York *Times*, July 20, 1930. The Home Study Department of the University of Chicago announces (1929–30): "Rarely is it necessary to examine an applicant for a home study course or to require proof of his previous training." (p. 7) "A student may do any number of the 15 units (of high school work required for admission to the University) through the Home Study Department" (p. 11).

avoid the social rift which is the great problem with which German educators are wrestling today. The importance of identifying school and society needed emphasizing a generation ago, as Professor Dewey perceived;[5] it needs no reiteration today. " Americans are boys," says Professor de Madariaga,[6] including even the grown-ups. The schools could well for the present direct their emphasis to another quarter. Of course, there are even now high schools and high school teachers that value brains and scholarship; high schools admirably equipped and well conducted; and in any event it is a great and hitherto unheard of achievement to keep the door open for all classes of the population for four years — from thirteen to seventeen — as the high school does. But the high school is too elementary, too broken up, and too miscellaneous to constitute for most students anything more than an elementary education. As to the quality of the achievement, no nation has ever so completely deceived itself. The present United States Commissioner of Education has just assured the assembled superintendents of the entire country[7] that the whole world is following in the wake of the United States; have we not introduced the radio and the " talkies " into the schools? Is not the percentage of the school population attending high schools several times as large as that in any other country? But what would happen to these statistics if the incompetently manned schools were dropped, as they should be, and if dabbling at cooking and typewriting were not reckoned as of equal importance with history or literature or science? Taxation for education has indeed gone

[5] John Dewey, *The School and Society* (Chicago, 1900).

[6] In a brilliant paper under the title, *Americans Are Boys* (*Harper's Magazine*, July 1928).

[7] See New York *Times*, Feb. 25, 1930.

forward by leaps and bounds; buildings and equipment have generally improved. None the less there are few states and still fewer large cities — though fortunately there are a few — in which the conduct of education is not tainted by politics and favouritism. And the largest cities are the worst. The schools of New York and Chicago are bedraggled in the mire.[8] There are, I have gladly admitted, here and there men and women on the superintending and teaching staffs who are cultivated and well educated. In strange ways, industry, ability, a fine spirit, and scholarship occasionally appear in a sea of mediocrity and incompetence; but it is unpardonable misrepresentation to attribute these characteristics to even a considerable portion of the rapidly changing teaching staff. In a vague way the general public wants education and believes in it; but of its difficulties and severities it has no comprehension. The inferiority of the product becomes obvious later, when a discriminating college professor or employer takes his lamp, like Diogenes, and starts the search for a high school or college graduate, who can write and spell,[9] and who is master of the elements of mathematics, a science, or a modern language.[10] There is no need to be surprised at this

[8] An upright and fearless Superintendent of Schools of Chicago, Mr. William McAndrew, has been recently driven from office by a shameless political intrigue; an equally courageous and intelligent district superintendent, demoted a few years ago because he had displayed courage and intelligence, Dr. John L. Tildsley, has exposed the shockingly low academic standards of the New York City schools — due largely, in his opinion, to "politics."

[9] "I have seen some English written by university students and even by graduate students which would have been severely criticized in an English elementary school." Edwin Deller, *Universities in the United States* (London, 1927), p. 36.

[10] All the tests made of the scholarship of the high school pupil concur in showing the inferiority of the product. See the examples cited by Professor Briggs, optimistic though he is. T. H. Briggs, *The Inglis Lecture, 1930* (Harvard University Press, 1930), pp. 124–136.

showing. It could not have been very different; trained teachers and intelligent parents supporting them could not possibly have been procured within a generation in a country teeming with material attractions; perhaps one ought not even to be discouraged; nor would one be, if one saw anything like a concerted effort on the part of the leading universities to uphold the essentially intellectual character of the educative process.

It is urged and rightly that the American high school cannot imitate the continental secondary school; it cannot concern itself merely with a limited group in pursuit of certain definite and highly respected ends. An increasingly large body of boys and girls wish a high school education, and they wish it for an ever greater variety of purposes. In a democratic country, this demand cannot and must not be ignored. But our school men fail, I think, to perceive another point. Let us grant that our high schools must do some things, with which European schools are not yet so deeply concerned. It is also true that European schools do something with which we Americans need to be greatly concerned. In our efforts to satisfy the varied and changeable tastes and needs of the many, we have for the time being to a considerable degree lost sight of the importance of solid and coherent — though not inflexible — training of the able. We have tried to include in the high school curriculum — we shall later learn that universities are liable to the same criticism — every kind of subject and activity, intellectual, vocational, and technical. It cannot be done; or it can only be done at the expense of genuine education. Thus the American high school is neither intelligent, selective, nor thorough; and it is the high school graduates of a given June — mostly untrained, mostly unselected, mostly equipped with discursive knowledge in a score of subjects, many of which possess no intellectual and practically no vocational value — it is these high school graduates of June, plus those furnished by extension and correspondence courses, who become the college students of the following autumn.

V I

The number of students who seek to enter college is far in excess of the number that can be admitted. Colleges therefore try to select. But it cannot be effectively done. In the first place, the colleges do not know what they wish: do they wish brains? do they wish industry? do they wish scholarship? do they wish character, or do they wish "qualities that fit for leadership" ? They swing blindly and helplessly from one to another. Even if they knew, they could not get what they wish. The high school is such a welter of subjects and activities, the high school teaching staff is so largely occupied in teaching subjects that the teachers themselves do not know,[11] that grading and certificates are well-nigh meaningless. Unable to rely on high school records of achievement or upon entrance examinations, lacking any reliable contact with high schools at large, the colleges are now experimenting with psychological tests. The experiments are regarded as hopeful and promising. Perhaps. But American educators so commonly count unhatched chickens that it may be as well to wait before becoming too enthusiastic.

The collegiate function of the American university

[11] E. A. Fitzpatrick and P. W. Hutson, *The Scholarship of Teachers in Secondary Schools* (New York, 1927).

has to do with the group which I have just described. They remain four years; they get during these four years for the most part the same sort of education that they got in the high school, though at a higher level, because they are older and know more. Another bargain-counter period is lived through in the college. On the counter, the student finds once more almost every imaginable article — Latin, Greek, history, science, business, journalism, domestic arts, engineering, agriculture, military training, and a miscellaneous aggregation of topics and activities that defy general characterization. Subject to a few more restrictions, latterly becoming in some institutions more rigid, and operating, though not always, at a higher level, he again nibbles at a confusing variety of " courses " — four months of this, six weeks of that, so many hours of this, so many hours of that, so many points here, so many there, with little, though happily increasing, continuity of purpose from year to year, until again, at the close of four years, he has won the number of " credits " or " points " that entitle him to the bachelor's degree. The sort of easy rubbish which may be counted towards an A.B. degree or the so-called combined degrees passes the limits of credibility. Education — college education, liberal education, call it what you will — should, one might suppose, concern itself primarily during adolescence and early manhood and womanhood with the liberation, organization, and direction of power and intelligence, with the development of taste, with *culture* — a perfectly good word that has unfortunately become odious in the ears of the professional educator in America — on the assumption that a trained mind, stored with knowledge, will readily enough find itself even in our complex world; that there are many things that do not

[53]

require teaching at all; and that there are many things of technical nature which may require teaching, but surely not in a college or university.

I shall not fail to point out the fact that a reaction against quantitative measurements, according to which an hour spent in military drill is as educative as an hour spent on calculus, has set in and that there are happily colleges which, while thoroughly alive and progressive, have not lost sight of cultural distinctions.[12] But for an overwhelming majority of colleges and college students the brief description I have given still holds.

VII

Once admitted to college, the student spends two years or more on work that should be included in a good high school — and is so included in countries whose secondary schools are soundly developed and staffed. Without, however, dwelling upon this point in this connection, I wish in the first place to emphasize the fact that an earnest student at, we will say, Columbia College, finds there ample opportunity to study science, mathematics, language, literature, history, philosophy, economics — indeed almost every imaginable subject of sound intellectual value — under competent and at times highly distinguished teachers and in reach of admirable laboratory and library facilities. To be sure, at the end of four years, when the students emerge as bachelors of arts or science, even those who have done their best usually betray signs of their inferior preliminary education or their barren environment. But in any event, Columbia College has done for the best of them all that it could. Here it should stop. Does it stop? By no means. The

[12] See pp. 64, 66–67.

process of adulteration and dilution began, as I have pointed out, before the student entered: the undergraduate student may have been enabled to satisfy a considerable portion of the matriculation requirements by extension courses or by correspondence courses taken under the Home Study Department.[13] Doubtless, now and then, an earnest student may safely dispense with continuous, full-time schooling; but it is absurd to suppose that to the hordes of extension and home study students registered at Columbia any such opportunity can be offered without lowering of standard, no matter what entrance examinations and psychological tests are subsequently employed. Abuse does not, however, end here. I have said that a student of Columbia College may study serious subjects in a serious fashion. But he may also complete the requirements for a bachelor's degree by including in his course of study "principles of advertising," "the writing of advertised copy," "advertising layouts," * " advertising research," "practical poultry raising," * " secretarial booking," * "business English," " elementary stenography," "newspaper practice," "reporting and copy editing," "feature writing," "book reviewing," "wrestling, judo and self-defence." * If an advanced student in the School of Practical Arts, he may count towards a Columbia degree courses taken in Teachers College — an independent corporation belonging to Columbia — " in cookery — fundamental processes," "fundamental problems in clothing," "clothing decoration," "family meals," "recent research in cookery," "food etiquette and hospitality," "principles of home laundering," "social life of the

---

[13] See Note 4, p. 48.

* Starred courses may be counted for degrees only if the approval of the dean or director has been previously obtained.

home," "gymnastics and dancing for men including practice in clog dancing," and "instruction (elementary or advanced) in school orchestras and bands."

Is not this an appalling situation? By the hundreds, crude, poorly taught, eager boys and girls eighteen to twenty years of age resort to Columbia to be educated. In the main it is of no importance what they think they want. The question is — what do they need? They need a solid, cultural secondary education. If they cannot be educated in this sense, if they cannot be intellectually and spiritually aroused and directed, they have no business at Columbia at all; they had better be at work learning a trade or a craft — where or how, is not Columbia's concern. Columbia College is not a vocational school; vocational training may be ever so important, but the confusion of all sorts of training — vocational, domestic, scientific, cultural, in high school and college — harms all alike and harms the highest most of all. It is defended on the ground already mentioned that America is a democratic country, which, for large social reasons, ignores distinctions. But America does not ignore all distinctions. It simply ignores the real distinctions; and not all the weight of its wealth and numbers can place cooking and wrestling and typewriting on an intellectual par with music, science, literature, and economics, or make it sound educational procedure to jumble them together.

In so far as business or journalism is concerned, Columbia can do nothing for undergraduates that is worth their time and money. Both are worse than wasted. For undergraduates do not even learn the tricks of business and journalism, though, in so far as they try, they fail to make a profitable use of the real opportunities for education which Columbia undeniably possesses. Does Columbia University, embodiment and protector of intellectual and spiritual ideals, tell them this? Not at all! It takes their money, consumes their time, and at the end of three or four years bestows upon them a bachelor's degree that represents neither a substantial secondary education nor a substantial vocational training. To be sure, there are, I repeat, those who have not been misled — who have worked at subjects that are worth while, under teachers able and earnest, though the unit and credit system makes it incredibly difficult to do so. But how does that help those who have obtained undergraduate degrees by working at subjects not worth while, under teachers not themselves really educated? And what sort of contribution is Columbia making towards a clearer apprehension of what education really is on the part of this conglomerate nation of ours, so sorely in need of illumination as to relative and genuine values when it admits that cooking and typewriting are proper training for an undergraduate degree?

One might suppose that Columbia College would find its problems with campus students of arts, business, and journalism sufficiently perplexing; for these problems have not been solved and are not even on the way to solution. But what of it? The University has an uneven teaching staff, an impossible and absurd teaching program, and inadequate funds. What is the remedy? Expansion! Achieving in New York City a limited success — the only sort of success, I grant, that is now possible — Columbia invades Brooklyn and requires the already over-burdened officers on Morningside Heights in New York to administer the newly formed Seth Low Junior College across the river, with a curriculum extensive enough to admit students after two years to any one of a dozen schools — professional, technical, or liberal — in the University itself. But not even thus is the administrative skill of the University officials or the pedagogical efficiency of the University ideals strained. Ninety-five miles from New York City an insignificant little college — St. Stephen's by name, one of hundreds scattered through the country, is gasping for breath. "The faculty and students wear the Oxford undergraduate gown to chapel, classes, and other official exercises " — the gown, by the way, *must* be purchased from the college store at the price of $8.00 — a subtle compliment by which Oxford's cool heart may well be thrilled! This remote seat of college education, long isolated " on the top of hills, overlooking the Catskill Mountains," now nestles snugly in the capacious bosom of Columbia University. Since July 1, 1928, it has " become an undergraduate college of Columbia University on a parity with Columbia College and Barnard College. The bachelor's degree granted will be that of Columbia University." But it is expressly stipulated that " the University is under no implied obligation, responsibility, or liability of any kind whatsoever, for the maintenance, support, direction, or management of St. Stephen's College or for the disbursement of the income thereof." The Columbia degree is thus bestowed upon students belonging to a remote institution " for the maintenance, direction, or management " of which Columbia expressly repudiates all responsibility! And this degree is "on a parity " with the degrees conferred by Columbia University upon students who, so to speak, work under its nose in Barnard College and Columbia College! A New York newspaper,[14] commenting on Columbia's

[14] The New York *Herald-Tribune*.

"Empire," intelligently remarks: "Columbia is already so various and conglomerate that one unit more or less cannot make much difference." And if Columbia's collegiate ideals, without financial or educational responsibility on the part of Columbia University, can thus subtly permeate remote colleges, one can readily understand that "there is not the least reason why a university should be confined to a single school of law, of medicine, or of engineering."[15] Not the least! Thus through Columbia and, as we shall see, the medical schools of the University of Chicago the "chain-store" concept enters the field of higher education in the United States.

VIII

Although Columbia is a flagrant, it is not by any means the only, offender. Fifteen "units" are required for admission to the Colleges of the University of Chicago, of which more than one-fourth (one, two, three, or four units) may be made up of stenography, typewriting, and bookkeeping — what a preparation for the intelligent use, cultural or professional, of four college years! Home economics and agriculture — as taught in high schools — are also "accepted." Now, to be frank, there is no more sense in "counting" stenography and bookkeeping towards college matriculation than there would be in counting manicuring, hair-bobbing, or toe-dancing. One has as much to do with intelligence and taste as another. In so far as these subjects "count," the University of Chicago admits to its college students who present eleven, instead of fifteen "points" — a calamitous situation, destructive of all uniformity or elevation of standard.

[15] *Columbia University Bulletin of Information, Report of the President, 1928,* p. 25.

Moreover, like Columbia, the University of Chicago is not above competing with the high schools of the state by offering correspondence courses of high school grade for matriculation. Of correspondence courses I shall speak more fully later; but at a time when the state is entirely capable of providing elementary and high school education, why should the University of Chicago complicate its own machinery and lower its dignity — for there really is such a thing as dignity in the intellectual realm — by accepting " credits," up to the full amount required for matriculation, obtained through correspondence work in bookkeeping, elementary French, Spanish, or German, elementary algebra, and other subjects? It must be a rare experience to listen to the pronunciation of a foreign language by a boy or girl who has qualified for matriculation in the University of Chicago by correspondence! Once admitted as candidates for a bachelor's degree, students may, as at Columbia, devote themselves to serious cultural or intellectual effort, for which, as at Columbia, the University provides abundantly. But it also provides and accepts for a bachelor's degree courses that belong in technical and vocational schools, not in a university — not even in a sound secondary school. With even greater consistency and liberality than prevails at Columbia, which does not count home study courses towards degrees, though they " are kept strictly up to the standard of those given in the classrooms of the University," [16] one-half of the "units" requisite to a bachelor's degree may be obtained by home study — among them numerous practical, cultural, and theoretic courses to which I shall shortly recur.

[16] Announcement 1927–28, p. 12.

IX

When endowed institutions, priding themselves that they are "pace-setters" in the realm of college education, so far forget themselves as to abandon education during the fruitful years of adolescence for such stuff, it is small wonder that state universities, dependent on taxation and "results," follow suit. The University of Wisconsin counts towards an A.B. degree courses in "newspaper reporting," "copy reading," "retail advertising," "community newspaper," and towards a B.S. degree courses in "nursing," "drug-store practice," "first aid to injured," "community recreation," "kinesiology," "elementary costume design," and "principles of coaching." The undergraduate student may indeed devote his time and energy to subjects of real substance, but he may also squander a large part of these precious and irretrievable years on the merest trifles — on "business letter-writing," "marketing methods," "sales administration," "retail advertising," "national advertising campaigns," "principles of journalism," "elementary pottery," "employe and leadership training problems," etc.[17] In order that he may be aware in advance of the pitfalls that menace the fullest enjoyment of these educational opportunities, the University officially greets the incoming freshman with a booklet of information [18] in which he is told that his "landlady" will "in nine cases out of ten" be "a right good sort, if you will play fairly with her." He is warned against loafing, cribbing, profanity, gambling, drinking, and lewdness — for a "skirt-chaser

[17] The recent White House Conference on Child Health and Protection suggests "Training for Parenthood" as a new college field. See Educational Supplement of the New York *Times*, July 13, 1930.
[18] Called *The Gray Book*.

is the scorn of a genuine he-man." Finally, "the up-to-the-minute den of iniquity, the more subtle and more vicious successor of the old time saloon is the modern roadhouse," which "caters to hippers." [19] From what sort of people do the students of the University of Wisconsin come? What high schools have they attended? What kind of parents and friends do they have? With what purposes or ideals do they seek the University?

Is it strange that the general American public is utterly at sea as to what education is, as to what purpose the college serves, as to where the line should be drawn between mere tricks, vocational training, practical experience, and intellectual development, when great universities descend to such humbug as to confer the degree of Bachelor of Arts or Bachelor of Science on the terms above described? For I am now speaking not of technical or professional education [20] superimposed upon the general education for which the college is responsible, but of undergraduate substitutes and equivalents for the college of arts and science on a par with the college of arts and science itself. Those responsible for the demoralization of the American college are not only lacking in intellectual rectitude, but — what is even more disastrous — they are utterly lacking in a sense of humour. Most of the absurdities which I have instanced need no teaching facilities at all; some of them might be taught to per-

---

[19] The word " hippers " does not find a place in the great Oxford Dictionary. For the benefit of some Americans and all non-Americans I must explain that a " hipper " is a person who carries a flask of whisky in the hip pocket of his trousers. In view of the use of such language in official documents and student publications, one may cease to marvel at the fact that the graduate of an American college rarely speaks or writes his native language with fluency, refinement, or dignity.

[20] With these departments as technical or professional schools, I deal later. See pp. 85 ff.

sons of inferior intelligence or deficient background in unpretentious technical schools; none of them deserves recognition by a college and least of all does any of them deserve a place in an institution of learning.

It seems to me no answer to say that those who so wish may still pursue the even tenor of their way. Can the intellectuals be really best trained cheek by jowl with students who may veer off into flimsy undergraduate courses in business or journalism? Is there no incongruity or incompatibility between the pursuit of culture and *ad hoc* training for a simple job? Do not teachers as well as students suffer, when simultaneously they address both? Utter idlers one might bear lightly; they do no more harm than empty benches; but the mixture of students of history or Greek with green reporters and immature bond salesmen is intolerable. An English writer, recalling his life at Eton, has raised the question as to whether it is possible " for brain to be stimulated and character fortified in one place, at one time, by the care of one and the same society of men. . . . If you look at them separately, . . . you may conclude that it is in their very nature to fly asunder." [21] Mr. Lubbock would take heart as to Eton, were he familiar with the Japanese juggling required of the college instructor in the United States, compelled, as he is, to keep not two, but a dozen balls in the air at once.

X

It is gratifying to be able to record the fact that there are American colleges which have not succumbed to nonsense. Harvard — I am now speaking

[21] Percy Lubbock, *Shades of Eton* (London, 1920), p. 219.

of the college work alone in all the institutions which
I am about to name — Yale, Princeton, Swarthmore,
Vanderbilt, Amherst, Williams, Barnard, Bryn
Mawr, Smith, and Wellesley, to select a small number
at random — give no credit towards admission or
graduation for any of the absurd courses which I have
above mentioned; they all offer a varied and solid cultural curriculum to undergraduate students who may
care to be educated. No premature or trivial vocational
studies confuse the pursuit of a liberal education.
Even these institutions are, to be sure, not free from
weaknesses — avoidable and unavoidable. They are
compelled to accept as college students graduates of
the high schools and preparatory schools which are
largely ineffective as training institutions; that they
cannot help. In the main the student body lacks intellectual background or outlook; that again they
cannot help. Their students are in the mass devoid
of cultural interests and develop little, for the most
part, during their four years at college; it is difficult
to say what they can or should do about that, though
increasing disquiet is at least a good sign. Where class
instruction is pursued, the classes are usually too
large; the young instructor's time is too largely consumed in correcting and grading papers, most of which
are badly written.[22] With certain important exceptions
which I shall mention later,[23] the colleges count points
and units and credits — an abominable system, destructive of disinterested and protracted intellectual
effort; any one of them could abolish it root and
branch without notice. They are all mad on the subject of competitive and intercollegiate athletics — too

[22] I have lately asked one of the most promising of our younger Greek
scholars, how many of his Greek students are " worth while." " Of graduate
students," he answered, " none; of undergraduates, less than 10%."
[23] See pp. 66–67.

timid to tell their respective alumni that excessive interest in intercollegiate athletics is proof of the cultural mediocrity of the college graduate, and a source of continuous demoralization to successive college classes, not a few members of which are forced to simulate an interest they do not feel. The colleges cannot except very slowly improve the secondary schools, for their own graduates — not usually the most vigorous, scholarly, or ambitious — become high school teachers; they cannot rapidly improve the quality of their own faculties, for that depends on education, salaries, and social prestige — all slow and difficult to change; but they could, given the courage and intelligence, frankly tell the world that their problem is infinitely complicated by giving loose rein to the athletic orgy in order to amuse and placate a populace, largely consisting of their own graduates.[24] There is not a college or university in America which has the courage to place athletics where every one perfectly well knows they belong. On the contrary, as we shall see, proportionately more money is spent on college athletics than on any legitimate college activity.[25] The football coach is better known to the student body and the general public than the president; and professors are, on the average, less highly remunerated. Does the college or university have to endure this? Of course not. But it does more than endure: it " advertises." At two of the most prominent crossings in Chicago, two years or more ago, huge painted sign boards fifteen feet high and fifty feet long were displayed, of which the following (page 66) is a reduced copy:

[24] See, for detailed evidence on this subject, *Carnegie Foundation for the Advancement of Teaching, American College Athletics, Bulletin Number Twenty-three.*
[25] See p. 206.

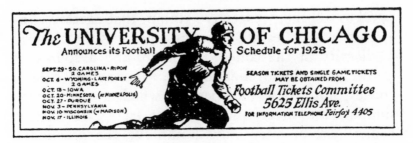

These advertisements were exhibited for two and a half months and cost the University $500 a month each.[26] Does the university tolerate an unavoidable evil or exploit a demoralizing appetite?

XI

I have just said that a few American colleges are endeavouring to break away from the absurd computation of degrees by arithmetical means and to encourage both concentration and scholarship. On paper, the number of institutions that have thus instituted "honours" work is impressively large; but the number so situated, financially or otherwise, as to be able to do it well, is relatively small. Without intending the list to be complete, special attention may be called to Swarthmore, Harvard, certain departments of Columbia, Barnard, Bryn Mawr, Smith, and the Experimental College at Wisconsin, as institutions in which by one method or another the more earnest or better endowed students are enabled to escape the deadly lockstep of the classroom, the deadly grip of the unit system, and to focus their energies on a limited field in close contact with the more competent instructors. Swarthmore, a small college, admitting annually about one hundred

[26] The expense is paid out of gate receipts, but this does not affect my point.

and seventy-five students, having made the most careful selection possible from over a thousand applicants, devotes, because it cannot be helped, as much as two years to patching, disciplining, and sorting out the student body before it can give during the last two years independence and concentrated opportunity to a small segregated group, known as candidates for honours; at the end of the last two years, external examiners pass upon their merits. Harvard has in many subjects appointed tutors, who direct the reading of the abler students and by means of a " comprehensive examination " force the student to read more widely than the " courses " above criticized. I do not imply that salvation lies only on this road. Just as one may make out a case for the tutor, so one may also make out a case for the lecture by means of which William James addressed a large group, some members of which certainly persisted in the study of philosophy — as, without such stimulus, they probably would not have done. There is no single, no royal road to knowledge, education, or culture; there is no single best way to teach at any stage. Over and above the colleges I have named, there are other institutions, some of them modest and inconspicuous where able students may obtain an education that runs beyond, sometimes far beyond, the secondary stage. But in the mass, it is still true that American college students are, at the close of four years, intellectually considered, an unselected and untrained body of attractive boys and girls, who have for the most part not yet received even a strenuous secondary school training.[27] Surely the Dean of Columbia College knows American college youth. " I am convinced," he has recently said, " that

[27] " I think that our French student works harder than the American student," remarked M. Henri Bergson on the occasion of a recent visit to American universities.

the youth of college age at the present time are as immature morally and as crude socially as they are undeveloped intellectually." In part this is true because, the high school having coddled them, the college continues the coddling process. Every jerk and shock must be eliminated; the students must be " oriented "; they must be " advised " as to what to " take "; they must be vocationally guided. How is it possible to educate persons who will never be permitted to burn their fingers, who must be dexterously and expensively housed, first as freshmen, then as upper classmen, so as to make the right sort of social connections and to establish the right sort of social relationships, who are protected against risk as they should be protected against plague, and who, even though " they work their way through," have no conception of the effort required to develop intellectual sinew?

XII

Some of the reasons for the low quality of college education I have already given, but there is one more, reflective of the tone and spirit of American life that is especially important. The American wants to get ahead; that is why our parents or grandparents emigrated to America. They were against a stone wall in their respective native countries. Hence, they came to America. They did get ahead, and they have bequeathed to their children some money and in an intense form the same motive. The children want to get ahead not only in respect to money, but in respect to other things, some of them dependent on the possession of a surplus; they want to gratify all the impulses that their parents could not gratify in the old world; they want friends, travel, power, amusement, excitement, position, education, self-development. Getting ahead intellectually is a simple matter if one has brains; hence the minority, endowed with brains and purpose, stick to their books and do actually get genuine intellectual advantages in the American college-university. But to get ahead in other ways one needs friends, contacts, social or athletic distinction. College is preëminently a place where one makes friends and contacts — partly through studies pursued in common, partly through clubs, societies, and fraternities, partly through becoming an indistinguishable unit, wearing the same clothes, and doing the same stupid things in a large mass dominated by "college spirit."

Obviously, the social motive in this sense, running beyond reasonable bounds, as it undoubtedly does, lowers the intellectual level. It is no exaggeration to say that most college students look upon college as a means of getting ahead in life; for them the college is largely a social and athletic affair. Intellectual concentration would take too much time; it would restrict the student's social contacts. Besides, it doesn't really matter. Hence, once more, the college is bound to keep, for most students, at a low level. Meanwhile, I repeat, a minority do indeed work — work hard and get education, culture, and inspiration. There exists, thus, a saving remnant. And this is especially true of students in the last two years of the college course. During the first two years there is a heavy mortality; during the last two, a more or less marked differentiation tends to occur; as a result, what we ought to call "pass-students" continue to nibble and play, while a small group of earnest workers are engaged in what may be, properly speaking, university work.

There is another strange feature that keeps our colleges down to a low intellectual level. As a nation we believe in initiative, as all pioneers must. Under pioneer conditions strong men must turn their strength now to this job, now to that. The nation has not yet lost the pioneer spirit. We believe — because we have had to believe — in native ability, rather than in trained expertness. A common workman, found to possess great ability, finds himself in a few years at the head of a great railway; a shrewd errand boy will at forty be the head of a great industry; a country lawyer is made president. Almost no one at the top has been deliberately trained for his post; anybody may, if really able, become anything — banker, executive, general, diplomat, scientist, editor — what not. But, more and more — and this, I say, is strange — precisely the opposite theory has invaded education from the high school up. What we call personnel workers and job analysts, having ascertained the shortest possible time and the fewest possible steps required to produce a plumber or a typist, have leaped to the conclusion that the technique of job analysis enables them to unravel the higher secrets of intelligence and personality and to ascertain the precise requirements of the most highly differentiated tasks.[28] To an amazing extent colleges of liberal arts and education, instead of training broadly and deeply typical minds, like the humanistic mind or the scientific mind, create departments and offer " courses " aiming to enable a given individual to do a highly specific thing. With these " *ad hoc* " courses, designed to teach tricks, devices, and conventions, the American university catalogue often teems. Apparently nothing can be left to chance, nothing to general training; every

[28] As to " personnel work," see pp. 104–07.

activity, trade, profession, vocation must be analysed so that curricula may be constructed, not to educate, but to train. Colleges and universities are hard put to it to keep their curricula up to the analysts, who, working through questionnaires, move very quickly. Can a girl's trained intelligence be trusted to learn how to wash, feed, or clothe a baby? Certainly not: there is apparently no fund of experience upon which an educated person may draw! The girl's education may therefore be interrupted, suspended, or confused, in order that under artificial conditions she may be taught such things, probably by spinsters. Can the trained intelligence of a young man be trusted to learn salesmanship, marketing, or advertising? Certainly not: the educational process has once more to be interrupted, suspended, or confused, in order that he may learn the "principles" of salesmanship from a Ph.D. who has never sold anything, or the "principles" of marketing from a Ph.D. who has never marketed anything.

"*Ad-hoc-ness*," if, in my extremity, I may be permitted to invent an indefensible word, is not confined to courses or curricula — existing or desired; it applies to chairs as well. Alongside of the chairs that would be found at Berlin or Cambridge, Columbia University — situated in the so-called "sophisticated East" — boasts in its Teachers College a professor of extra-curricular activities;[29] Rollins College, a professor of books;[30] the University of Chicago, a professor of police administration; Dartmouth College, a professor of biography, as if an educated boy could not through intelligence, initiative, and associa-

[29] Listed as professor of education.

[30] The Minneapolis *Journal*, alive to this absurdity, gravely suggests that "one lecture at least should be devoted to the noble art of returning them."

tion find his way to a library, a bookshop, or a playing field, or as if proper presentation of subjects would not arouse curiosity. The University of Michigan has set up a professorship of bio-linguistics. Vassar College, whose students are girls from eighteen to twenty-two years of age, has established an " Institute of Euthenics." Well, what is " euthenics "? Euthenics is the " science of efficient living "; and the " science " is artificially pieced together of bits of mental hygiene, child guidance, nutrition, speech development and correction, family problems, wealth consumption, food preparation, household technology, and horticulture. A nursery school and a school for little children are also included. The institute is actually justified in an official publication [31] by the profound question of a girl student who is reported as asking, "What is the connection of Shakespeare with having a baby? " The Vassar Institute of Euthenics bridges this gap!

To these *ad hoc* courses I shall have occasion to revert later. I mention them in this connection for two reasons: first, because they show the confusion in our colleges of education with training; second, because, as an inevitable result of the untimely invasion of the practical and the immediate, they illustrate the low intellectual level at which the college may operate. I say " may," for the same college that gives one youth a course in " kinesiology " or " scoutcraft " gives another the opportunity to study any substantial subject under thoroughly competent guidance. And let us not forget the group of colleges that still follow a somewhat steep and narrow path.

[31] *The Meaning of Euthenics, Vassar College, 1929, p. 7.*

XIII

I come next to the graduate school, which is by far the most meritorious part of the American university. Considerable parts of the work done in a considerable number of graduate schools are of genuine university quality, in the strictest sense of the term.

The most distinctive American graduate school[32] was started in Baltimore in 1876, largely under the influence of the German universities. It began with a faculty of philosophy and shortly afterwards with a single professional faculty, that of medicine, both under the leadership of a great and scholarly president. At its beginning and for twenty years thereafter the Johns Hopkins University was the nearest thing to a university and practically nothing else that America has yet possessed.[33] The faculty was small, but eminent; the student body was also small, but eager. The whole group was afire with the zeal to learn. Instruction proceeded, as in Germany, through lectures to larger groups, and seminars in which the professor and a limited number of students pursued intensively advanced studies and research, methods now in common use in all American graduate schools. The most stimulating influence that higher education in America has ever known came from the Johns Hopkins of those days, an influence out of all re-

[32] The Harvard Graduate School was established in name in 1872; but its definite development began in 1877–78. C. H. Haskins in Morison's *The Development of Harvard University, 1869–1929* (Harvard University Press, 1930), p. 454. At Yale, the Graduate School was established in 1847.

[33] An inconspicuous undergraduate department was also started because of the lack of undergraduate training in the sciences in other institutions. It has, however, outlived its purpose and its usefulness and today harms rather than benefits the University, for it has quite destroyed the unique character of the institution. Had the college been abolished and the graduate school soundly developed, the story I am telling would have been a different one.

[73]

lation to the size of the institution and due solely to the impact of a small, homogeneous group, operating uncompromisingly at the highest possible level. Its doctors of philosophy were sought as teachers in all sections of the country. Graduate instruction was thereafter developed by many institutions; and the development has gone on with amazing rapidity. Following the success of the Baltimore experiment, graduate schools were developed out of or intertwined with the colleges at Harvard, Yale, Columbia, Princeton, and elsewhere; the University of Chicago, founded in the early nineties, established strong departments for graduate work. Since that date the quality of graduate opportunity and study has at its best indubitably improved, not deteriorated; its extent has indubitably increased, not decreased. Mathematics, physics, English, history, economics, even mediaeval and classical studies have attained heights that fifty years ago could not possibly have been dreamed of; witness the names of Charles Peirce, Willard Gibbs, Michelson, Moore, Breasted, Manly, Millikan, Richards, Gildersleeve, Turner, Shapley, Rostovtzeff, Capps, R. L. Jones, and scores of others. In some fields, we have been at once sound and original — among them, economics, sanitation, biology, and experimental medicine, in connection with which, to select a few names at random, Taussig, Wesley Mitchell, Welch, Abel, Mall, Morgan, Van Slyke, and Loeb spring to mind. A distinguished English Chaucerian has recently said that not London or Oxford but Chicago is the most productive centre of Chaucerian study today; and the great Scottish scholar, Sir William Craigie, who with Professor Onions brought the Oxford Dictionary to completion, is now compiling a Scottish Dictionary, not at Aberdeen or Edinburgh, but at the University of Chicago. To be sure, these men were mainly trained abroad; but with avidity America welcomed them and created for them congenial centres of teaching and research. Amazing progress has been made in providing scientists with laboratories and scholars with books. The great scientific laboratories of Harvard, Yale, Columbia, Chicago, Pasadena, Michigan, California, Wisconsin, and other state universities are not surpassed in respect to adequacy by the laboratories of any other country. They might be criticized as being too complete, too commodious, too well equipped rather than the reverse; good men have not infrequently been swamped by the expansion and complexities of their facilities and by the burdens of teaching, supervision, and administration connected therewith.[34]

In the established sciences — mathematics, physics, chemistry, and biology — we have, of course, pursued the paths that are followed in other countries, for these sciences assumed their modern form everywhere within the last century. The same is true of the humanistic disciplines, in which, however, the handicap due to our remoteness from Europe and Asia has been to a remarkable degree overcome by the purchase of manuscripts and old editions, by photostatic or other reproductions, by the establishment of schools at Rome, Athens, Baghdad, Jerusalem, and Luxor, and by the sending of expeditions to Italy, Greece, Egypt, and Mesopotamia. Harvard, Chicago, Yale, Princeton, Pennsylvania, and Michigan have, among others, thus actively fostered archaeological and mediaeval studies. The best work in the social sciences may, however, almost be called an original contribu-

[34] *" Es kommt nicht auf den Käfig an*
Ob ein Vogel singen kann."

tion of high importance: psychologists, breaking away from philosophy, have studied children's growth, educational development, and the reaction of the mature man to his environment; economists, abandoning abstractions, are studying trade cycles, unemployment, and finance; political theorists, abandoning the philosophic and historic methods, are studying the workings of government in every phase. The modernization of the university shows nowhere else to better advantage. I do not mean to imply that this movement in the social sciences is wholly American; but the vigour with which it has swept on, and the extent to which it has gone cannot — I am assured by foreign authorities — be quite matched in any other country.

On the whole, therefore, contrasting the situation in 1876 with the present situation, little more than half a century later, one cannot but be struck by the enormous and unpredictable improvement in respect to opportunities and facilities requisite to advanced teaching and research in new as well as in generally accepted subjects.

A special paragraph should be devoted to libraries. The true university, Carlyle maintained, was a collection of books. But the larger the collection, the more necessary that it be properly housed, properly arranged, and readily accessible. Half a century ago, roughly speaking, America was practically without libraries. It is less than sixty years since Daniel C. Gilman, destined soon to be President of Johns Hopkins University, resigned the librarianship of Yale University, because he could not obtain an assistant and had himself to light the fire in the stove every morning. No staff of experts, no central heating — a stove fire, in a combustible building, so recently as that! Today, universities, municipalities, secondary and elementary schools emulate one another in providing admirable collections of books and journals, made available to readers and borrowers quickly, freely, and comfortably. A library technique has been developed that is genuinely helpful; library construction has steadily improved. And university libraries have been so woven into the texture of university life and activity that, as far as physical arrangements go, work at every legitimate level is relieved of drudgery, inconvenience, and delay. Sound educational ideals have thus been embodied in steel and stone. The advanced worker needs access to catalogue and shelves; he has it. He wants a quiet nook in which he can work secure from interruption; he has it. The professor who meets his students in a common lecture room, equipped with chairs, a rostrum, and a blackboard, might as well lecture in a public hall; he needs, especially for his advanced students, a seminar room, adjoining the stacks devoted to his subject. Thus books are at hand; a workshop for him and his students in a congenial atmosphere is created. The American university has achieved this result better than any other university anywhere. It is not too much to say that no university should embark upon library construction without studying the successive and continually improving American contributions to the solution of the problem of the university library. A great English scholar, the late Professor T. F. Tout, comments [35] on " the excellence and accessibility of American libraries and the gradual accumulation in the American continent of great masses of manuscript material for European, and especially for British, history. Among the things for which I envied the American scholar most

[35] *History and Historians in America*, being the Presidential Address of the Royal Historical Society, Feb. 14, 1929 (London, 1929), pp. 10–11.

was the admirable organization of the great University Libraries of the New World. We on this side may have more precious rarities, but they, on the other side, know better than we do how to order a library so that the research student can have the greatest facilities for his work. I know of no university library which does more to help forward research than the great library at Harvard, where every professor has his study and the humbler research student has his little cubicle, where the earnest worker can gather around himself the indispensable tools that he has in constant use, while all have access to the well-arranged stacks, so disposed that books dealing with particular subjects are grouped together with a maximum degree of accessibility. And at New Haven I was privileged to see plans for an even more magnificent and convenient library building for Yale University which, I feel confident, are now rapidly being carried out in stone with the faith and enthusiasm that characterizes all the great American seats of learning. Nor are these standing by themselves. In the newest of Western and Middle Western universities the library is fostered with a zeal, and at an expense, which put to shame the newer university libraries of England. As far as printed books go, the greater American libraries are exceedingly well equipped, and if some gaps must still be there, there is always the wonderful Library of Congress at Washington and the huge Public Library of New York, itself a synthesis of a whole group of collections, and the impressive Library of Columbia University. In these great collections of books the American student can generally find what printed volumes he is in search of. The deficiency is rather in manuscripts and in older and rarer volumes, which are everywhere extremely difficult to procure. But these deficiencies are being rapidly supplied, and there are many public authorities and many millionaires who are doing their best to fill up the gaps."

The university press has also been developed, so that, to a far greater extent than previously, publication can be obtained. Two comments should, however, be made. The university press in America is almost wholly without endowment. It must therefore be conducted as a commercial enterprise. The result is that much trash is printed for no better reason than an expected profit; and — what may be even more unfortunate — important works, particularly in the field of scholarship, remain unpublished, unless they are taken under the wing of some foreign publication agency.

Extended and improved as they have been, the university libraries cannot keep pace with the demands made upon them by the ever swelling miscellaneous student body. No reading room will long suffice for the hordes of students, summer and winter, graduate and undergraduate; nor can any university library possibly provide duplicate copies enough to answer their calls.

Again, work of advanced university grade is often ingeniously favoured. The men whom I have already mentioned and their compeers introduced seminars and individual research, in which the individual worker found all the freedom that he could use. As the pressure of numbers increased — for reasons that I shall shortly discuss — steps have been taken in many instances to protect the real university professor. Occasionally, he is called a research professor and removed from the maelstrom of the college and the graduate school; in other instances, his teaching hours have been cut down. Chicago has recently acquired separate buildings in which modern language scholars and social scientists concentrate their advanced teaching and research; Michigan is similarly equipped in physics and biology; the formation of " islands " is thus taking place.

In one way or other science and scholarship have thus greatly advanced. The extent to which they have thriven may be gathered from the volume of publications in the form of books, monographs, journals, and transactions, and from the number and enthusiasm of learned and scientific societies. Once more, the Johns Hopkins was the pioneer: it started the American Journal of Philology, the American Journal of Mathematics, Modern Language Notes, Studies in Historical and Political Science, and the Journal of Experimental Medicine. There is hardly a field in which American publications must not now be reckoned with, scarcely a field in which American scholars and thinkers have not come together for the purpose of conference, discussion, and the promotion of learning.[36]

But there is, alas, another side that one may not ignore. To begin with, the American graduate school suffers from the curious cultural meagreness of American life. One studies Greek, philosophy, or medicine under great masters; but there is something lacking, something subtle and elusive, but vitally real and substantial. An able student at the American Academy in Rome once told me that he " found it necessary to go abroad for a year every few years, else he would

[36] Professor Tout (*loc. cit.*, p. 2) calls attention to the fact that out of 800 fellows of the Royal (British) Historical Society over 100 are Americans and Canadians; that out of 300 subscribing and exchanging libraries one-third lie " beyond the Atlantic "; of the *Bibliography of Modern History*, one of " our most ambitious undertakings," Philadelphia is " responsible for the sixteenth century," and the seventeenth-century volume was " finished in Chicago."

suffocate." It could not be otherwise; time may provide the remedy; but we may perhaps expedite the process by acknowledging the situation and by opposing certain dominant currents of American life. Cultivated persons have emigrated to America. But their children are soon bleached — reduced to the standard American pattern. The melting pot has its advantages; but it has cost us dearly.

In addition to this general defect, the graduate school suffers gravely from the inferior training of the high school and the college. So kindly and sympathetic a critic as Professor Tout feels himself bound to note [37] that " American schools seem, according to American testimony, less thorough and the results of their work less permanent, than is the case with the better sorts of British schools. The absence or rarity of compulsions, both at school and college, leads to a neglect of languages, and one of the weak points of the American historical student is that he is even often less familiar with the tongues in which his sources are written than his English counterpart. In making this statement please do not think that I hold any illusions as to the adequacy of the linguistic equipment of many English aspirants to historical fame! But I am bound to confess that foreign languages, and especially Latin, are for many Americans a worse stumbling-block than even the lack of that broad basis of general historical knowledge that the honour school of almost any British university affords. Perhaps one grows more conservative as one gets older, but America certainly made me see that there was more to be said for honour schools and compulsory language subjects than in my hot youth I had ever dreamed was the case. It also taught me that the

[37] *Loc. cit.*, pp. 4–5.

[81]

thesis, though a good servant, is a bad master, and that the cult of the repeated thesis is sometimes a mistake. If America had something like an English honour course for her M.A., and reserved her thesis for the Ph.D., the advantages of both systems might be retained and the disadvantages minimized. In adopting, rather too whole-heartedly, the German thesis system, the American reformers of a generation or two ago forgot that the German youth, when he went to the university, had had in his *Gymnasium* a good old-fashioned, well-rounded education, and had passed an examination that might well be compared to the British or American pass degree."

I have alluded to the intertwining of the graduate school and college. This is a consequence of the inferior training of which Professor Tout has been speaking. A student receives his bachelor's degree; he ought to be ready for graduate work. In some cases, he is; in others, he has through industry or good fortune become ready for graduate work even before he obtains his undergraduate degree; but in a majority of cases, the graduate student is unfit for advanced work. Lectures and courses are therefore of three kinds: those designed primarily for undergraduates; those designed primarily for graduates; those open to both. A single institution, a single faculty, a single professor cannot discharge these three separate functions satisfactorily.

The Dean of the Graduate School of the University of Chicago concedes that in some universities advanced " work is done fairly well " (I should myself go further) — " one university showing strength in one department, another in another — but in none of them, not even in the best, is the graduate work on the scale or of the quality that would be possible if the institution were entirely free from undergraduate entanglements." [38]

We have not learned Sorby's maxim: "Make a machine do its own special work to perfection, and do not try to make it do several different things all badly." [39]

And, finally, there is the question of sheer numbers, to which I shall later recur.[40] In vast throngs, American boys and girls go to college for social or prudential reasons; and so for prudential reasons they pass on to the graduate schools — for an A.M. or a Ph.D. degree is a merchantable asset in the educational market, because with higher degrees go higher salaries. The mere seekers for degrees throng the graduate school; and in order to meet the needs of the unfit, the graduate school has adopted a type of organization and administration that is quite irrelevant to higher education. In so far as this body of students is concerned, the graduate school is merely a kind of advanced teachers college with courses, requirements, methods of instruction and accounting, just as the college is something of an advanced high school. Dean Laing writes:

"I do not think that I am exaggerating when I say that scores of Masters are graduating each year without having attained even the slightest appreciation of the higher culture. Nor do they accquire it later. Large numbers of them regard the degree as a gilt-edged teacher's certificate, and having obtained it they do not pursue their studies further. They are through. If you doubt my statement, study the published output of the secondary school teachers of this country (and it is in the secondary

[38] Dean Gordon J. Laing, *The Standards of Graduate Work* (address included in *Problems in Education*, Western Reserve University Press, 1927), p. 201.

[39] *The Endowment of Research* by various writers (London, 1876), p. 165.

[40] See pp. 188 ff.

[83]

schools that the Masters are for the most part to be found) and compare it with the publications of secondary school teachers in England, Germany or France. You will find that our secondary teachers make but a pitiful showing beside the others. Only in the field of method are they productive. I know positively that this is true in my own field, the Classics, and I have no reason for thinking that it is not true in other subjects. There are, of course, notable and distinguished exceptions, but they are few in numbers." [41]

Of course, such students, so trained, do not even make good high school or college teachers. For the unsatisfactory results " specialization " and " lack of training in methods of high school and college teaching " are blamed. Unjustly, in my opinion. Specialization at the graduate level is inescapable — but it ought to rest on a broad cultural foundation; " methods " are futile at a stage when mastery of subject-matter and personality can alone count. If the precedent set by the Johns Hopkins in establishing a chair of chemical education is followed, the graduate school will become worse, not better; and a scholarly career will still further lose whatever attractiveness remains to it. The graduate school need not worry about training teachers; that is only another indication of our over-anxiety to make things easy for secondary and college students. More wholesome, far, would it be to make things difficult, by forcing the student to help himself. He may fairly ask that his teacher be a scholar and a person; that is enough. [42]

Touching the question of numbers, university administrators have latterly spoken plainly. " The

[41] *Loc. cit.*, p. 199.

[42] Mr. Graham Wallas' *The Art of Thought* (London, 1926) is an invaluable contribution to this subject. Especially important for Americans are the points that " industry " is not necessarily synonymous with thought and that periods of incubation, " free from conscious thought on the particular problem " are of vital importance to thinking.

graduate school," writes President Lowell of Harvard,[43] " contains, of course, a good number of real scholars and some of high intellectual distinction, but in the majority mediocre men who had better not be there." And to the same effect Professor Woodbridge, long the Dean of the Graduate School of Columbia: " Only a fourth (of the graduate students) needs to be considered seriously in the interest of scholarship and research." [44]

XIV

It is impossible — and in addition I am not qualified — to discuss separately all the graduate professional schools of the American university; but I may permit myself to speak of the medical faculty and the faculty of education.[45] Medical schools were long merely groups of local practitioners, nominally, if at all, associated with universities. A distinct upward movement began at Harvard with the advent of Mr. Eliot in 1869. Mr. Eliot first clearly perceived the need and during his long and splendid career brought the Harvard Medical School from a wretched, almost didactic, school without the most elementary matriculation requirements to its present eminent position. In his *Harvard Memories*,[46] describing his first efforts at reform, he tells of the opposition he encountered on the ground that written examinations were impracticable. The professor of surgery "who had

[43] In a personal letter, dated January 8, 1930, and quoted by permission; President Lowell discusses the subject of numbers and proposes limitation in his *Annual Report* for 1927–28, pp. 16–18.

[44] *Annual Report of the Dean of the Graduate Faculties, Columbia University,* 1927, p. 14.

[45] I ignore engineering, because it is not invariably a university faculty and because I am unfamiliar with schools of engineering alike in America and abroad; and, for the same reason, the legal faculty.

[46] *Harvard Memories* (Harvard University Press, 1923), p. 28.

complete charge of the medical school " told the young president "that he knew nothing about the quality of the Harvard medical students; more than half of them can barely write; of course they can't pass written examinations. . . . Dr. Bigelow's observation of the quality of the then medical students was somewhat exaggerated, but not grossly so."

Largely in consequence of Mr. Eliot's wise counsel, a sound and brilliant beginning was made at the Johns Hopkins, when, between the middle eighties and early nineties of the last century, there was assembled a medical faculty, incomplete, to be sure, but consisting, as far as it went, of perhaps the most uniformly distinguished group ever assembled in the United States at one time for an academic purpose. Men trained in medicine at Johns Hopkins have been influential in founding and developing the Rockefeller Institute for Medical Research and university faculties of medicine throughout the country. Medical scientists have indeed been drawn from other countries; and in recent years, other institutions, notably Harvard, have contributed. Within a single generation, a transformation has been accomplished, the like of which has taken place in no other country in so brief a period.

Nevertheless, even in respect to medicine, we must not deceive ourselves. The pre-clinical sciences were, indeed, rapidly and generally improved in respect to both facilities and personnel in the two decades following the opening of the Johns Hopkins Medical School, and in many universities are not only competently but admirably represented. On the clinical side, the front is, however, much more uneven. The relationship between universities and the hospitals in which their clinical teaching is done is sound and real — *i.e.*, the university chooses the staff — at Harvard, Yale, Chicago, Rochester, Cornell, Vanderbilt, Washington (St. Louis), and certain other institutions. Whether the hospital actually belongs to the university, as at Rochester and Vanderbilt, or is contractually connected with it as at Yale and Cornell, university ideas and methods may prevail in the selection of professors of medicine as completely as in the selection of the professor of Greek; the entire world is the field from which men may be drawn and the university has only itself to blame, if it fails to choose the best, as of course sometimes happens. But the sound relation of university and hospital, even when expressed on paper, is nominal rather than real in fully four-fifths of the clinical faculties of the country, which are still made up of local practitioners. Undoubtedly, the clinical teachers very generally devote more time, energy, and conscience to teaching than was usually the case a generation ago. Again, so called "full-time" units, consisting of groups on salary devoting themselves solely to teaching, research, and the care of hospital patients,[47] have been introduced in the important clinical subjects in several universities. An adequate and competent part-time staff assists in teaching and in the care of patients — sometimes also in research. The "full-time" plan, inaugurated at Johns Hopkins, and subsequently taken up by Yale, Rochester, Iowa, Cornell, and others,[48] provides comfortable salaries for a group of workers in each of the most important clinical de-

[47] I have described the "full-time" plan and discussed its results thus far in *Medical Education, A Comparative Study* (New York, 1925), pp. 55-58, 322-23.

[48] The medical clinics at Columbia and Vanderbilt are also organized on the "full-time" basis in the sense in which I employ the term in the text.

partments; it does not restrict in any wise their freedom to attend patients who are of educational or scientific interest. It provides that, should such patients be well-to-do, they may pay a modest fee that goes into the general medical school fund; but the educational staff is left free to do its proper university work, and in consequence the income from this source is negligible. The full-time organization at the Johns Hopkins Medical School has been operative for almost fifteen years; its receipts in surgery during the year 1928–29 were $4,770; at Yale, after almost ten years, the receipts were $10,241; at the University of Rochester, after six years, $6,650; at Washington University, St. Louis, after thirteen years, $4,680.

The term " full time " is, however, in America unfortunately applied to modifications of the Hopkins scheme, which are, in my judgment, quite capable of destroying its unique character. At Stanford University clinical professors carry on their private practice in the private wards of the Stanford Hospital, each on his own responsibility as to the number of patients he will see; in addition to his salary as university professor, he collects fees for his private work. Thus the professors on " full time " give full time to the hospital, but only part time to the medical school. The one safeguard is the privilege of the University to discontinue a professorship in case of abuse — a step which has been taken in two or three instances. At Harvard, it is difficult to speak of a " system " at all. Certain professors in medicine, surgery, and pediatrics have a limited consulting practice — in some instances amounting to practically nothing at all; others have a few beds at one hospital or another. In effect, therefore, some individuals are on the strict or nearly strict full-time basis, as I use the words, while others of equal rank derive most of their income from practice. Of the younger men there are fortunately many who give their entire time to academic medicine and surgery.

The situation in respect to medical education at the University of Chicago is unlike that which, as far as I know, exists anywhere else in the world. It can be understood only in the light of its history. Rush Medical College was established as an independent or proprietary institution in 1837. It had the usual history of the more prosperous American proprietary schools. Many of the more prominent members of the local profession formed its "faculty"; between 1875 and 1895 it acquired certain laboratory facilities. In 1887, it became the Medical Department of Lake Forest University, a merely nominal relationship to an insignificant college, for the school retained its autonomy. In 1898, the University of Chicago having been established meanwhile, Rush severed its connection with Lake Forest and immediately "affiliated" with the University of Chicago, which was already providing instruction in the pre-clinical sciences. In effect, therefore, the University of Chicago was conducting a divided school: it offered genuine university instruction on the University campus in anatomy, physiology, bio-chemistry, and pathology. On the clinical side, it accepted the work in medicine, surgery, and other branches done at Rush Medical College, conducted by the local profession and situated in a remote part of the city.

The arrangement was never sound; as the work of the laboratories and clinics became more and more involved with one another and funds for clinical teaching and research were needed, its defects were more and more acutely felt. During the last thirty years, two things have become more and more plain: first, anatomists, physiologists, and bio-chemists cannot be geographically detached from the clinics without damage to both parties concerned; second, clinical teaching and research require endowment. Hence the previously divided medical schools living on student fees have striven to bring laboratories and clinics into close geographical connection, to select the clinical staff, not from the local profession, but from the country at large, and to procure adequate endowments for clinical as well as laboratory work.

To achieve these ends at Chicago it was in 1916 proposed to abandon Rush as the clinical portion of the school by converting it into a post-graduate school to which physicians in the field might resort from time to time for special training, and to complete the school on the University campus by building a genuine university hospital in closest possible contact with all the sciences affecting medicine. The campus clinics, thus intimately associated with excellent laboratories in both medical and non-medical sciences, would not only be in position to train physicians at a high level, but to prosecute the study of disease as a science without any immediate reference to practice. In no other American university is the situation quite so happy in this important respect. Within a brief period, following the announcement of the plans to round out the medical school on the campus, funds were secured with which to start; far more rapidly than anyone could have dreamed, additional funds with which to expand the facilities planned at the outset have been most generously contributed. To be sure, these facilities are not yet complete, so that instruction in certain specialties still needs to be improvised; but this, as we shall soon see, is true of every other American medical school to greater or less extent.

The sums originally given to the University were intended for the purpose above described. To carry out the plan, the assent of the courts was necessary, and this was duly procured.[49] Had the University adhered to its purpose as expressed to the original donors and as approved by the Supreme Court of the State, the University of Chicago would possess across the city a well-equipped hospital in which so-called postgraduate courses would be given, and on its own campus a series of modern clinics in immediate touch with all the sciences, engaged in training physicians and in scientific research. Instead, however, the plan has been wretchedly compromised, for the University now conducts on the clinical side two medical schools of distinctly different calibre and confers two medical degrees — one mentioning Rush Medical College, the other emanating from the Ogden Graduate School of Science. If Rush and its affiliation with the University of Chicago are good enough for an M. D. degree sanctioned by the University of Chicago, it was absurd to create on the campus another medical school conferring the M. D. degree; if it is not good enough — and on that presumption the entire original campaign was conducted — it should have been discarded and utilized in the manner agreed upon.

But on the campus itself unexpected modifications in the full-time plan have been made, in advance of experience which might or might not have justified them. The hospitals forming the University clinics aim to admit patients who can pay part or all of their hospital charges, the admitting officer, however, be-

[49] Trustees of Rush Medical College *v*. University of Chicago, Illinois Report, Vol. 312, p. 109.

ing instructed to coöperate with the clinical staff so as
to exclude patients who are of no scientific or educational interest. On the other hand, patients once admitted under this limitation are all cared for by the
salaried teaching clinical staff, and fees are charged
according to the nature of the service rendered and
the capacity of the patient to pay; ample provision
has, however, been made for the admission of interesting patients unable to pay at all. Under this arrangement within a single year the Department of Surgery
earned for the Medical School upwards of $80,000.
The salaries paid are not excessive, but the arrangement seems to me so easily capable of abuse or de-
terioration that it cannot be classed with the full-
time arrangement adopted in Baltimore, New Haven,
and elsewhere. It was, as I have said, the purpose of the
full-time organization to free clinicians from routine
of any kind, to make them absolutely independent
judges as to whether they would or would not look
after this or that patient, and to give them the largest
possible latitude for teaching and research. I do not
believe that this state can permanently prevail unless
the endowment of the department is sufficient to make
its earnings negligible. Nominal fees must indeed be
charged for patients who can pay, out of prudential
considerations touching the local medical profession;
but if the fees thus earned are more than nominal,
there is grave danger that the academic point of view
may be imperilled. If the scientific budget of a clinical
department is once dependent upon the earnings of
the clinical staff, that staff will in all probability have
to earn the requisite amount — by doing what it is interested in, if it can, by doing other things, should
that become necessary. There is, in my opinion, no
safety for academic or scientific medicine unless

money enough is provided to make men on full time as independent of their earning power as if they were professors of Sanskrit. Surely a rich country like America that wishes to promote scientific medicine can afford the funds with which to carry it on at the highest possible scientific level without any of the compromises which have been adopted in order to make it relatively easy to do.

The modifications of the full-time system — perhaps, to be frank, I should call them compromises — are the strongest testimony to the importance of the type of full-time organization set up in Baltimore, Rochester, New Haven, and St. Louis. In my judgment, none of the modifications would have come into being but for the stimulus and example of the severer type; and, in my judgment, none of them is likely to remain as good as it now is, unless the severer type is upheld in complete integrity. We are not likely to relapse into conditions common twenty years ago; but the academic battle in clinical medicine is not yet won. For that reason it is as important as ever to make distinctions and to call things by their right names.

What I here say of the medical faculty is just as true of other faculties; professorships of law, engineering, literature, and economics will not attract the highest type of ability, will not procure concentration on legitimate university objects unless the incumbents are freed from the necessity of earning incidental income whether for themselves or for the university. To this point I shall recur when I discuss the question of salaries.

In respect to clinical facilities and equipment many institutions make a brave showing; and the personnel is at times worthy of its setting. General statements cannot, however, be made. To be as accurate as possible, one may say that a medical clinic of solid university character exists in ten or twelve institutions; surgical and pediatric clinics in the German sense of the term are distinctly fewer in number; obstetrics and psychiatry and ophthalmology have been soundly developed in two or three places; neurology and dermatology are just beginning. The most nearly complete of American medical schools — the Johns Hopkins — lacks an ear and throat clinic, a neurological clinic, a dermatological clinic, and funds for other important purposes. Other schools, many of them excellent as far as they go, are even more defective. A small, but promising beginning has been made at Vanderbilt University, Nashville, Tennessee; something similar is in process at Duke University, Durham, North Carolina; improvements are under way at Tulane University, New Orleans, Louisiana. That is, in the entire South, there are at most three institutions of promise. No other medical faculty or partial faculty, worthy of mention, exists in that section, comprising thirteen states and a population of 28,987,285. West of the Mississippi, beginnings and strivings are also in evidence at several state universities. Excellent faculties with admirable equipment and steadily increasing support have been established at Washington University (St. Louis), and at Iowa City; but in a region consisting of twenty states, inhabited by 26,107,571 persons, there are few other faculties fairly comparable with those above named. We have got rid well-nigh wholly of the scandals that disgraced the country as recently as twenty years ago. Positive and immense progress has thus been made. Foreigners, who knew conditions as late as 1914 and revisit the country now, are amazed at the change. But their favourable impressions and comments should not blind us to the fact that America as a whole has not yet advanced far beyond the beginning of a significant era in medical education. We are not yet quite convinced that, on its clinical side, medicine is science at all.[50]

Moreover, and I am now speaking of American medicine at its best, unaccountable lapses occur. For reasons that defy comprehension, important posts in the best endowed faculties are from time to time filled with inferior or sterile men; side by side with its full-time clinics, the Johns Hopkins tolerates a urological clinic conducted on the basis that the full-time organization was intended to supersede. As I write, a weak, independent medical school in Brooklyn has suddenly expanded into a " medical centre " by separating a " medical school " from the hospital to which it had luckily been attached, annexing a Methodist, a Jewish, and other hospitals, undertaking to raise a small sum of money now, and hoping " when conditions improve," to raise more — a return, in the leading state of the Union, to the sort of thing that medical educators have spent the last two decades in combating! Finally, the very intensity with which scientific medicine is cultivated threatens to cost us at times the mellow judgment and broad culture of the older generation at its best. Osler, Janeway, and Halsted have not been replaced. As a matter of fact, scientists — medical as well as other — owe something to themselves as human beings, something to the traditions and heirlooms of history, something to the unity and integrity of all science. The recent

[50] See Alfred E. Cohn, *Medicine and Science* (*Journal of Philosophy*, Vol. XXV, July 19, 1928). Also, Rufus Cole, *Progress of Medicine During the Past Twenty-five years as exemplified in the Harvey Society Lectures* (*Science*, Vol. LXXI).

founding of the Institute of Medical History at Johns Hopkins indicates appreciation of the fact that, even though a university faculty of medicine trains mainly practitioners, too often vocational practitioners, the roots of medicine go deep into cultural soil; its ideals are fundamentally humanistic, scientific, and philosophic.

X V

The American school or faculty of education has made an unquestionable contribution of genuine value to American, perhaps one might add without exaggeration, to modern education. A generation ago elementary and secondary schools were a treadmill. The curricula were dead; the discipline was unintelligent; the world of reality and action hardly existed for the schools. Rousseau and Froebel and Pestalozzi had dreamed dreams of immense inspirational importance. They had had no general effect. A tremendous change in practice has, however, recently taken place though, to be sure, not in America alone. The curricula, especially in the elementary school, are alive. This wholesome transformation has not been accomplished wholly through colleges of education; but they have been important, perhaps the main agencies, in bringing it about. There are so many problems, specifically educational closely bound up with psychology, philosophy, economics, and government — without falling into any one of these categories — that education may make some claim to constituting a profession with cultural roots and high ideals in the university sense of the term. In this American development Teachers College at Columbia led the way; others — at Chicago, at Harvard, and at the state universities — have followed. For their accomplishment in vitalizing elementary and high schools they deserve high commendation.

Unfortunately, like the universities to which they belong, faculties of education have lost their heads. In the first place, in discarding what was dead or irrelevant, they have lost sight of much that was alive and relevant. They have failed to heed the fact that, as human beings mature, schools must shift the emphasis from the individual to the task itself. "Respect for persons," writes Professor Woodbridge, "is what the old education neglected. It would be a pity, would it not, if the new should neglect respect for learning?" [51]

"Past" and "dead" are very different words.[52] More and more, philosophy, scholarship, and history have tended to fade much too far into the background; technique, administration, "socialization" have more and more come to the fore; more and more, by means of "combined degrees" and otherwise the need of taking courses in "education" interferes with the mastery of subject-matter. Because one type of discipline was barren and repellent, it does not follow that "ease," "spontaneity," "self-expression" are sound guides. Civilization is an artificial thing; it is inseparable from ideals deliberately adopted; these ideals often involve effort that runs against the stream. Without ideals, without effort, without scholarship, without philosophical continuity, there is no such thing as education, no such thing as culture. The college for teachers has become less and less sensitive to these considerations. It has run into all kinds of ex-

[51] *Loc. cit.*, p. 50.

[52] The most influential and important philosopher of the new movement has recently spoken contemptuously of "the vaunted culture of Europe." More unwise words could hardly be addressed to professors of education in the United States.

cesses, all kinds of superficiality and immediacy, all kinds of "rabbit paths." It is undertaking to tell "how" to persons who mainly do not know "what." Of course, there are profound individual differences impelling individuals in different directions, and these must be respected. But, the choice once made, the individual who at the high school, college, or university stage, requires that his teachers employ an insinuating technique so as to guide him happily and painlessly towards the mastery of a subject belongs not in school but somewhere else. Teachers will, of course, vary in their powers and methods of presentation and inspiration. That seems to me, at the higher levels, of relatively slight importance, if they are masters of their respective subjects. Let the onus rest mainly on the student, for there it belongs and thus only will his powers be brought out. The very acme of absurdity has been attained at the Johns Hopkins in the creation of a professorship of chemical education.[53] Remsen was a distinguished chemist. His influence was felt throughout the entire country. What might he not have accomplished, had he possessed as running mate a mediocre or unsuccessful investigator who would have been professor of chemical education? But, hold! If the university professor of chemistry needs at his side a professor of chemical education, so do physics, mathematics, history, English, Greek, Latin, and other chairs. American universities, all under-financed, and few in weaker financial condition than the Johns Hopkins,[54] must thus create, parallel with chairs of subject-matter, professorships of education. Truly the

[53] The official description is as follows: "This course will cover theory, observation, and practice in the teaching of chemistry. It is especially designed for students who are planning to teach chemistry in universities, colleges, or large high schools."

[54] See p. 199 ff.

Johns Hopkins has once more opened a new vista —
even if in the wrong direction!

One is thus led to ask whether schools of education
are capable of coördination in the university with such
professions as law and medicine. The American teachers college has not yet proved the affirmative. And it
seems on the whole less impressive at the moment
than when it was proposed a generation ago. And
this, because the American college of education, not
wholly, but largely oblivious of the really important,
is devoting itself more and more to the technical,
trivial, and sometimes absurd. In education, there are
things that require doing, but it does not follow that
it is the business of the university to do them all.
The members of the first teachers colleges in the
United States were themselves scholars; but scholars
and scientists are now scarce, very scarce, in these
faculties. In their place, one finds hordes of professors
and instructors possessing meagre intellectual background whose interests centre in technique and administration viewed in a narrow *ad hoc* fashion. The
staff of Teachers College, Columbia University, requires 26 pages for mere enumeration: the roster
contains 303 instructors;[55] the catalogue lists over
19,000 " students " of one kind or another. A few instructors offer courses in educational philosophy, in
foreign or comparative education; problems of elementary and secondary education are not slighted.
But why do not these substantial and interesting
fields suffice? Why should not an educated person,
broadly and deeply versed in educational philosophy
and experience, help himself from that point on? Why
should his attention be diverted during these pregnant

[55] Not including scores of teachers in the Extension Department, Summer School, etc.

years to the trivialities and applications with which common sense can deal adequately when the time comes? Most of 200 pages, filled with mere cataloguing, are devoted to trivial, obvious, and inconsequential subjects, which could safely be left to the common sense or intelligence of any fairly well educated person. Atomistic training — the provision of endless special courses, instead of a small number of opportunities that are at once broad and deep — is hostile to the development of intellectual grasp. A Negro preacher in a popular play declares: "The Lord expects us to figure out a few things for ourselves;" but Teachers College is organized on the opposite principle. Thus in this huge institution thousands are trained "*ad hoc*," instead of being educated and encouraged to use their wits and their senses. Among the hundreds of courses thus offered, I cite as fair examples "manuscript writing," "teaching of educational sociology," "administrative procedures in curriculum construction," "research in the history of school instruction in history," "music for teachers of literature and history," "methods used in counseling individuals," "research in college administration," "psychology of higher education," "teaching English to foreigners," "teaching the individual," "extra-curricular activities, including school clubs, excursions, athletic insignia, class parties and dances, extra-curricular finances, and a record card for pupil activity"!

The School of Education of the University of Chicago is a more modest affair: it has a teaching staff of only 33 [56] and about 800 students, and its list of courses occupies only 40 pages. I find one course devoted to "educational progress in Europe and the United

[56] Not including teachers in the Summer School, etc.

States from 1400 to the present." As for the rest, the School avoids the detailed absurdities in which the Columbia list abounds and pays relatively far more attention to psychological problems. But absurdities and trivialities are not absent, as, for example, separate courses in " the supervision of the teaching staff," " duties of school officers," " awareness of situations and planning of behaviour," " reflective thought as a basis for teaching method," " supervision of instruction " under eight separate heads, " study and supervision of the high school girl," etc. In the main, however, its attention is devoted to tests, measurements, organization, administration — including administration of the teaching staff and how to organize for planning the curriculum! Of testing, the psychologists appear to have practically lost control. It may have a limited field of usefulness; but the length to which it may go is shown in a formula devised at the University of Chicago, showing "the relation of scholarship to a combination of all tests ":

$$R_s.12345678$$
$$\sqrt{1-(1-R^2S\ 1)\ (1-R^2S\ 2.1)\ (1-R^2S.4.123)\ (1-R\ S.\ 6.12345)}$$
$$(1-R^2S\ 7.123456)\ (1-R^2S\ 8.1234567)$$

Thus neatly and simply can a tester dispose of all the personal factors on which good teaching really depends!

By the side of this formula, Professor Spaulding's is a very modest one indeed: [57]

If A_r = average of class-enrolments in required subjects
X = the number of hours of combined classes
T = the total number of class-hours
G = the average number of pupils per grade, then
$$A_r = \frac{X.2\,G+(T-X).G}{T} \text{ and } X = T.\frac{A_r-G}{G}$$

[57] Francis T. Spaulding, *The Small Junior High School* (*Harvard Studies in Education*, Volume IX, Harvard University Press, 1927), p. 31.

The Harvard Graduate School of Education has a staff of 37 instructors, a few devoting themselves to large fundamental issues, while most of them deal with simple practical problems, which would quickly yield to experience, reading, common sense, and a good general education. Among the latter are special courses in the teaching of different subjects, courses for specialists in play and recreation, supervisors of recreation parks, social centres, summer camps, festivals, pageants, commercial education, community recreation, and singing in schools and communities. Obviously, Harvard, too, leaves as little as possible to intelligence, individual initiative, chance, and technical non-university training, and is at least partially blind to the significance of history and philosophy.

The calibre of the persons who are attracted to this sort of thing and its upshot may be gathered from the trivial and uninteresting character of educational periodicals and the subjects of the dissertations submitted for higher degrees. The topics discussed in the current literature are so unimportant as compared with the subjects discussed by physicists, chemists, or political scientists that it may well seem as though they were devised to frighten off intelligence. And that the unconscious effort to frighten away intelligence is usually quite successful is demonstrated by the theses which crown the student with the A.M. or Ph.D. degree. At random I select from the Chicago and Columbia lists: " The City School District," " The Experience Variables: A Study of the Variable Factors in Experience contributing to the Formation of Personality," " Measuring Efficiency in Supervision and Teaching," "City School Attendance Service," " Pupil Participation in High School Control," " Administrative Problems of the High School Cafeteria,"

" Personnel Studies of Scientists in the United States,"
" Suggestion in Education," " Social Background and
Activities of Teachers College Students," [58] " Qualities
related to Success in Teaching," " The Technique of
estimating School Equipment Costs," " Public School
Plumbing Equipment," " An Analysis of Janitor Serv-
ice in Elementary Schools," [59] " The Equipment of
the School Theatre," " Concerning our Girls and What
They Tell Us," " Evidences of the Need of Education
for Efficient Purchasing," " Motor Achievements of
Children of Five, Six, and Seven Years of Age," " A
Scale for Measuring Antero-Posterior Posture of
Ninth Grade Boys," " A Study of School Postures and
Desk Dimensions," " The Technique of Activity and
Trait Analysis Applied to Y. M. C. A. Executive
Secretaries as a Basis for Curricular Materials," and
" Statistical Methods for Utilizing Personal Judg-
ments to Evaluate Activities for Teacher Training
Curricula." Harvard is in danger of following the
same course: it has recently bestowed the Ph.D. de-
gree for theses on " Vocational Activities and Social
Understanding in the Curriculum for Stenographer-
Clerks," " Guidance in Colleges for Women," " The

[58] In this production, the author of which is a dean of women at a
teachers college, account is taken of whether in the homes from which the
students came there is a lawn mower, a desk set, a rag carpet, a built-in
bookcase, potted plants, company dishes. Among the leisure activities investigated are " shopping," " heart-to-heart talks," " just sit alone," " think
and dream," " going to picnics," " idle conversation (talking about just
anything)," " having ' dates ' with men," " telling jokes," " teasing some-
body," " doing almost anything so you are with the gang," " reading."

[59] I pause for a moment to contemplate the thesis on " An Analysis of
Janitor Service in Elementary Schools." Why elementary? There are
reasons: first, obviously, the title suggests other theses — and new subjects
are in demand, as students multiply — the duties of a junior high school
janitor, of a high school janitor, of a college janitor, etc. " Are these
really different subjects? " I once asked a professor of school administration.

" Oh, yes," he replied, " the lavatory problem, for example, is with
small boys quite different from the same problem at the high school level! "

Intelligence of Orphan Children in Texas." (Why orphans? Why Texas?) On the other hand, a minority of the theses deal with serious and worthy subjects. That I have not mistaken the drift of intelligence and scholarship away from schools of education is admitted by the head of an important faculty of education, who permits me to quote, from an unpublished memorandum, the following:

> " There is in the United States no University School of Education in which a faculty of marked power and distinction is devoting its full time to a highly selected body of graduate students under a program of ample scope systematically directed toward professional leadership."

Closely related to testers are the job and personnel analysts who are springing up in schools of education and departments of sociology. A professor of education, successively at Pittsburgh, Chicago, and Ohio State University, began his career by analysing pharmacists and secretaries, in order that all lost motions might be excluded from their training and curricula neatly calculated to turn out the desired product might be devised. Professor Charters' analysis of secretaries [60] reveals two points of profound social, scientific, and vocational importance: (1) that there are 871 secretarial duties, among them taking dictation (!), winding the clock, locking the desk, weighing mail, getting rid of cranks and beggars, answering the telephone, dusting, and opening the mail; and (2) that secretaries should possess 44 traits, among them, charm, imagination, graciousness, humour (sense of only), modesty (not conceit), poise, and self-respect. Are the 871 duties hard or easy? Should

[60] The volume is entitled *Analysis of Secretarial Duties and Traits* by W. W. Charters and I. B. Whitley. It can be procured from the publishers, Williams & Wilkins Company, Baltimore, for $2.50.

they be acquired in the training school or "on the job"? Two formulae furnish the answer: $\dfrac{H}{H+E}$, $\dfrac{S}{S+J}$. The study, printed in a volume of 183 pages, concludes with the pregnant sentences:

"Just what may be obtained from a further use of the $\dfrac{H}{H+E}$ formula is not clear, but very great value is attached by the investigators to the further use of the $\dfrac{S}{S+J}$ formula.

On the basis of the information contained in this study, the investigators feel that a rather exact determination of the content of the curriculum for secretaries would be possible."

The same method has been applied to the study of teacher-training by Professor Charters at the expenditure of three years of time and $42,000 in money, under the guidance of a general committee including the Presidents of Yale University, the University of Buffalo, the University of Minnesota, and the Director of the Department of Education of the University of Chicago, and with the coöperation of scores of " school men " throughout the country. Despite the array of names contained in the preface and introduction " there was no final committee review or revision of the document "; the author of the introduction did not himself read the volume through — no one possibly could — and confesses that it " looks like a delegated job " and that the " delegate did not know what to leave out." The result of this uncritical dragnet questionnaire " research " is therefore an admirably printed volume of 666 pages, which disclose the important facts that teachers are called on to do 1,001 [61]

[61] I am not meaning to imply that teachers do not have a thousand and one things to do!

things, variously subdivided, and that they should possess 83 traits, which may fortunately be so apportioned that a senior high school teacher need possess only 26, a junior high school teacher 26, an intermediate grade teacher 26, and a primary grade teacher 24. Among the 1,001 activities, it is revealed that teachers must concern themselves with "helping pupils to find errors" (p. 319), "asking questions" (p. 324), "giving new problems" (p. 330), "creating proper atmosphere by humorous remarks when appropriate" (p. 334), restraining pupils "from applying cosmetics in classroom" (p. 355), and taking care that pupils go quietly "to drinking fountains, lavatories, and other rooms" (p. 358); among the "traits" are accuracy, attractive personal appearance, conventionality, discretion, fluency, magnetism, and sobriety (pp. 56–61). It is hoped that this exhaustive analysis, based, apparently, upon the assumption that American teachers have neither native sense nor ordinary good breeding, "might provide the necessary basis for determining systematically what teachers should be taught." [62]

A quarto volume of 194 pages, that is almost equally impressive, has just emanated from Yale. In a "research" into "Incentives to Study," based on a "Survey of Student Opinion," Mr. A. B. Crawford, Director of the Department of Personnel Study, seeking "to collect data of importance to future educational and administrative policies of the University" (Preface), has discovered that "the subjective opinion and judgment of the superior student would presumably have more than average reliability." Page after page of tables, percentages, graphs, bibliography, and ques-

[62] The volume is called *The Commonwealth Teacher-Training Study.* It is published by the University of Chicago Press and is sold for $4.00.

tionnaires leads to ten conclusions which would all have been matter-of-fact to plain common sense, though, to be sure, the language employed is not precisely that in which a cultivated American or Englishman would ordinarily express quite obvious facts:

"Certain secondary factors of influence (Economic Status, Definiteness of Orientation, etc.) tend to motivate students academically. Together with measures of capacity such as scholastic aptitude test ratings, these indices may be advantageously used as supplementary criteria in selective admission."

And again:

"The influence exercised by these various factors is attributable to the purposive motivation of which they are all expressions and which underlies them as a basic motivating force."[63] (p. 125)

Following this, what further can be said regarding incentives to study? In fairness, attention should be called to the fact that the author of this perspicacious document has been assisted by a senior student in computing the "correspondence ratios" which are somewhat less intelligible than profuse, by three professors of psychology, a member of the Department of Education, the President of the University, and divers and sundry other individuals.[64]

[63] My former chief, the late Dr. Wallace Buttrick, for more than twenty years head of the General Education Board, was accustomed to designate English of this kind as "pedagese."

[64] As a sample of the form and substance of the questionnaire, I quote the following: "Judging from your courses at Yale, what do you consider the most important characteristics in a successful teacher?

Professional reputation	Scholarship and research	Method of presentation
Knowledge of subject- matter	Enthusiasm Personality	of material Teaching experience
Devotion to teaching for its own sake		Teaching technique

1.................. 2.................. 3..................

What extra-curriculum activities do you regard as most valuable to the development of an individual?

At this point, faculties of education and faculties of sociology fade into each other, occasionally drawing a psychologist or two into the vortex. Two professors at the University of Chicago are, for example, engaged in making " A Study of the Psychological Differences between Leaders and Non-Leaders," and another one has made " A Study of Executive Talent." Another — a professor in the Department of Political Science — has published a sagacious volume on the *Prestige Value of Public Employment in Chicago* with eighty elaborate tables and sixteen graphs. The technique employed is sufficiently delicate to distinguish between the prestige value of employment as elevator starter at the City Hall and elevator starter at the Wrigley Building. A professor in Syracuse University believes " the most needed directions of investigation " to be as follows:

" We require, first, the close observational study of leaders over a long period of time, with biographical data extending back into infancy, in order to discover the fundamental traits and drives. Combined with this longitudinal observation we need an improvement of the cross-sectional method of rating and measuring the crucial traits. Such measurements, however, will be of service only when the *fundamental* traits have been discovered and formulated. The main need, however, lies in a field heretofore scarcely touched, namely, that of devising a technic to discover and formulate the way in which the various traits are working *together,* some kind of symbol, qualitative though it may be, to express the kind of integration which the personality exhibits. To achieve this, we must observe the individual in all his social and vocational relationships. For it is out of the varying situations of life that we can discern a common denominator expressive of the central integration of the personality."

Which do you regard as most valuable to the life of the university community?
Why? "

A Columbia professor, greatly concerned with the personal characteristics of industrial leaders, suggests an interview so framed " as to bring to light the emotional conditioning or the types of experience which have led one man to become bitter, another pugnacious, another very diplomatic and still another frank and open in a coöperative way."

Of course, things having gone so far, a psychoanalytic approach to the mind of the executive is inevitable, and it is to include not only executives but head nurses, supervisors, heads of departments, as well as the official head of the institution as a whole. The hopeful soul writes:

" I suspect that there is implied here a principle which might profitably be teased out by appropriate research and applied in the field of industrial relations." [65]

Quite plainly, the tester, the questionnaire addict, and the mechanician have no patience with the subtleties, accidents, and nuances of personality and inspiration. One may venture to commend to them a brief dialogue which they have apparently overlooked:

[65] In passing it would be a pity to lose the chance of calling attention to such works as Strong and Uhrbrook's *Job Analysis and the Curriculum*, which tells how to train " young men for executive and supervisory positions." Perhaps even more significant because issued by the Bureau of Publications of Teachers College, Columbia University, are the following volumes:

Sturtevant and Strang, *A Personnel Study of Deans of Girls in High Schools*

Buckton, *College and University Bands, Their Organization and Administration*

Goodwin Watson, *Happiness Among Adult Students of Education*

It would be obviously unfair to call attention to the absurdities I have mentioned but for the fact that they are so numerous as to be representative of a large part of the literature of sociology and education — so large as to imperil the development of a scientific spirit in either field. Nonsense is also published in other fields — even in the so-called " exact sciences "; but it carries no weight and soon disappears. Its authors do not usually become professors in leading universities.

"Ham. Will you play upon this pipe?

Guil. My lord, I cannot.

Ham. I pray you.

Guil. Believe me, I cannot.

Ham. I do beseech you.

Guil. I know no touch of it, my lord.

Ham. It is as easy as lying: govern these ventages with your fingers and thumb, give it breath with your mouth, and it will discourse most eloquent music. Look you, these are the stops.

Guil. But these cannot I command to any utterance of harmony; I have not the skill.

Ham. Why, look you now, how unworthy a thing you make of me! You would play upon me; you would seem to know my stops; you would pluck out the heart of my mystery; you would sound me from the lowest note to the top of my compass; and there is much music, excellent voice, in this little organ; yet cannot you make it speak. Do you think I am easier to be played on than a pipe? Call me what instrument you will, though you can fret me, yet you cannot play upon me."

XVI

As if the machinery were not already sufficiently complicated — perhaps in part because it has become so complicated — a new movement not, let me add, necessarily unsound, has in recent years led to the creation of " Institutes " within the university. What is an " Institute "? The word was taken over from German nomenclature where it means a laboratory or a group of laboratories. In America it may mean something or nothing. At the University of Chicago, the Oriental Institute denotes the group of instructors who deal with oriental subjects. The " Institute " has no other existence — it is not a group detached from the faculty, it has no autonomy, it is merely a number of persons or departments, supported, like others, partially out of general funds, partially by special funds held by the university for their use. Harvard has in its faculty of law an Institute of Criminal Law, which would appear to be simply the name for the research activities of the chair devoted to that subject — a dubious departure, since it implies a possible separation of teaching and research within the limits of a university chair. The Johns Hopkins has created an Institute of Medical History — a happy name, first, because it implies identity of aim with the great Institute founded by Professor Sudhoff at Leipzig, and, again, because the subject, as conceived by Dr. Welch, is something more than a department of the Medical School.

In respect to institutes, Columbia has outstripped all competitors. In its Teachers College there is an Institute of Educational Research, an Institute of School Experimentation, an International Institute, which is an administrative group, an Institute of Child Welfare Research, about which the less said, the better,[66] and also a Division of Field Studies, which is a " service " group, available to the country at large on a profitable financial basis, with the result that the individuals concerned are for an unduly large part of their time absent doing odd jobs, which they have no business to be doing, because they should be training their students to perform them when they go out into their respective posts. The epigraphist, who among other heavy duties manages the Columbia University School of Business, suggests in

---

[66] As a specimen of its output see *An Inventory of the Habits of Children from Two to Five Years of Age* by the Acting Director, issued by the Bureau of Publications, Teachers College, 1928. Children may have, it appears, a maximum of 2,325 habits (emotional, mental, motor, and social-moral). A child's score in each division is found through the formula $\frac{T}{S-3X} \times 100$ — it matters little what T, S, and X stand for. Like the publications of the personnel experts, this study is seriously intended; it is not, as one might infer, a burlesque of the statistical method.

his recent report the establishment of an Institute of Distribution, which would, of course, be nothing more than a disproportionate, tumorous growth within the Faculty of Commerce or the Department of Economics. The Institute of Distribution would embrace " the nature of the changes taking place in consumer demand, the relative efficiency of various distributive methods, the foreign trade situation, the economic costs of distribution, foreign trade and the debt situation, our tariff policy and foreign trade, the economic and social aspects of advertising and instalment buying and its effect on credit."

The most recent — and to my thinking the most incomprehensible — development in the way of an Institute has latterly taken place at Yale. Yale had long possessed an inferior medical school; in recent years the school has, under the highly intelligent, enthusiastic, and energetic leadership of its present dean, Professor Winternitz, rapidly improved its facilities, personnel, and resources. Its development is, however, far from complete; its resources are far from adequate. While, therefore, it belongs among the small number of American medical schools to which great praise is due, it has not reached a state of stability or equilibrium; for the next decade or two, at least, it requires the same sort of leadership that it has enjoyed during the past ten years. Yale has also long possessed a school of law, which has in late years become academic rather than merely vocational in quality; and it also possesses the usual chairs of economics, sociology, psychology, etc. Now it is proposed to form a " Human Welfare Group," which will include the Yale School of Medicine, the Yale School of Law, the Yale Divinity School, the Division of Industrial Engineering, portions of the University departments dealing with human life in its mental, physical, and social aspects and with comparative studies of other living organisms, and, finally, to add thereto an Institute of Human Relations. The whole is officially described as " a centre for the intensive investigation of problems bearing upon mental, physical, and social well-being." And it is gravely maintained that " existing educational procedure " will be simplified through the coördination of activities including child-development, psycho-biology, psychology, and the social sciences generally with law and medicine: " light will be thrown upon questions such as the connection between physical health and family income, mental stability and occupation, crime and recreational facilities, child training and mental growth, economic conditions and divorce, and legal procedure and respect for the law. It may be possible in many instances to bring about a readjustment between the individual and his environment which will lead to greater happiness " — a practical task, which, in so far as it goes beyond what is required for teaching and research, is no concern of the University as such whatsoever. That, like " field " surveys of education, touched on above, is the concern of persons trained by the University, rather than the concern of the University itself.

For the Institute of Human Relations a handsome new building has been erected, and considerable sums have been obtained. But what will the building contain? Generous facilities for " child-development," mental hygiene, psychology, and psychiatry, a small amount of space for anthropology, and the statistical division of the Social Science Department. The name of the building and its contents do not correspond.

A steady stream of literature aiming to explain the

idea and to elicit financial support, emphasizes the importance of breaking down " departmentalization." Within the space at my disposal I cannot adequately deal with the confusion of thought involved in the use of such phraseology. Knowledge advances in the first instance only by artificial simplification; departments are set up, not because life or the physical world is simple, but because no progress can be made by observation or experiment unless one's field is circumscribed. Once results are thus obtained, cautious integration takes place. Thus, for example, it is at this day absurd to speak of medicine as unduly departmentalized in theory or in practice, whatever may happen as a consequence of individual stupidity in this or that case. Chemistry, physics, biology, and social science are in the most intimate and effective interplay in the modern hospital; on the other hand, little progress would have been made in diagnosis or therapeutics, unless rigidly enforced simplification had prevailed and unless it were still possible to effect such tentative simplification whenever a problem is to be unravelled. Dr. Rufus Cole, in a recent address on the progress of medicine, has, without having this in mind, completely demolished the theory on which, as far as medicine is concerned, the Human Welfare Group was conceived. " Virchow was wise enough," he says, " to see that ' each department of medicine must have its own field and must be investigated by itself. . . . Pathology cannot be constructed by physiologists, therapeutics not by pathological anatomists, medicine not by rationalists ' " — nor, as Cole himself adds, "by chemists, physicists, or mathematicians." Having thus established the importance of *order* in the field of medicine, the remainder of this admirable discourse is devoted largely to showing by concrete illustrations how clinical science has in its progress absorbed and utilized physics, chemistry, and the pre-clinical disciplines.[67]

I am not contending that legal education or training has done so well as medicine; but the remedy lies not in physical or compulsory breaking down of lines between law and economics nor in establishing under one roof bits of several subjects, nor in the graphical representation of interrelationships; but rather in the development of intelligence and flexibility to the end that workers will, as there is need and opportunity, rove freely over a wide territory, to return, at their pleasure, to their own narrower hunting grounds.

As a matter of fact, there is nothing new in the proposed Yale Institute — not even " integration." Every good modern hospital looks upon its patients as social problems, as well as individual cases. If the staff of a hospital or medical school is indifferent to social and economic factors, the remedy is not a " clearing-house " which will take into account factors neglected at the point at which they should be considered — but a new staff, which has a modern point of view. The same is true of law. Justice Holmes and Justice Brandeis "integrate" law, economics, and philosophy. Where did they acquire their point of view? Not in a special institute of human relations. As a result of education and contacts, they read, observe, inquire. Their point of view is percolating through courts, the profession, and the law schools. It will be finally established when law school faculties are composed of large-minded men, not when a separate institute is created. Our bewilderment is not relieved by the draughtsman (see page 116). This chart is necessarily incomplete and serves simply, by taking the School of

[67] *Loc. cit.*, pp. 617–27.

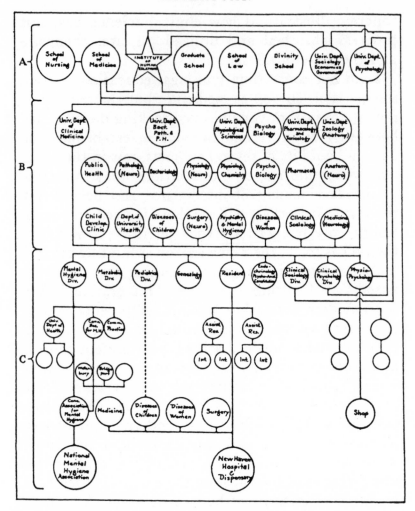

ORGANIZATION OF THE HUMAN WELFARE GROUP

In this chart only the biological and psychiatric aspects are elaborated because of space limitations. Obviously the activities of any of the Schools indicated in section " A " of the chart might be similarly outlined. Section " B " shows, therefore, only the departments affecting the School of Medicine. These are also operative in the Graduate School. The lower line of this section shows the sub-divisions of the University department of Clinical Medicine. Section " C " is an elaboration simply of the psychiatry and mental hygiene sub-division of clinical medicine. Any of the other sub-divisions, such as the diseases of women, the diseases of children, or surgery, could be outlined in the same way.

Medicine and the Department of Psychiatry and Mental Hygiene as examples, to indicate the manner in which related activities in the pure and applied sciences are tied together to form a unified group of which the Institute of Human Relations is the activating center and correlating agent. For if the Human Welfare Group includes law, does not law draw with it history? And if the Human Welfare Group includes divinity, will divinity fail to require philosophy? And if the Group requires physiological chemistry, what about physics and chemistry and mathematics? And is it conceivable that a Human Welfare Group can omit education? And when all these implications, quite as essential as those represented on the chart, are followed, what result do we reach? The Human Welfare Group is identical with Yale University! And we are precisely where we started, enriched not by an idea but by a building and funds.

The initial projects of the Yale Institute of Human Relations, tentative in form though they admittedly are, show either the inevitable need of " departmentalization " in the study of certain problems or the confusion and irrelevancy attendant on the artificial effort " to break down barriers." The Institute began with a study of unemployment based originally on a questionnaire. The study does not in the course of its fourteen pages of inquiry go beyond the scope of an ordinary department of economics. Why is it necessary to dislocate the department of economics in order to present a study of this kind under the aegis of a new institute? The subject is economic; the questions are economic; the literature referred to is economic. I pointed out this fact to the persons in charge of the study and requested enlightenment; but my request for an appointment at which the subject could be discussed was courteously evaded.

Still worse fares the inquiry into 1,500 cases of bankruptcy in New Jersey by questionnaire and personal " follow-up." To be sure, the questionnaire is called " tentative " and has doubtless undergone modification. But the significant facts are these: that the inquiry divides itself sharply into three parts — all highly departmentalized: a legal part, an economic part, and a sociological part. Among the sociological inquiries one reads:

> Does the bankrupt live in an apartment, a flat,[68] or lodgings?
> How many rooms?
> State whether the majority are on an air shaft.
> Number of hours of sleep?
> Is he inclined to worry?
> On the block in which he resides — ditto as to the block on which he does business — is there a car barn, a theatre, a cemetery, a garage, a stable, a police station, or a pool room?

Now, can any one believe that, whatever the subtle connection may be, the plight of a New Jersey bankrupt is going to be illuminated by knowledge of how many of his rooms open on an air shaft or whether he lives near a cemetery? Are these facts needed in order to ascertain his standard of living? And imagine the sources of waste and failure to which lack of success may be attributable, but which delicacy and tact forbid the investigators to explore!

Again, the Institute of Human Relations ignores the necessarily individualistic character of genuine thinking. It would be as easy to write a poem or a symphony by a committee as to promote the study of human problems by physically arranged groups. Can really first-rate minds, working in various fields, be

[68] I have been unable to find anyone who knows the difference between an apartment and a flat.

artificially and mechanically brought to coöperate in their study, or is anything new likely to be accomplished, if quite ordinary persons mechanically pool their activities in a " clearing house " ? " Science," wrote the great scholar who heads the *Kaiser Wilhelm Gesellschaft*, " is fundamentally and in the end always an affair of the individual. No possible development can change that. But there are tasks, which stretch beyond a single life; tasks, requiring such prolonged preparation that one person can never really get to them; others, so complex, that division of labour is required. Nay, more, one can even say that, on a close view, all scientific tasks are part of a larger task, and that, as long as they are handled in isolation, progress is impossible. Thus we come upon one of the paradoxes by which our spiritual life is hemmed in: science is an affair of the individual, yet scientific problems can never be solved by an individual. How are we to escape? We cannot leave science exclusively to the study or laboratory of one person, still less can we carry it on *in a common workshop*. We can at best work in ever widening concentric circles, bring workers into *informal* contact and endeavour to reach some sort of systematic progress on the basis of the freedom of the individual." [69] In other words, too much planning, too conscious planning, too much articulation, too conscious articulation will destroy the freedom of the individual upon which in the last resort progress depends. The advancement of knowledge and practice requires specialization and departmentalization as well as free and easy cross-fertilization. The President of Yale University is not unaware of this;

[69] A. Harnack, *Vom Grossbetrieb der Wissenschaft* (*Preussische Jahrbücher*, 1905), pp. 193–94. Since the above was written, Professor Harnack has died. The *italics* are mine.

but he thinks that the new Institute will provide for all.[70] I cannot share his favourable expectation. The history of thought is against it. Easy-going contacts within the university are stimulating and helpful; at deliberately arranged coöperation the really gifted shy. That attracts only the inferior, never the original mind. "The true scholar," writes Professor Zinsser, "the true scholar — an incorrigible individualist if he is worth his salt — will not become a mere tenant, but will make the soil he cultivates his own." [71]

The plans of the Human Welfare Group, in so far as they have been stated, seem to me to shipwreck at this point. The members of the medical faculty have endless tasks; the members of the legal faculty have endless tasks; it seems to me absurd to suppose that the gaps can or should be as neatly bridged in fact as they can be filled out on paper. Here, as elsewhere, the budget is revealing. The Institute of Human Relations is, as I have said, a building mainly devoted to "child-development," psychiatry, and psychology;

[70] "In the first place, there will doubtless be always more or less of the individualistic research which now is carried on by the members of existing Departments. A scholar in psychology, or sociology, for example, would not be expected to interrupt, or abandon, any piece of research upon which he might have embarked, simply because he became a member of the Institute. Nor would he be coercively compelled to inaugurate research which did not appeal to him, simply because it was of interest to the staff of the Institute; although, in the nature of the case, the members of the Institute will always be working in fields which are closely related to one another. But, on the other hand, it is distinctly intended to foster from the outset coöperative research in fundamental fields affecting the fuller understanding of human behaviour and social organization. Such basic research may be carried on by scholars only temporarily attached to the staff for the purpose of carrying out some specific part of such a program, or it may, and generally will, be prosecuted entirely by permanent members of the Faculty and their assistants. An illustration may be drawn from one of the first fields which it is now planned to study — the family." James R. Angell, *Yale's Institute of Human Relations* (*The Yale Alumni Weekly*, April 29, 1929).

[71] Hans Zinsser, *In Defense of Scholarship* (*Brown University Papers VII*, published by the University, 1929), p. 12.

for these purposes annual grants amounting to $300,000 have been obtained. Everything else is medical and should be so called. The further needs of the project are stated thus:

Summary of Financial Needs of the Human Welfare Group

Women's Pavilion	$500,000
Surgical Pavilion	600,000
Isolation Pavilion	450,000
Private Patient Pavilion Addition	650,000
Hospital Endowment	2,000,000
School of Nursing Endowment	1,000,000
Clinical Sociology Endowment	1,000,000
Positive Health Endowment	500,000
Medical Education Research Endowment	150,000

If " the financial needs " are carefully examined, it would seem that Yale has perhaps purposely confused a simple situation with rhetoric on the subject of breaking down departmentalization.[72] Only one apparent novelty is proposed: a professor of clinical sociology. But what good hospital lacks its social workers, who work instead of lecturing? What Yale needs, what the country needs is not a new Institute, but the development of fundamental disciplines in easy, helpful, and varying contact through the enlistment of first-rate intelligence, as Professor Harnack points out. Among these are psychiatry, neurology, criminology, etc. Assuredly, these subjects are sufficiently complex already, involving as they do all kinds of anatomical, physiological, social, economic, and educational factors. Is the psychiatrist going to be most helped, if left

[72] In *Science* (No. LXXI, 1930, pp. 235–36) the following language is attributed to one of the promoters of the enterprise: " The institute will serve as a dynamo and assembling plant for those university organizations concerned from the view-point of research, teaching, or treatment with problems of human well-being." A " dynamo " and an " assembling plant " ! The confusion of metaphor corresponds with the confusion of thought.

to his own devices, making from time to time both such combinations and such simplifications as seem to him worth while, or is he going to be most helped if he feels himself part of a huge organization, involving law, medicine, the social sciences, etc.? [73]

An Institute set up at Johns Hopkins deals with law. A faculty of jurisprudence was ruled out; a separate institute had to be set up. Very well. What is the program of the Institute? " Constructive research on broad problems of such a character that *the results of investigating them may be expected to be of immediate value.*" Subjects are to be chosen for investigation by the savants of the Johns Hopkins Institute of Law, not because they are profoundly significant, not because they are of fundamental importance, not because they interest that " incorrigible individualist " the real scholar, but because they are " of immediate value." It was, of course, because Rowland and Sylvester and Gildersleeve and Herbert Adams and Mall chose topics the results of investigating which could be expected to be of " immediate value " that the Johns Hopkins University became famous and influential! But this is not all. The Institute has already issued its first publication — a volume of more than 200 pages, listing, on the basis of replies to a questionnaire, *Current Research in Law, 1928–29.* " Research " in law would appear to be practically synonymous with publication or intended publication: for the volume enumerates text-books, new and revised, case books, new and revised, digests, law review articles, translations, " tentative findings as to Negro lawyers," and reports of almost every conceivable variety.

[73] A Yale professor, distinguished for his scientific achievements, writes: " I really do not dare to put on paper a statement of the way that I, and I believe many others here, feel over the latest and largest expansion for quite intangible objects."

One feature must fill the physicist, astronomer, humanist, or medical scientist with envy: for not infrequently the legal researcher can predict in advance when his investigations will terminate (in six months, one year, two years) and how much paper their publication will require — one volume, two volumes, a book, an article, etc.

The Yale Institute of Human Relations and the Hopkins Institute of Law possess one feature in common: national advisory committees — strange aggregations both, of lawyers, doctors, editors, and public personages of all sorts. What is their function? Are the members of the staffs of the two Institutes so uncertain of their purposes that they need advice? And are they likely to get it in this way? The members of the Yale Advisory Group were told that neither time nor effort would be required of them; the members of the Hopkins Group " will meet at dinner in the coming February." I have asked some members of both Committees what they conceived their function to be. No two persons gave the same answer; some admitted that they did not yet know; and one — a prominent lawyer on the Hopkins Committee — asked me to tell him when I found out.[74] As a matter of fact, no university is entitled to appeal to the public in behalf of a new and questionable departure by citing in its support prominent persons who have amiably lent their names to projects that they do not understand or merely do not wish to oppose. Specific investigations and innovations in an uncharted country should proceed quietly, without the beating of tom-

[74] A member of the Yale Committee writes me that he had supposed he would be asked to advise: " However, we have not been asked. Instead, the recent publicity gives me an uneasy feeling that it may be mere ' window-dressing.' "

toms. Both the Yale and Hopkins Institutes are issuing through the press and directly from the universities a series of "releases" for publicity purposes. They make claims that are premature and unjustified. In the realm of higher learning at least it should not pay to advertise; the great man who made the Johns Hopkins, proud as he rightly was of the distinguished group he had assembled, made no predictions as to what they would achieve in this or that field.

XVII

I began by saying that the graduate school is the most creditable part of the American university; and I cited men, laboratories, and libraries in support of that statement. But what with overcrowding, vagaries especially in the fields of education and sociology, and incomprehensible institutes, the graduate school is in imminent danger of being overwhelmed. Fifty years ago, the degree of Ph. D. had a meaning in the United States; today, it has practically no significance. The same is true of research. It meant something to do or coöperate in doing research at Johns Hopkins or Harvard a generation ago. Unquestionably, the quantitative increase of publications, especially in the United States and Germany, has lowered the standard. Cole quotes the Danish physiologist, Krogh, as stating that "too many experiments and observations are being made and published and too little thought bestowed upon them."[75] Professor Krogh speaks of "experiments and observations"; what would he say of the amount and quality of "research" that is now being conducted in the United States by means of questionnaires, mailed by the thou-

[75] *Loc. cit.*, p. 624.

sands, often thrown into the waste-basket, sometimes "followed up," after a while filled out carelessly or critically, as the case may be, the data then tabulated with infinite pains and at enormous expense, and finally made to yield conclusions obvious to common sense at the start or unsupported by reliable evidence at the end. Now, the questionnaire is not a scientific implement: it is only a cheap, easy, and rapid method of obtaining information or non-information — one never knows which. No effort has been made to use it in experimental sciences; it is worth hardly more in education, law, and the other social sciences, for words never mean precisely the same things to different persons, and there is no possible way of discounting poor analytic capacity or the practical joker. The post office is, therefore, no substitute for trouble and thought; and it becomes a more and more inadequate substitute as questionnaires increase daily in number, complexity, and size. Human problems can be studied only if information is ferreted out; and to ferret out facts, a trained and educated mind must go to the source, employing all possible tact, knowledge, insight, and ingenuity. It is not too much to say that a competent inquirer will never ask the same questions of any two persons. For every answer is unique and may suggest a clue that opens up hitherto unsuspected sources of inquiry.[76]

The question is thus raised as to what precisely constitutes research. The gathering of information — even though accurate — is not research. The massing of con-

[76] The defect of the questionnaire is clearly expressed by a writer in the *School Review:* " Long experience has made it clear to careful workers in social science that they cannot safely rely on testimony collected through questionnaires. Very few people are skilled in analysing their own experiences and in arriving at valid conclusions as to what has really contributed to their present modes of thinking."

glomerate descriptive material, so common in domestic science, in the social sciences, and in education, is not research. Unanalysed and unanalysable data, no matter how skilfully put together, do not constitute research; reports are not research; surveys are not research; sympathetic accounts of salesladies, stenographers, waitresses, deans, bankrupts, litigants, school systems, happy and unhappy students of education, matriculating students in doubt as to whether they love their father more than their mother or vice versa,[77] with or without graphs, curves, and percentages, are not research and would not be called research anywhere except in the United States.

What, then, is research? It is a quiet, painstaking effort on the part of an individual himself, not through someone hired by him, though intellectual coöperation is, of course, not barred,[78] an effort, I say, to reach the truth, the severest that the human mind with all available apparatus and resources, is capable of making at the moment. The subject must be serious or have serious implications; the object must be disinterested; no matter how closely the outcome may affect wealth, income, or appetite, the observer must preserve an objective attitude. In the physical and biological sciences, controls must be set up under the most rigorous conditions; predictability is vitally important, if practicable. In the social sciences, neither control nor predictability is feasible. Serious question has been raised as to whether, such being the case, the social sciences are sciences at all. Let us assume that they are. Precisely because they

[77] This question was actually asked of the incoming freshman class at Columbia University (1930) in a questionnaire prepared by a member of the University Department of Psychology.

[78] I emphasize intellectual coöperation: this excludes the technician working under orders.

are thus handicapped, they must be more critical
rather than less critical. The mere accumulation of
measurements, of data, of facts (which may not really
be facts after all) may be a worthless expenditure of
time, energy, and money. To be sure, there are problems which are up to the present time susceptible of
study only by the inductive method; but it is of the
very essence of science that the investigator have an
idea, though he hold ever so lightly to it. He must
be ready to modify it or to drop it if the facts go against
him, but endless counting will produce no theory, no
principle, no ideas. A very large part of the literature
now emanating from departments of sociology, departments of education, social science committees, and
educational commissions is absolutely without significance and without inspirational value.[79] It is mainly
superficial; its subjects are trivial; as a rule nothing is
added to the results reached by the rule of thumb or the
conclusions which would be reached by ordinary common sense. I have already given abundant examples in
support of the position; page after page could be filled
with additional examples, furnished by universities,
social congresses, educational assemblages,[80] etc. I do

[79] At the conclusion of a paper read before the assembled sociologists
of the country, the author says: " I am by no means sure of just what, if
anything, we have been measuring."

[80] I cannot forbear referring to a few learned disquisitions, not mentioned in the text: a paper on " Experimentation in Face to Face Interaction," read before the American Sociological Society, Dec. 1929, and
another entitled " Susceptibility to Accidents " by a professor in Syracuse
University, " Family Bereavement " — a new field of research, by a professor at Northwestern University, " The Cultural Approach to the Study
of Personality Problems " (University of Chicago), " Case Skills in the
Development of Family Life " (Tulane University). I am inclined to
award the palm to a questionnaire research into " the origin and nature
of common annoyances " by Professor Cason of the University of Rochester.
Professor Cason read this important paper at the Ninth International Congress of Psychology in Sept. 1929. After several years' work, he compiled
a list of 21,000 annoyances, but finding duplication and *many instances of*

not mean to imply that the physical and biological sciences have not also suffered. Poorly trained workers, ambitious to announce "results," are abundant enough in those branches, too. But, at least, standards have been created, and there exist effective agencies, that ultimately — as a rule quickly — separate wheat from chaff. No such critical sense has as yet asserted itself in the social sciences; the leaders, instead of restraining the rank and file, are too often "promoters" whose own productions will not bear scrutiny; and the variety of tasks they undertake shows the low esteem in which they hold scientific workmanship.

XVIII

I approach now the "service" activities of American universities, partly separate from undergraduate and graduate departments, partly, as I have already indicated, intertwined with one or both of them. Let me begin by calling attention to the widespread thirst for knowledge, information, or training — a

---

spurious annoyances, he boiled the list down to 507, which he arranged on a scale marked from 30 to 0. "To find hair in food I am eating" is marked 26, "a dirty bed" 28, "cockroaches" 24, "to see a bald-headed man" 2, etc.! This "research" has now been printed as a monograph by the Psychological Review Company; price, $3.25.

On the other hand, absurdities are not confined to the social sciences and education. As I write, a dissertation submitted in partial fulfilment of the requirements of the Kansas State Agricultural College for the degree of Doctor of Science reaches me. It is entitled "A Study of the Bacterial Content of Cotton Undershirts." Externally it conforms to academic type — states its problem, reviews the literature, describes the investigation, and closes with summary and conclusions; there are the requisite graphs, tables, references, etc. From the conclusions I quote briefly: "From the results obtained, it is reasonable to believe that underwear worn next to the skin does contain varying numbers of micro-organisms. . . . On a hot day the body might perspire freely which in all probability would encourage rapid growth of organisms. . . . A comparison of the shirts worn various lengths of time shows that the number of bacteria tends to increase with the length of time garments are worn."

thirst partly sound and spontaneous, partly unsound and contrived. It is of course a good thing that a democracy wants to be informed or improved — fundamentally, if feasible, superficially, if nothing better is at the moment possible, since the superficial improvement of one generation may lead to the fundamental improvement of the next. America abounds in individuals and families who really want something better than they were born into; and its loosely organized institutional structure enables energy and capacity to find a level of expression higher than is readily accessible in the old world. Whatever can be done to evoke and train effort that would not otherwise be aroused, or that would otherwise be misdirected or even worse directed, or that would otherwise discharge rebelliously at a lower level, is therefore all to the good — provided it does not incidentally do the university, the individual concerned, or society at large more harm than good.

But precisely because it is relatively easy for an American to rise or to change, the maintenance of clean standards and a sense of values is in America important. Naïve and uneducated people can be easily fooled; the practice is in the highest degree reprehensible. Naïve and uneducated people cannot possibly know what education is — what is the difference between education, information, training, tricks, technique, etc. Ideals are in the custody of universities. Universities are morally and intellectually bound to be honest and consistent. They can plead nothing in extenuation, if they mislead. Perhaps organizations should be set up to create and to meet every demand; there is, for example, indisputably a field for adult education; perhaps there should be set up institutes for adult education, that respond in elastic fashion to the varying needs of a society made up of adults with every conceivable kind of educational and social past and every conceivable kind of present desire. Surely, however, adult education must reach a high level before the university is justified in taking cognizance of it. And if in any wise a university takes advantage of popular gullibility, the whole " service " organization is exposed to grave suspicion.

XIX

Why do certain American universities feel themselves under pressure to develop their " service " functions, even to call themselves " public service " institutions? There are many reasons. State universities have to make themselves " useful "—or they think they do—in order to justify themselves to the man in the street or on the farm, since income depends on appropriations of the state legislature; thus large numbers—some resident, others non-resident—get the kind of information or training, which they need or think they need, and from which they feel themselves competent to profit—though, as I have urged and shall continue to urge, this sort of thing does not deserve to be called college or university education at all; endowed institutions think they must be useful in order that alumni, local communities, and the general public may be encouraged to contribute gifts, and in order that they may not be reproached for being aristocratic or " highbrow " or careless of the needs of the general public. And when I say, " useful," I mean directly, immediately useful, for Americans like to see " results." I believe that the intelligence and generosity of the American public—including alumni—are thus underestimated and undermined. But whether this is true or not, universities have a duty to perform and a function to discharge.[81] On this point, an able and experienced university president has recently written me: " I am inclined to think most Americans do value education as a business asset, but not as the entrance into the joy of intellectual experience or acquaintance with the best that has been said and done in the past. They value it not as an experience, but as a tool. Possibly Americans value everything in that way — value church and religion and marriage and travel and war and peace, never for the sake of themselves, but always for the sake of something just around the corner. The sense of tomorrow has amazing power in our American life. Never was there a people so careless of the past and even so careless of the present, except as a stepping-stone into a tomorrow which shall bring wealth and dynamic and material progress. All this has its good side and its very bad side as well." [82]

We can, fortunately, illustrate the correct attitude of the university professor towards practice. Pasteur was a professor of chemistry. In the course of his professional career, the prosperity and well-being of France were threatened by silk-worm disease, by difficulties in the making of wines, in the brewing of beer, by chicken cholera, hydrophobia, etc. Pasteur permitted himself to be diverted from his work in

[81] The new president of a state university, who, to quote his own language, " innocently " began to study the curriculum and discovered that " courses had been divided and subdivided until they had reached a point of attenuation that did not justify recognition on the part of a university. In the professional schools and departments we found emaciation rampant, for the departments had taken in courses that belong to trade and technical schools." (Quotation slightly abridged.)

[82] Letter (Jan. 16, 1928) from the late President W. H. P. Faunce of Brown University (quoted by permission).

order to solve these problems, one after another; having done so, he published his results and returned to his laboratory. His approach was intellectual, no matter whether the subject was poultry, brewing, or chemistry. He did not become consultant to silk-worm growers, wine makers, brewers, or poultry men; he did not give courses in silk-worm growing, wine making, or chicken raising. The problem solved, his interest and activity ceased. He had indeed served, but he had served like a scientist, and there his service ended. This is not the usual way in which the American university does service. To be sure, there are scientists, economists, and others, who are thus interested in pressing practical problems, and who, having reached a scientific result, communicate it to the world and pass on to other problems. These are, as I take it, genuine university workers. I am not therefore making a plea for scholasticism or gerund grinding — only a plea for the use of judgment, dignity, a sense of value, and a sense of humour.

The absurdities into which the ambition to be of " service " has led certain universities will be regarded as incredible outside, at times inside, the United States — yes, at times, I suspect, within the universities which are themselves guilty. Let me begin by admitting that under the conditions of modern life there are thoroughly competent people who are strongly moved to study; and the younger men connected with universities can learn something of the world in which they live and something of the art of teaching by expending a moderate amount of time and strength in conducting classes for mature, competent, and serious persons in subjects worthy of a place within the framework of a university. The conditions which I have incidentally inserted are, however, important: the subjects must be substantial, the students must be competent and serious, the instructors of high quality and thoroughly protected against exploitation. In so far as I know university extension in America, no university that engages in " service " work observes these or any other ascertainable limits. There are of course serious students, who work year after year, whose persistence is more significant than regular college attendance might be; but there are thousands of drifters, floating in and out, and getting nothing. Columbia University in 1928–29 enrolled about 12,000 extension students, over 10,000 of whom were " resident," the rest nonresident. Substantial courses are indeed offered—courses in Shakespeare, economics, modern languages, philosophy, etc. This is, if kept within bounds and upon a high basis, legitimate, though an entirely separate and independent institute of adult education might do even this as well or better. But what is one to say of the ideals of Columbia University when it befuddles the public and lowers its own dignity by offering extension courses to misguided people in " juvenile story writing," " critical writing," " magazine articles," " persuasive speaking," " advertising layouts," " practical advertising writing," " retail advertising and sales promotion," " advertising research," " individual problems in fiction writing," " writing the one-act play," " book selection," " story telling," and " direct-by-mail selling and advertising? " If there is a country in the world, in which the advertiser is destroying individuality and compelling almost everybody, regardless of needs, wants, and solvency, to buy the same things, it is the United States; and Columbia University, which should be a bulwark against uniformity and the home of intellectual and cultural integrity, independence, and idiosyncrasy, plays the purely commercial game of the merchant whose sole concern is profit or of the shop assistant who thinks that an academic certificate in a business subject may bring him an increased salary. The director of this strange and unworthy conglomeration of sense and nonsense is simultaneously professor of Latin epigraphy, director of university extension, director of the school of business, and president of the reactionary medical school in Brooklyn, of which I have spoken above. Of the value and importance which the University attributes to Latin epigraphy, a layman may venture a guess on the basis of the professor's executive responsibility for 20,000 extension and home study students in every imaginable field, not to mention his sallies into the fields of medical education and business education.

The university, which tries to keep pace with the times in the sense in which Columbia tries, leads a restless life. I have, for example, mentioned the fact that the University offers a course in " photoplay composition "; but the ordinary photoplay has been displaced by the so-called " talkie," as a result of which I am informed that the course has just been abandoned and that the lady who gave the course is now at Hollywood where she is spending a year studying the " new technique." The University will, I assume, offer a course in " talkies " when this young woman forsakes the alluring precincts of Hollywood and returns to the academic groves on Morningside Heights.

Nor is this all. There are persons who cannot come to the University or one of its centres for extension work. They may lack " previous academic work " altogether. Shall they be left out in the cold? Not at all.

To them — a miscellaneous group made up of probably a relatively small number of persons desiring some guidance for their scant leisure and a much larger group ready to "fall for" an alluring advertisement that promises quick culture or quick *ad hoc* training at a slight monetary expenditure, Columbia appeals in full-page newspaper and periodical advertisements, guaranteed by the seal of the university (see next page).

One cannot, however, do full justice to this publicity material without reproducing the type and arrangement, so skilfully drawn up to attract the attention of the ingenuous.[83] To these "home students" Columbia offers by mail home study courses, covering "the same ground as courses given in residence." "Instructors are members of the staff" of the University, though there are reasons to suspect that they are at times appointed to the staff in order that in its advertisements the University may be enabled to make this claim. During the year 1928–29, Columbia University registered over 7,500 home study students, a goodly number, if, as the advertisements claim, the instruction is "of university grade." Inconsistently enough,

[83] A showy pamphlet issued in 1929 states that 7,519 persons are enrolled in home study courses. The care with which the "individual" is "personally" studied may be gathered from the fact that of this number, 884 are "undetermined" in respect to age, 794 are "undetermined" in respect to previous education, and 1,361 are "undetermined" as respects occupation. The "personal" note is invariably struck. A leaflet, left at the New York Public Library to be picked up like a handbill, contains the following:

COLUMBIA UNIVERSITY has adopted the policy of offering, for home study, regular University courses adapted to the special requirements of instruction by mail. This extends the educational advantages of a great University to men and women everywhere who cannot undertake class room study.

PERSONAL INSTRUCTION. Home Study is conducted by carefully designed methods that assure to the student every advantage that lies in instruction of University grade, in thoroughness of teaching, in the constant guidance, suggestion, and criticism by University instructors.

no " credit " is allowed for home study work. Why not, if the work is of " university grade " and the instructors are regular " members of the University staff "? The "offerings " in the home study department include serious subjects like art, ancient and modern languages, economics, mathematics, etc., but also " scoutmastership," " elementary English composition," " composition of lyric poetry," " fire insurance," " juvenile story writing," " magazine article writing," " philosophy," " photoplay composition," " elementary typewriting," " manufactured gas," " personnel administration, including how to get personnel policies introduced," " secretarial correspondence," down to such subtleties as " expressing personality in a letter," " business," and finally the " A. K. Cross Method of Vision-Training in Art Study," respecting which the instructor writes from Boothbay Harbor, Maine: [84]

"Columbia University now offers a method for the home study of art that makes an hour at home more profitable than days of art school attendance."

and further:

" I enclose information of a new method of visual training that will give child or adult, amateur or artist, the same visual and mental images of Nature's appearances. This may be accomplished without study of theory and without personal instruction, through the use of a simple device for determining perspective and color appearances."

And that there may be no doubt about it, the University, operating from Maine, supplies the inquirer with scores of testimonials of the patent medicine variety, from among the wealth of which I quote the enthusiastic tribute of Mrs. N. P. W. of Buffalo to the assidity of her husband:

[84] Logically enough: if the student may live in Oklahoma, why should not the instructor correspond with him from Maine? But how does the Director maintain " university standards " under such conditions?

"My husband is getting on fine, that is what *I* say, but I think his work is much more artistic than it was when he started the course with you. . . . We paid the course fully since October. . . . My husband is a very fine character, but not real happy with the work he has to do for his living. I believe that does not bring the real joy in his pictures. . . . God bless you." [85]

It is interesting to observe that the Home Study Department of Columbia University is thus able to offer "instruction of university grade" by mail to any one without respect to age or previous education — a thing which the University itself on the campus does not attempt. On the contrary, on its campus psychological and other tests are employed for the purpose of eliminating the unfit. It is clear that the mails automatically do as well. Could not the University save money and simplify its task if, in place of psychological tests and other means of determining fitness, applications by mail were alone required? And why, if instruction of "university grade" can be given by Columbia University from remote points to applicants living anywhere, should an expensive plant be maintained on Morningside Heights in the City of New York?

One cannot but admire the businesslike methods which Columbia University employs in order to render "service." Having inserted a full-page advertisement in Sunday newspapers and certain monthly magazines with a coupon to be filled out by any one thirsting for information, prospective customers are requested to "mention subjects, even if they are not

[85] These testimonials cover several pages. One wonders why so many of the testimonials selected for distribution by a member of the "regular staff" of the University should be ungrammatical.

"The University gives assurance that from a material standpoint many of the courses prove a profitable investment in a short time." Announcement, Oct. 1930, p. 10.

listed." At my suggestion, a lady living in a quite inaccessible village in the extreme portion of northern New York filled out a coupon. In due course, the pamphlets requested arrived. Subsequently, she received a personal letter from the University, assuring her that the University's concern for her was quite as acute as if she were one of " the campus students " — which may, of course, be the case, though not in precisely the sense in which it was designed to impress her! To this communication she made no reply. A university, bent upon rendering " service," is not to be thus daunted. A " follow-up " letter headed, " Shall we retain your name? ", regrets that the University has " up to this time not had the pleasure of welcoming you as a student." It goes on to say:

" Columbia University is a public service institution and it is desirous of serving you in any way it can. At the same time, seventy-five thousand persons have inquired for this work this year, over-taxing our limited facilities."

Now I confess myself puzzled: if the University is already over-taxed, why should it so assiduously pursue? But a really modern university doubtless feels its responsibility for minds much as the mediaeval church felt itself responsible for souls. The erring children must not be suffered lightly to wander in darkness — when a home study course, distinctly profitable to the University, can provide illumination. Later, no response to the anxious University having been made, a " nice-looking gentleman " in an attractive motor car appeared in this out-of-the-way place to " follow up " personally what American bond salesmen call a " prospect." I possess the engraved card, bearing his name and the magic words, " Columbia University, New York." Persons who value repose must therefore be careful not to indulge their curiosity by writing to

Columbia University for information about home study courses; they will not be allowed to escape if vigilance and effort can save them. Students are also assured that "they are encouraged to ask questions and submit problems. Often the service received in connection with a single question is worth far more than the tuition fee. The home student's problems are as personal as his medical problems."

Another friend, having received a University Home Study Circular, enclosing a postcard for reply, at my request signed and returned the card. She has been bombarded ever since. The Home Study Department is obviously gifted with second sight, or, perhaps a signature and an address convey profound meaning to those versed in the subtleties of chirography. In any case the following note was received shortly afterwards:

COLUMBIA UNIVERSITY
in the City of New York
University Extension
Home Study

Dear Student: —

Do I anticipate? Among the many inquiries that come to my desk daily, I often select a few to whom, with the regular assignment blank, I am glad to send this little "form" letter.

Frankly, I think that I see, in certain ones, evidence of real desire and sincere interest, in fact, just the kind of student that we gladly welcome.

I wish you could see the letters of appreciation for the "open door" providing mind enrichment through home study.

If I have not misjudged your inquiry and the good impulse prompting it, I shall doubtless receive, by early mail, the coupon asking personal conference at this office.

I anticipate it with pleasure.

No reply was sent, but the incident was not ended. The following plaintive and touching appeal coming a few days later indicates a certain apprehension:

COLUMBIA UNIVERSITY
in the City of New York
University Extension
Home Study

Dear Inquirer: —

When I was a little fellow Mother would often send me on an errand and tie a string on my finger "lest I forget."

All of us, big and little, are apt to forget. This little note may serve to remind you of your good impulse to enrich your mind in spare time through home study.

We were glad to offer you free consultation service.

Now translate your good impulse into prompt action and let us have your early request for interview.

We enclose another appointment coupon. Maybe you mislaid the first one. Do not delay, please, others are waiting.

Are others really waiting? How many others? How long does Columbia keep them upon its list of inquirers in order to pursue them with circulars, pressing novelties upon their attention? As I write, a friend whose address changed almost three years ago receives an appeal sent to the old address! And if others are waiting, why should a great University assume so heavy a responsibility in behalf of a casual and unknown inquirer? The answer is plain: Columbia, untaxed because it is an educational institution, is in business: it has education " to sell."

But the incident was not even then closed. Appeals to intelligence having brought no response, conscience was invoked, as the following communication received a week later indicates:

COLUMBIA UNIVERSITY
in the City of New York
University Extension
Home Study

Final Notice
Dear Delinquent: —

Do you not owe us something? Yesterday died last night, leaving many unpaid obligations.

"The most enduring pleasures," says Professor Phelps of Yale, "are those of the mind and the happiest persons are those who have the most interesting thoughts."

We were glad, therefore, to note your interest in further culture and to send you descriptive pamphlets and prompt assignment to our advisory service.

We have had no response from you and we find this hard to understand. Is not some response due yourself and us? What could have caused you to overlook this courtesy?

Let us have an early appointment, or at least a line stating your lack of interest in this most important matter.

The recipient of this appeal finally wrote to express lack of time and interest. Did Columbia thereupon abandon the chase? By no means. The telephone came into play. The " delinquent " was recalcitrant; but the " professor " left his name and telephone number in the event of a change of heart.

In its zeal to be of service in times of crisis, Columbia could not rest at this point. Another circular was shortly afterwards sent broadcast through the mails, entitled *A Message to Investors*. The recipient was informed that "March fifteenth is the investor's New Year's Day." Why so? Because " his income tax return makes him review his current position and his past achievements. It brings to his attention his gains and keeps him from forgetting his losses. It instills in his mind a resolve to extend his profits further through the current year and to recoup his losses. . . . One thing only is certain; the investor who bases his moves on knowledge of fundamental principles will, as usual, show a good profit and loss statement March fifteenth a year hence. No such assurance can be given those who act on 'hunches' or tips, or on superficial data. The Columbia University course in Investments is strong in fundamentals. . . . It is a practical course, written and taught by experienced men. It is an up-to-date service, completed late in 1929 and revised in February 1930. It brings to the investor Columbia's experience of more than ten years in teaching by mail. Over one thousand investors have already enrolled. . . . Perhaps the Department can help you."

Is there any "service" that Columbia University will shirk? From the heart of the national metropolis, it has announced its readiness to organize an institute of rural life. It offers a course on the merchandising of drug products, running into such details as the "individually owned rural drug store" and "variety stores." The city of skyscrapers must, of course, have a course in "building management," separate divisions of which are devoted to "office buildings" with special attention to "janitor service," "apartment houses," "loft buildings," "financial buildings," etc. On the other hand, situated in the City of New York where there is scarcely an inch of open space, Columbia offers to resident extension students, by way of adjusting a modern university to its environment, courses in "practical poultry raising," "bee keeping," and "home vegetable and fruit growing." No wonder then that it has proposed systematic instruction on part time in "fire insurance" and a two weeks' institute at which commercial leaders may discuss the "problems created by the high degree of prosperity." The latter announcement was made some two years ago. In view of the recent speculative panic, the "institute" might now turn its attention for a fortnight in precisely the opposite direction! And so Columbia, has indeed done. On the heels of the recent stock market crash, the University issued the following printed circular:

ANNOUNCING THE NEW COLUMBIA UNIVERSITY
HOME STUDY COURSE IN INVESTMENTS

These are days of uncertainty for the investor.

The past few years have been good ones. Market prices for nearly all kinds of securities have been advancing continually with the result that profits have been almost inevitable. Anyone could make money under such conditions.

Now all this has been changed. The events of the past few weeks have proved that prices can fall as well as rise. They have brought home to the investor the sober truth that one can lose as well as gain in the market.

These are uncertain times. Few investors really know whether to buy securities, or to sell, or to await developments. Few know whether the field for future profit is the field of common stock or that of bonds.

. . . .

Perhaps you would be interested in knowing more about this course. If so, please return the enclosed post card.

Of course, the " service " of Columbia University is for the most part not education. No single institution can educate twenty thousand people by " extension " or by mail or indeed in any other way. The whole thing is business, not education; and it is a business out of which Columbia University has made in a single year a profit of $300,000! [86]

Despite the claptrap which I have exposed, I repeat that Columbia does serious work and possesses serious students in substantial subjects. But this does not meet the point. Culture cannot flourish in the feverish atmosphere of a university which draws no distinctions, sets up no criteria, and engages in every miscellaneous activity. The whole American public may never be civilized; but America's contribution to civilization depends not upon the whole public, but upon a gifted, earnest, and agglutinated minority. This minority needs to be protected against the beat-

[86] See *Treasurer's Report, 1929.*

ing waves of mediocrity and humbug. The university which fails in its responsibility to them must answer heavily at the bar of history. It ought to mean something to be a Columbia student; but when students registered in such courses as I have instanced can truthfully say, "I am a student at Columbia," when in the *Annual Report* they are enumerated as students, what does the word " student " mean? Is not Columbia engaged in lowering American culture as well as in building it up? Is it answering a spontaneous demand or manufacturing a spurious demand?

X X

The University of Chicago is quite as eager as Columbia to " serve," and the Home Study Department is quite as " efficiently " conducted by means of extravagant and misleading advertisements, form letters, circulars, etc. The following advertisement may be regarded as the opening gun of a campaign for students:

DEVELOP POWER

AT HOME

to *initiate, persevere, achieve;* carry on through life
your education; earn credit toward a Bachelor degree, by
using the 450 courses

The University of Chicago

Gives by Correspondence

Inquire, or check the advertisement to show desire and mail
to 329 Ellis Hall, University of Chicago, Chicago, Illinois.

" The privileges of our home study courses are open primarily to students." But, as a matter of fact, " they are helping persons of widely differing needs and attainments in many walks of life," and all applicants for information receive a letter assuring them that

they "will find some of them *serviceable* " — the inevitable word. They are further assured that they can
by mail acquire one half of the credits requisite to the
bachelor's degree. "Our courses " also "permit the
maximum of personal instruction." And the University of Chicago, like Columbia, exhibits its solicitude
for the most casual inquirer : " May we not hear from
you soon? " If the University does not hear, it sends
and keeps on sending as a reminder picture postcards
and form letters "to recall our previous correspondence." Moreover, the University would appear to en-
tertain a rather humble opinion of the instruction
given on its costly campus, for it circulates a leaflet in
which a home study student who apparently knows
the campus is quoted as saying: " I have found the
work (home study) superior to resident work in
several ways. . . . The ideals of true education are
more nearly met in this way than in resident work.
Contrast reading and thinking and making orderly
notes with sitting in a class taking notes from a more
or less well organized lecture, often poorly delivered."
And another: " I feel that the material of this course
is far better learned than many of the classroom subjects I hold credit for." Still another: " Contrasting
the value derived from this major by correspondence
and one I recently took in residence, I am 'strong'
for the work as you have organized it; " and another:
" The University of Chicago's work in that line is the
best given anywhere in America. A fellow has to de-
liver the goods, and he also receives more goods than
from any other such department that I know of." Let
Columbia and the state universities dare to take up
this gauntlet!

Meanwhile, needing revenue and space, Chicago,
like Columbia, might, if its own circulars be true,

convert its dormitories into paying apartments and a few laboratories into offices for correspondence courses. The offerings include a liberal abundance of substantial subjects and undoubtedly avoid the worst atrocities perpetrated by Columbia, but the list is even so sufficiently absurd; as examples, I may cite at random "psychology of advertising and selling," "guidance for investors," "advanced design," "architectural drawing," "field studies (in sociology)," "costume design," "proofreading," "copy-editing," "versification," "play-writing and stagecraft," "organic chemistry, covering the aliphatic series and the aromatic series," "technical methods of library science" (*sic!*), the "training of children," and to cap the climax, "French," "Italian," and "Spanish" in which "the student may obtain a *thoroughly* adequate reading and writing command" of the language in question; for a "knowledge of sound" he is directed to "phonograph recordings and special phonetic material in French." Now, correspondence courses may have their uses; and in a country where postage is cheap and superficiality rampant, they are likely to spring up; but that the prestige of the University of Chicago should be used to bamboozle well-meaning but untrained persons with the notion that they can thus receive a high school or a college education is scandalous. It is only fair to say that resentment is rife among the genuine scholars and scientists on the faculties of Columbia, Chicago, and other institutions.

XXI

When strong, independent institutions, such as Chicago and Columbia, priding themselves on the assumption — unwarranted, to my thinking — that they set the pace for the unfortunates who derive their income from legislatures,[87] are thus guilty, one cannot be surprised by anything that emanates from state universities. The University of Wisconsin offers instruction by correspondence at almost every level from " elementary and grammar school studies " to university studies " taken for credit toward a degree." The range of opportunity is broad, including, as it does, " ancient and modern languages " (pronunciation comes singularly easy to correspondence students!), " comparative literature," " engineering (civil, electrical, structural, or mechanical)," " science," " business," " mathematics," " library methods," " speech," " pharmacy," " physical education," etc., etc. Among the special courses to be found under these general headings, one may single out " retail advertising," " show-card writing," " vocational guidance," " shop arithmetic," " cupola practice," " the prospective mother," " the child in disease," " cooking for rural schools," " sewing," " elementary school library methods," " community music," " prescription practice," " speech writing," " debate," and " speech teaching problems." Nor is the " service " of a state university limited to trivial instruction by mail or " institutes." To a certain extent, contacts between faculty and business, industry, health, sanitation, or philanthropy are essential to the faculty itself. To that extent — and to that extent only — such contacts should take place. But as the function of the university is the increase of knowledge and the training of men, contacts and responsibilities are harmful to the uni-

[87] The " pace " may be set for better or worse. The Ann Arbor *Daily News* (August 25, 1930) announces that the University of Michigan is about to offer " correspondence courses patterned after the Columbia plan."

versity, and hence to society, as soon as they multiply beyond the point I have indicated. Such harmful and disorganizing multiplication is abundantly in evidence: it takes place in endowed institutions, when professors are at the beck and call of industries, conferences, governments, with or without remuneration and regardless of the relation between the effort expended and real results achieved; it takes place, perhaps even more freely and, if this be so, more disastrously in tax-supported institutions whose economists may be disturbed by anxious corporations, whose chemists and agriculturists are made to bear more than a disinterested and scientific responsibility for cattle and crops, and whose educational staff may be called on to render routine service in connection with state or local school problems. I admit that the line is hard to draw. But meanwhile the university should by precept and by example endeavour to convince the public that in the long run it will suffer, not gain, if it treats its universities largely as service institutions. And in any event, universities, among them Ohio, Michigan, and Wisconsin, cannot be excused when they actually retard the development of proper governmental agencies by themselves reaching out for practical responsibilities that do not belong to universities at all. Instead of doing all they can, they should be doing as little as they can — training men competent to hold the posts which the present activities of the universities themselves really keep from developing.

On inquiry I find some difference of opinion as to the merits of the persons who carry the main burden of " service." The executive head of the home study department of one university assured me that the work was done by the " best young men " always suggested by the department appealed to. But a distinguished economist in the same institution assured me that no "first-rate man" was ever detailed for such duty: "We suggest poorly paid third-rate men, whose income needs supplementing." The difference in point of view is not without significance to the students, whether they be competent and earnest or merely victims of adroit advertising.

I have intimated a doubt as to the extent to which the rage for "credits" in American education really represents a desire on the part of persons to be educated or an unworthy effort on the part of colleges and universities to "sell education" [88] — at a profit, whenever possible. Under date of December 9, 1929, the permanent secretary of the Association of American Colleges addressed a letter to every "dear colleague" — and that includes *over four hundred colleges* — to the effect that an "exhibit of various forms of publicity material used by colleges" was planned "as a feature of the annual meetings." He desired to obtain "representative samples of material found valuable both as regular college publicity and in connection with money-raising, recruiting and good-will campaigns"; among other things he desired typi-

[88] This phrase is actually in a report of the Special Curriculum Committee to the Trustees of Trinity College (June 15, 1929): "One of them (apparently the Faculty) prefaced his views by the postulate that the College is a business corporation with education to sell." To its credit be it said, the New York *Times* made an editorial protest: "It (Trinity College) is a cultural institution and its function is not commercial." But the report in question told the truth — though, fortunately, not the whole truth. Columbia, Harvard, Chicago, the state universities, and many institutions of equal and lesser prominence and importance are "selling" education; but the business plane is lower than that of reputable commercial establishments, for the latter return the buyer's money, if the "goods" fail to correspond with the terms of the advertisement. It has apparently not yet occurred to our universities that "religion" was once "sold" and with the same consequences to the church that are likely to overtake the universities. Some day the "money-changers" will be driven — or laughed — out of the university temple.

cal "news releases, including samples of stories," "posters for use in street cars," "sample speeches," etc. So genuine and spontaneous is the uprising of the American populace by which the universities complain that they have been overwhelmed! [89]

XXII

It is idle to labour the point further; but one may comment on a flagrant and apparently unnoticed contradiction. The current literature of college education emphasizes the importance of contact between instructor and student and attributes no small part of the failure of the college to mass-education on the campus. The dictum of Mark Hopkins is frequently recalled: the ideal college consists of a log of wood with an instructor at one end and a student at the other. The preceptorial system introduced at Princeton by President Wilson, the honours work at Harvard and Swarthmore, the tutorial system at Harvard — all are efforts to establish close, informal contacts between members of the student body and the instructing staff. If the difficulties thus attacked are real — and no one disputes the fact — in what terms is one to characterize the advertising of Chicago, Columbia, and other institutions which spread before thousands the alluring prospect of obtaining just as good an education — an education of "university grade" (Columbia) — by mail? The problem of America is not "Main Street"; there are Main Streets in all countries. The hopelessness of America lies in the inability and unwillingness of those occupying seats of intel-

[89] This organization includes 422 colleges in the United States, among them Stanford, Yale, University of Chicago, Amherst, Williams, Harvard, Radcliffe, Dartmouth, Princeton, Columbia, Cornell, Bryn Mawr, Swarthmore, Vanderbilt, etc.

ligence to distinguish between genuine culture and superficial veneer, in the lowering of institutions which should exemplify intellectual distinctions to the level of the venders of patent medicines. So, too, there are Babbitts in all countries, not only in the United States; but "Babbittry" in the presidency of great universities is an exclusively — as it is a wide-spread — American phenomenon. No nation responds to exacting leadership more readily than the United States: witness the response to the Johns Hopkins at its founding, to the advanced work of the California Institute of Technology, to the reorganization of Swarthmore; but the lessons of history, even of recent history, are for the most part lost upon the eminent university heads of our own time. To be sure, universities might be too remote, too cloistral, too academic. But American universities have yet to learn that participation is wholesome only when subordinated to educational function, only when it takes place at a high, disinterested, intellectual level.[90]

XXIII

With the "service" functions which many American universities have undertaken, I class certain "schools" or "departments" of a vocational character — schools of domestic science or household arts, schools of journalism, business, library science or librarianship, optometry, hotel management, etc., none of which belongs within a university. I cannot hope, within the limits of this volume, to discuss them all

[90] Of the great American universities that I have mentioned, one, Princeton, still largely a college though in some departments important graduate groups are developing, does no "service" work whatsoever of the type which I have described; another, Yale, mostly a college, does little and "has no ambitions in that direction." (Letter from the President.)

separately or fully; but I can at least raise the question of the propriety of including them in a modern university and give reasons for my scepticism — to use no stronger word.

Let us turn for a moment to schools of domestic science. One wonders what " science " means to the university authorities who conduct or condone faculties of domestic science. The departments bloom like the cedars of Lebanon at Columbia, Chicago, and the state universities. Despite the difficulty experienced by universities and their medical faculties in obtaining professors of bio-chemistry, the departments of domestic science or household arts at Columbia and Chicago boast staffs that undertake to deal with nutritional problems and to offer advanced degrees (A.M., Ph.D.) indifferently to persons who write theses on underwear and on topics in the field of physiological chemistry. A course on catering is found side by side with research in food and nutrition. It is of course absurd to suppose that either competent teachers or competent students can be found in departments of this kind, at a time when there is a strong and unsatisfied demand for both in academic and medical departments of superior dignity and importance. None the less Chicago has in the Department of Home Economics and Household Administration given Ph.D. degrees for theses on the " Basal Metabolism and Urinary Creatinine, Creatine and Uric Acid of School Children," the " Coefficient of Digestibility and Specific Dynamic Action of a Simple Mixed Diet in Contrasting Types of Individuals," "Variations in Demand for Clothing at Different Income Levels — A Study in the Behaviour of the Consumer," and M.A. degrees for theses on " Photographic Studies on Boiled Icing," " Trends in Hosiery

Advertising," "An Analysis of Paring Knives in Terms of Time and Material Wastes in Paring Potatoes," "A Study of Controlled Conditions in Cooking Hams," "Buying Women's Garments by Mail," "Style Cycles in Women's Undergarments," and finally "A Time and Motion Comparison on Four Methods of Dishwashing." In form and aspect nothing could be more impressive. The last-mentioned thesis, for example, bears the title page:

THE UNIVERSITY OF CHICAGO

A TIME AND MOTION COMPARISON ON FOUR
METHODS OF DISHWASHING

A DISSERTATION
SUBMITTED TO THE GRADUATE FACULTY
IN CANDIDACY FOR THE DEGREE OF
MASTER OF ARTS

Nor does the resemblance to scientific research cease with the title page. The dissertation includes: Introduction, Review of Literature, Purpose, Limitations, Method of Procedure, Results and Comparisons, Conclusions and Recommendations, Conclusions (once more!), Bibliography. Time was kept and motions counted for "the removal of dishes from table to tea cart" and similar operations. In the washing of dishes, motions were counted and tabulated for "approach stove, grasp teakettle, remove lid at stove," "travel to sink, turn hot water faucet on," "turn hot water faucet partially off," "travel to stove, replace lid, turn fuel on," "approach sink," etc., over a total of a hundred typewritten pages of tables and explanatory comment, such as "stooping and lifting are fatiguing." In the effort to find subjects for dissertations the ingenuity of teachers is taxed to the uttermost and every nook and corner of home and school ransacked for the merest scrap of a suggestion. The conclusion of the research on dishwashing is therefore perhaps less important than its suggestiveness. A departmental head, bound to find subjects for research, may rejoice in the fact that the same method of "job-analysis" ought to be applied to "all the three hundred plus processes" that are part of the housewife's activities. Thus there loom in the near distance three hundred theses, and how many additional theses will be suggested by each of the three hundred it staggers the imagination of a professional mathematician to contemplate. Now of course the young housewife, who is doing her own work, must not only read and apply the thesis on dishwashing but each of the "the three hundred plus" others. If she reads a thesis a day, she will be busy for a year; but, fortunately for her, the dissertation in question has not yet been printed.

The citations above made open new vistas to "research"; for if the comparative merits of various ways of washing dishes make a worthy subject of academic recognition and expenditure, why not the comparative merits of freezing cream, mixing soft drinks — or hard, etc.? And if bacteria in men's undershirts, why not bacteria in men's socks or in each of the diminishing number of garments, male and female — nowadays, alas, a more limited field than in the Victorian era! The fear that the conquests of science may shortly leave research nothing to do vanishes before the new Alexanders, who have discovered in the inane and trivial inexhaustible worlds to conquer!

I should not like it to be supposed that I have treated the Department of Home Economics and

Household Administration of the University with levity. Fully cognizant of the fact that I am not a cook, a chemist, or a dressmaker, I submitted the list of Chicago theses to two eminent authorities in the fields of bio-chemistry and nutrition. They have favoured me with thoughtful opinions. The chemist writes:

"I feel that the standard of research for dissertations for a doctor's degree should be the same for all departments. Of the problems enumerated, perhaps two require the technique which would be the minimum required by a scientific department from a candidate for the Ph.D. degree."

The other wrote:

"One has the feeling that the whole thing is superficial and that the subjects are worked up merely because it is necessary to write a thesis in order to get a degree. You could get no idea of the 'Extent of Breast Feeding' by a 'Statistical Study of Two Hundred Maternity Hospital Cases,' nor can you get anywhere by studying 'Likes and Dislikes of Two Hundred and Sixty Pre-School Children.' And then: 'Changes in Fat Constants in Fats Used for Frying Doughnuts.' Why doughnuts? For myself, I hope that nothing comes of this study, because otherwise the logical thing to do would be to study the same result in relation to fried bananas, egg plant, oysters, etc. The whole thing deepens the impression that we live in a machine age and in an era of mass production."

Columbia's showing does not differ in kind. Through Teachers College, Columbia offers courses in "methods of experimental and comparative cookery"; credit may also be obtained through courses in "tea room cookery,"[91] in "food etiquette and hospitality," in the "principles of home laundering." Among subjects accepted as theses for Ph.D. degrees may be

[91] The University of Wisconsin offers an unusually attractive course in "tea room and cafeteria management," because "a field trip to Chicago is required."

instanced " Some Attempts to Standardize Oven Temperatures for Cookery Processes " and " Some Sugar-Saving Sweets for Every Day." [92] "Abstracts on Recent Research in Cookery and Allied Subjects" prepared by an instructor, but introduced by a professor, deals in Part I with " refrigeration." [93] As evidence of the scientific depth of the " research " I quote the following:

" The theory of refrigeration implies the reduction of the temperature of a body below that of the surrounding environment."

" Frequent opening and closing of the doors of the food chamber causes an increase in ice consumption and a temporary rise in the temperature of the food chamber."

" A good refrigerator should have a temperature satisfactory for the preservation of food."

In Part II of the same series of " Research Abstracts," devoted to " ice cream," an expectant public is informed, that as respects " the influence of sugar," the primary function of sugar in ice cream is to sweeten it. [94] Secondary and tertiary functions are not enumerated. And I must not forget to call attention to the bibliography by means of which these recondite facts are buttressed — among the eighty-one cited being a goodly number of advertising circulars!

Now I grant that in America there may be need of training some persons in cooking, clothing, and housekeeping; and need, also, to train persons to teach those subjects, though I suspect strongly that a basi-

[92] The activity of the Johns Hopkins University in home economics appears to be limited to " a survey course of the new *trends* (Italics mine) in home economics, including subject-matter, methods and lesson plans for foods and cookery, clothing and textiles, household management and child care." One wonders what would happen to higher education in the United States if the word " trend " were expunged from the academic vocabulary. There is no telling how much futile effort and expenditure would thereby be saved.

[93] *Teachers College Record*, January 1930, pp. 320–331.

[94] *Teachers College Record*, February 1930, p. 472.

cally good general education, even if limited, would in the end produce better cooks and teachers of cooking, than ever emerge from these premature and narrowing *ad hoc* efforts. But, however this may be, neither from cultural, practical, nor scientific standpoints, are the persons who need the training, the persons who give the training, or the subjects themselves of university calibre. Separate modest, inexpensive, and unpretentious institutions, conducted by teachers who are graduates of the school of experience will achieve the end far more effectively than the pretentious establishments that now encumber many universities; and once these activities, like " extension " and " home study," have been put in their proper place, there is a somewhat increased possibility that sound concepts of science and culture may become definite and obtain authority. As a matter of fact, today children " learn " domestic science in the elementary schools; they " learn " it again in the high schools; and now we find students " learning " it in college and graduate school. And what can they really do at the end? Two of the great universities in the Middle West have after disastrous experience with annual deficits found it impossible to find a Ph.D. in domestic science who could handle their own food problems and balance their budgets; one of them has therefore placed in charge a woman who had had only an ordinary education but had successfully managed a boarding-house, with the prompt result that the deficit at once disappeared and the students were better fed. Another, similarly discouraged, turned from its graduates in domestic science and gave the problem to a young man who had been an instructor in French but wished employment on the administrative side of the university. Instead of a deficit, the department showed a profit approximating $50,000 at the end of the very first year. Thus, schools, colleges, and universities throw away the opportunity really to *educate*, for the sake of a flimsy and unpractical "training" that for the most part does not even *train*. If this investigation were carried into the teaching of agriculture in elementary schools, high schools, and colleges, an even greater waste of funds would be disclosed, with, if possible, even less in the way of concrete results. The truth is that educated women when suddenly confronted with domestic problems solve them happily and easily. In his *Life* of his wife Professor George Herbert Palmer sums up the whole thing in a single paragraph:

"In all this domestic side of life she took great pleasure, becoming a joyous expert not merely in that cheap thing, 'domestic science,' but in the subtler matters of domestic art. Powers trained elsewhere were quickly adjusted to the home and used for the comfort of those she loved. When at one time she was struggling with a new cook on the subject of bad bread, and after encountering the usual excuses of oven, flour, and yeast, had invaded the kitchen and herself produced an excellent loaf, astonished Bridget summed up the situation in an epigram which deserves to be recorded: 'That's what education means — to be able to do what you've never done before.'" [95]

The theory of education has never been more incisively stated; Bridget's words may be unreservedly commended to university and college presidents and to heads of schools of business, journalism, and domestic science. But there are college presidents in America who are as intelligent as "Bridget." Professors of English or Latin or philosophy, stepping into a college presidency, have had to deal in short order with problems of drainage, power house, food,

[95] George Herbert Palmer, *The Life of Alice Freeman Palmer* (Boston, 1908), pp. 225–26.

athletics, money, leaking roofs, new buildings, and educational reorganization. They have successfully turned their trained minds to one after another easily, sensibly, and good-humouredly.

XXIV

On a par with university faculties of cookery and clothing, I place university schools of journalism. The staff is usually made up of journalists, sometimes retired, sometimes still active as night editors, managing editors, book editors, or theatrical critics. From these facts, the scholarly level of the university school of journalism may be surmised. At Columbia the course consumes four years, the first two of which comprise the usual elements of a college education, that is, they are of secondary school range. The opportunities thus offered to the prospective young journalist are excellent as far as they go; if he is sensible, lucky, capable, and industrious, he may obtain good instruction in English, modern languages, politics, or economics. But beginning with the third year — the first in the School of Journalism itself — a dismal period — the " professional " courses concern themselves with such topics as " newspaper practice," " psychology of news interest," " reporting," " the law of libel," " feature writing," and the " graduate " courses with " book reviewing," " dramatic criticism," and " Sunday supplement work." It has even been proposed somewhere to offer a course in the technique of utilization of the press and other media for the distribution of news and feature articles — a course against which newspapers have themselves protested on the ground that it lowers the dignity and reliability of the press. Interspersed with technical courses are elective courses in " modern European fiction " and " international relations," during which the fog may rise.

"There was in my day," writes a student who passed through the Columbia School a few years ago, " no course or seminar in which critical or constructive evaluations of the profession as such were in order. An individual attempt to deal with newspapers as a social institution with responsibilities and opportunities was frowned on by the instructors, who, with two notable exceptions (one of them the present Director of the School) were 'hard-boiled' practising or retired newspaper men. There were the newspapers; if you knew how, you could get a job on them; 'high brows' were not wanted; but of course in this age you must be 'trained' to get on. . . . The School of Journalism leaves ' the profession ' unchanged."

At the end of his discipline the student usually receives the degree of B. Lit.; but an additional year, at the end of which a " substantial article of not less than 15,000 words on a journalistic subject " must be produced, entitles the candidate to the higher degree of Master of Science.

The University of Wisconsin has somewhat outstripped Columbia. In order to be modern, one must specialize: hence Wisconsin outlines five sets of courses, one for the daily newspaper group, the second for the community newspaper group, the third for the advertising group, and the fourth for the magazine group. The final set of courses is provided for prospective teachers of journalism!

The net result is the further dilution of an already diluted education by the effort to teach under the guise of a profession a few practical tricks and adjustments that an educated or clever youth would rapidly pick up " on the job." His newspaper training and value will of course come only with time. The student whom I quoted above writes further: " I am ' dead ' certain that it does not require two years to acquire the technical equipment and indeed I doubt whether it can be acquired at all ' off the job.' " On the absurdities to which I have called attention, further comment is wasted. The newspaper is a social phenomenon of tremendous importance, the critical study of which is well worthy of a university department of social science. But journalism is not a profession in the sense in which law and medicine are professions. The " professional " training of the school of journalism simply cuts short the possibility of genuine culture at its most important moment. Assuredly no make-believe under the label of "professional" training will in the long run compensate for the loss of a substantial education in history, politics, literature, science, and philosophy.

XXV

Undergraduate schools of commerce or business have long existed at Chicago, Columbia,[96] the state universities, and elsewhere. They are, in my opinion, poor substitutes for a sound general college education and in the long run would seem likely to be of little importance even from a vocational point of view. More pretentious and for that reason more dangerous is the Harvard Graduate School of Business Adminis-

[96] In this connection, I may once more call attention to the fact that the Director of the School of Business at Columbia University is simultaneously Director of Extension Teaching and Professor of Latin (Epigraphy). Consider for a moment the smile that would traverse all Europe if Professor Gilbert Murray were made Director of a School of Business at Oxford or Professor Wilamowitz made Director of the *Handelshochschule* at Berlin. What does a university really think of either classics or business when any such ridiculous combination of functions is made?

tration, which is in theory a professional school. To this enterprise I shall confine myself.[97]

Is business a profession? In a loose way, the term "profession" is used merely as the antithesis to "amateur"; hence one may speak of a professional cook or a professional football player, a professional barber, dancer, or business man. But, from the standpoint of the university, though cooks and business men have in many institutions ensconced themselves comfortably in the academic groves, a day of reckoning is at hand. Times change, to be sure, and the academically unprofessional barber of former days legitimately finds himself the full-time professor of surgery today. Whatever our decision at this moment, we shall not maintain that a changed social and economic order, a changed system of ethical values, a deeper knowledge of economics may not some day convert business into a profession. But is it a profession today in any other than the amateur sense above described? Is the Harvard Business School helping or hampering a genuinely professional evolution?

I have already pointed out the fact that professions are learned professions, that they have cultural roots and a code embodying an ideal; that in the long course of their history, one can make out the essentially intellectual nature of their attack on problems. The case is different with business.[98] The profit-making motive must dominate; advertising is an element indispensable to success. The ways of carrying on business

[97] Graduate work with advanced degrees is also offered by the other schools of business or commerce mentioned in the text.

[98] Substantially the same criteria are set up by Professor Edwin F. Gay, *Social Progress and Business Education, Proceedings of Northwestern University Conference on Business Education*, June 1927, p. 84. Professor Gay, the first Dean of the Harvard School, takes a hopeful — perhaps one should rather say a prayerful — view of both business and schools of business; but he avoids details.

have changed — and in many ways for the better. Occasionally, a business man conducts his business like an artist or a philosopher, but, in general, business is business today, as it has ever been; only, to an extent never before known, it dominates the world, invades with its standards alien realms, and draws into its vortex spirits that might otherwise be creative in government, science, or art.

Now I am not supposing that the world should try to rid itself of business. Business has always been with us; it always will be; it always should be. Among other results, it both " serves " and civilizes. Through business the world will be made happier and more comfortable; through business culture and intelligence may be brought within reach of millions who would otherwise be only hewers of wood and drawers of water. But is business today in itself an end fine enough, impersonal enough, intelligent enough, fastidious enough, to deserve to be called a profession? I do not myself think so; nor is such the prevalent view in older civilizations in which modern business, cultivated with vigour as it is, is compelled to measure itself against a rich culture supported by the thick soil of centuries. Alas, in present-day America, the soil is thin; on a thin soil, art and science and philosophy do not readily thrive; business does.

Modern business does not satisfy the criteria of a profession; it is shrewd, energetic, and clever, rather than intellectual in character; it aims — and under our present social organization must aim — at its own advantage, rather than at noble purpose within itself. The fact that many successful business men generously contribute funds to philanthropy does not prove that present-day business as business has, can have, or should have as its object anything other than success; though, on the other hand, financial success does not disprove a high conception of effort on the part of individuals whose commercial efforts are deeply imbued with the aesthetic, scientific, and altruistic marks characteristic of professions rightly esteemed as such.

That business is a phenomenon of major importance is undeniable; that, therefore, it behooves universities interested in phenomena and in problems to study the phenomena and problems of business is clear. It is one thing, however, for economists and sociologists to study the phenomena of modern business in a school of business or in a department of economics, and it is quite another thing — and, in my judgment, an irrelevant and unworthy thing — for a modern university to undertake to " shortcircuit " experience and to furnish advertisers, salesmen, or handy men for banks, department stores, or transportation companies. Let the economists study banking, trade cycles, and transportation; let the chemists study textiles and foods; and let the psychologists study advertising, not in order to train business men to attract the public but in order to understand what takes place when a jingle like " not a cough in a carload " persuades a nation to buy a new brand of cigarettes. Technical accomplishments such as salesmanship, etc. belong to technological schools or must be left to apprenticeship.

Thus Professor Wesley Mitchell and Professor Seligman and their associates at Columbia University are quite as legitimately in place in a university as the astronomers who are studying sun spots or historians and ethnologists who are puzzling over the Balkans; but neither of these distinguished students of taxation or economics has any part in the Columbia School of Business. There are in the Harvard School of Business men of scientific turn of mind — students of economic history, of the phenomena of economics, transportation, and banking, for example. While then the scholars on the staff of the Harvard Business School are really and critically interested in phenomena, the main emphasis of the School from the standpoint of its administration is concentrated on " getting on " — the canker of American life. A pamphlet of 145 pages describes the School; from beginning to end there is not a sentence or a word indicative of professional or scientific conception. " In former times the man who worked up from the bottom had a better chance " (p. 11) ; " today a business school provides the training needed for use " (p. 11) ; " properly taught, the graduate can go into business with a preparation which permits rapid progress " (p. 12) ; " the commonly satisfactory progress in business made by men who have recently completed the course " (pp. 14, 15). What university school of medicine would dare to define its ideals and results in such terms? Contrast these wretched *ad hoc* appeals with the incisive utterance of an Oxford professor, who is at once a scholar and a man of affairs :

"Most of the facts which are necessary to the business man can be acquired either before the student enters the university — if they are elements of general information — or after he goes into business — if they happen to be of special value for his walk of life." [99]

From the standpoint of business itself, the Harvard School of Business takes a narrow view. Is modern business to be accepted at its own claim, or has a civilized society some critical responsibility in respect to it? The Harvard Business School raises neither ethical

[99] De Madariaga, *loc. cit.*, p. 8.

nor social questions; it does not put business on the
defensive as the Harvard Faculty of Medicine puts
empirical medicine on the defensive; it does not even
take a broad view of business as business.[100] For example, it describes its department devoted to foreign
trade without one word as to the importance of mas-
tering foreign languages [101] or acquiring a sympathetic knowledge of the history and " *mores* " of foreign
countries; attention is concentrated on superficial
tricks, really to be acquired only by contact and experience, "the organization of the export department," " advertising," " sales personnel," " selection
and management of the export sales force." This is
not only to waste cultural opportunities; it is un-
imaginative and short-sighted from the sheer business point of view. In precisely the same base and
narrow spirit does this pretentious graduate school
of America's oldest and still on the whole greatest
university deal with advertising "as a tool to be
used in the promotion of sales." Does the course in
advertising raise any real questions? Not at all. It accepts the thing and learnedly proceeds to train " executives " to " consider the use and application of advertising to accomplish certain results." The School even

[100] A student of the Business School writes of it as follows: " I have
been disappointed to find that in the first year at least the student body is
not encouraged to weigh the system they are studying in any scheme of
values. . . . The point of view is still analytical with a view to action.
The capitalistic system is assumed as the necessary point of departure. Too
many professors are inclined to snicker at ' philosophizing,' as one called
it in my presence. ' Hard-boiled ' thinking as to ' How ' is called for; thinking as to the ' Why ' is considered academic."

[101] The pamphlet contains two brief references to modern languages:
in describing " preparatory studies," it speaks mildly of modern languages
as "beneficial "; to obtain the doctorate (not the Master's degree), "the
candidate must be able to use *in his special field* at least one modern
foreign language " — a merely technical requirement and that only in reference to the highest degree bestowed. In 1926–27, two such degrees were
awarded; the student body numbered 785.

offers annual advertising awards.[102] A prize of $2,000 was recently bestowed upon a young woman who organized a Campaign for Pet Milk. Is it a proper concern of Harvard University to coöperate with business to market a product of this or any other kind? In 1929 a prize was awarded for an advertisement entitled " The Call That Will Wake Any Mother "; the year before, for one entitled " Kill My Cow for an Editor? I should say not! " " An award of One Thousand Dollars ($1,000.00) will be given for the advertising research . . . conspicuous in furthering the knowledge and science of advertising." [103] " Advertising *research!* " The " *science* of advertising! " What do the real scholars and scientists on the Faculty of Harvard University think of the company in which the University thus places them? The question does not seem to have occurred to the trustees of an institution whose seal continues to contain the word, " *Veritas.*" " *Veritas*" has little to do with the case! The new seal of Harvard University may some day contain the words — *Veritas et Ars Venditoria!* [104]

Faced suddenly with the problem of training for business a thousand students — graduate students — the School had to manufacture a literature. Texts and reference books existed in the field of economics, which was, of course, already cultivated on the campus of

[102] The Harvard Advertising Awards are paid from a fund set up in 1923. The awards are made annually by a jury composed of advertising managers, publicity directors, and certain members of the faculty of the Business School.

[103] *Harvard Advertising Awards for 1930,* p. 9.

[104] While I have singled out the Harvard School of Business, I should call attention to the fact that other university schools of business are no better and no different. Thus Columbia teaches the psychology of salesmanship, aiming " to present in a *scientific* manner those facts of psychology that bear on the sales process " ; " the work of the spring session (in ' advertising research ') will consist . . . of a series of tests of advertisements, slogans, logotype," etc.

the University. But the School of Business had to do something that was not already being done by the economists and statisticians of the University — some of whom it lured into the new adventure — or by an ordinary school of accounting. The head of the institution had an inspiration. The great Langdell had conceived the idea of using case books for instruction in law; why not case books in business? Of the fact that the case book in law had developed unexpected shortcomings from the University point of view he was perhaps not cognizant; anyway the Harvard Graduate School of Business has in short order ground out a series of case books in business. Research had also to be gotten under way.[105] One can gather something as to the intelligence and sense of humour characteristic of those who out of hand contrived the School from the titles of the literature emanating from the Research Department. Here are specimens: "Operating Accounts for Retail Drug Stores," "Operating Accounts for Retail Grocery Stores," "Record Sheets for Retail Hardware Stores," "Merchandise Control in Women's Shoe Departments of Department Stores," "Operating Expenses in Retail Jewelry Stores" (a separate volume for each year from 1919 to 1928), "Methods of Paying Salesmen and Operating Expenses in the Wholesale Grocery Business in 1918."[106]

[105] Though the Business Faculty had managed its own finances so badly that no money was left for the purpose. See p. 171.

[106] In less than ten years, fifteen large volumes on "Problems" in Advertising, Sales Management, etc., have been produced by the School. "Within a period of ten months no less than eight books in this series have been brought from the press." (*The Harvard Problem Books* — inside cover.) Can this be matched for productivity? They range in size from 386 to 1,050 pages. Their purpose is baldly stated: "to prepare the student for actual business." There is not the faintest glimmer of social, ethical, philosophical, historic, or cultural interest in the entire document. It is "advertising," in neither letter nor spirit differing from the type of advertising employed to sell Paris garters, patent medicines, or rayon stockings.

If an educated man, a Harvard graduate, really wishes to become a retail drug or hardware merchant or a wholesale grocery salesman, does not Harvard put a low valuation on its training and his capacity when it provides him with special graduate training for the career? Cannot something be left to wit, to experience, and to the vocational "business college?" And how, once more, does this sort of thing react on the University at large and on American culture and civilization? One is told on the campus that it has stimulated the desire for studies that will lead to a " job " — not quite the purpose that Harvard University should serve.

But there are other respects in which the organization of the Harvard Graduate School of Business Administration resembles the ordinary vocational business college. On the occasion of a visit to the School, I copied from the bulletin board the following notice:

"Requisite graphs have not been received from the following:

(a list of more than 70 names)

These must be submitted without delay or the grades will be recorded as zero."

The students in question are, be it remembered, college graduates from among whom " executives " are to be obtained. To my inquiry as to why such school-boy methods are employed, the reply was made that " the faculty would not know otherwise how to grade (and hence recommend) them." It had apparently not occurred to the faculty that failure to do his duty without coercion is perhaps the most significant fact that could possibly be recorded respecting a candidate in training for a responsible business post! How much light does a coerced graph throw on the maturity and fitness of a graduate student?

The School of Business was founded by a New York financier who gave $6,000,000 for the purpose. Of this sum, $5,000,000 were at once invested in buildings, calculated to accommodate 1,000 students. The sum of $1,000,000, increased by subsequent gifts to $2,700,000, was retained as a permanent fund. The dormitories now show a profit of $100,000 a year; an income of $125,000 is yielded by endowment; the School is thus mainly carried by fees. But the School, as I have shown above, does " research "; and research, even research in advertising, is expensive. Hitherto " research " has been financed by " hand-to-mouth " [107] methods. There has resulted " financial uncertainty " and the " library program presents serious problems." Is it too much to ask that the persons who conduct the Harvard Graduate School of Business Administration should themselves pursue fairly sound business methods? Would a sound business man invest five-sixths of his original capital in bricks and mortar and trust to luck for the money needed to give substance and vitality to the enterprise? One wonders whether the Faculty should not itself be sent to school — preferably the school of experience! In order to relieve the situation created by unsound business procedure, a voluntary committee has now undertaken to form an association of two hundred and fifty, each of whom will contribute $1,000 a year " to stabilize and promote research and the collection of material for the teaching of business." The management of the Fund is vested in a Board of Trustees, elected by the subscribers, who characterize themselves as " selected business leaders."

[107] Phrases quoted are all from a recently published document entitled " The Two Hundred Fifty Associates of the Harvard Business School."

Their intentions are undoubtedly innocent and honourable — but what becomes of academic freedom and scientific spirit, when the research funds of a School operating in the social and economic realm and working " in finance, government, labour relations, . . . and public utilities " are not only year by year derived from but managed by " selected business leaders " and by them alone? [108] Could anything more naïve be imagined? Harvard University has nothing to do with it. Neither the President, the Corporation, nor the Faculty is mentioned in the twelve pages of the document explaining the project! " The Dean of the School hopes to make membership in the Associates a source of real satisfaction." And this at Harvard!

XXVI

The point that I have been trying to stress, viz., that universities need not and should not concern themselves with miscellaneous training at or near the vocational level could be illustrated further, if I had time and space in which to discuss schools of pharmacy, library science,[109] town-planning, social service, etc.

[108] " Opportunities will be accorded all members to observe the experiments of the School at first hand and, in so far as may be practicable, to participate in them."

[109] Does library training belong to a university? And if it does not necessarily belong there, it has no business there at all — such is the importance of preserving university ideals pure and undefiled. The Carnegie Corporation has — unwisely, in my opinion — appropriated $1,410,000 to the Graduate School of Library Service at the University of Chicago, and similar schools have been established at Columbia, Western Reserve, and the state universities. Nevertheless, the President of the Carnegie Corporation in his latest *Annual Report* (1929) pp. 12, 13, says:

" Pratt Institute, it may be pointed out, offers no degree at all, and still maintains its place as one of the best schools for the professional study of librarianship " — thus giving the " university " case completely away.

And again — and here President Keppel not only destroys the university school of library science but puts his finger on the spot:

" The way should be made easy for able men with scholarly tastes and

In so far as training schools are really needed in these branches, they belong elsewhere than on the university campus. I venture, however, in bringing the consideration of these " service " schools to an end, to call attention to two more — perhaps the most amusing and reprehensible of all these academic efforts to modernize universities.

A few years ago, the New York Legislature created the practice of optometry, as a thing in itself, quite distinct from ophthalmology. Is the mere measurement of vision apart from a study of the entire eye a safe or sound procedure? There is high scientific authority for a negative answer. But Columbia must " serve." It immediately established courses in optometry devised not on the basis of the merits of the case, but in strict conformity with the New York law. The law required two years of study on the basis of an ordinary high school education; so did Columbia. The University Extension Announcement for 1927–28 announced a " two-year course leading to the certificate of graduation in optometry "; the announcement claimed only that it was as " nearly satisfactory " as possible under the circumstances. Nor was this cheap and easy training something that sprang up in the " pioneer days " which are usually urged in America in extenuation of academic absurdity; it is but a matter of yesterday. Simultaneously a " four-year course leading to the degree of B.Sc." plus a certificate in optometry was offered among the professional courses of the University. To make matters simpler, students who had not received the meagre education requisite for matriculation could obtain additional preliminary education through late afternoon or evening classes. Thus the

---

training in letters to shift from the overcrowded field of English teaching (or, I should add, any other) to librarianship, etc."

net was flung as widely as was humanly possible. Latterly, the law has changed; so therefore has Columbia. Indeed, the University states that "the optometry courses in Columbia University have been planned and modified always in accordance with the New York State Optometry Law." [110] Originally a two-year course sufficed. Now, "the two-year course is no longer given." [111] Has the human eye changed? No, only the New York law. Thus in this department Columbia abdicated responsibility in favour of the New York State Legislature! A distinguished ophthalmologist of international scientific reputation assures me — what ordinary common sense must of itself perceive — that "there is always danger that the optometrists will not discover lesions that are just beginning," adding the equally fatal comment, "there are other objections to their methods." But what does Columbia University care about that?

The second of the schools or departments with which I close this imperfect account of the "service" activities of American universities is to be found at Cornell University. Cornell, striking out into a hitherto uncharted sea, has discovered that the "profession (not the vocation, be it noted) of hotel management has gained recognition from educators. Through the coöperation and financial assistance of the American Hotel Association," the University is enabled to offer an undergraduate course made up of four years of "academic" work and "three summer periods of supervised work at regular pay-roll jobs in approved hotels." At the end of this exacting intellectual and practical training, the student enters life as a bachelor of science! The curriculum includes courses in "meat

[110] *Bulletin of Information — Professional Courses in Optometry, 1929–1930,* p. 5.
[111] *Loc. cit.,* p. 6.

cutting," "auxiliary equipment," "psychology," "personnel management," "front office practice," "mechanism of hotel machines," etc. "To illustrate the type of experience for which credit" towards the degree of Bachelor of Science is given, "a few of the jobs held last summer by Cornell hotel students are listed" — among them, waiter captain, room clerk, bus boy, bellman, front office clerk, key and mail clerk, pantry man, food checker — all quite plainly liberalizing experiences which no prospective hotel manager or employe can afford to miss during the fateful college years! Bachelors of science who have devoted four precious years to this stimulating, enlightening, and broadening collegiate training have already risen to elevated posts — among them, that of room clerk at Swampscott, Massachusetts, assistant steward at one of the Pennsylvania Railroad Station restaurants, bell captain at Star Lake, New York, and manager of a "lodge" at Towanda, Pennsylvania, (population 4609) wherever that may be.

XXVII

In concluding the discussion of "service" activities, I may make one final observation. Does anyone really suppose that Yale and Princeton, having no schools of business, will for that reason in future be less conspicuous in business and banking than Harvard and Columbia which have? Or that Harvard, having no school of journalism, will in coming years furnish fewer editors, reviewers, and reporters than Columbia which has? Will the graduates of the Harvard School of Business crowd Yale and Princeton men out of industry, transportation, and commerce? Will the graduates of the Columbia School of Journalism crowd Harvard, Yale, and Princeton men out of journalism? Will the significant contributions to economics come from business schools rather than faculties of economics? Will critical and fundamental thinking come from researchers who live on annual contributions that come from and are managed by " business leaders " ? These questions answer themselves; they dispose of the present schools of journalism and business as genuine university enterprises.

Suppose one should ask similar questions in respect to law or medicine. Will the lawyers and the students of law in coming years come from the Harvard Law School or the Brooklyn Law School? Will the physicians and the scientific students of disease come from Harvard, Cornell, and Johns Hopkins or from a school that trains " practical " men? Once more, these questions answer themselves; and in so doing draw a sharp line between the type of conception embodied in the Harvard and Columbia Schools of Business and the type of conception embodied in the Harvard Faculties of Law and Medicine and the Johns Hopkins Faculty of Medicine.

One may push the matter one step further. I am writing in the year 1930; let us project ourselves a decade or fifteen years hence. It is 1940 or 1945. We are examining the academic history of the prominent journalists and business men of the day. Will they be graduates of technical schools of journalism and business or educated men who without any such technical training in the problems of today have turned full minds and enlarged vision on the changing problems of their own times? And of the two sets, which will have added more to American civilizations? Which will represent in their individual lives the riper cultural fruit?

Now let us ask the same question as respects medicine and law. If the experience of Europe during the preceding century and of America during the preceding half-century is of any significance, medicine and law will depend for their advancement on university graduates in the medical and legal faculties; for medicine and law are professions, essentially intellectual and learned in character and requiring for their cultivation the traditions, resources, facilities, and contacts which exist within a university and nowhere else; business and journalism are not; and they make no such requirements. Long ago Germany learned that industry needs universities, not merely because the universities train chemists and physicists for their research laboratories, but because universities train intelligence, capable of being applied in any field whatsoever. That lesson the American university has yet to master.

XXVIII

It may be urged that in the picture I have painted the shadows are too dark.[112] Perhaps they are.[113] No one knows the relative proportion of sense and nonsense in American education at any stage. I have again and again insisted that there are first-rate American scholars and scientists — more today than ever before — who contrive to do work that is internationally respected; and I have dwelt with emphasis upon the novelty and importance of our contribution to mod-

[112] Let me call attention in this connection to the fact that I have practically limited myself to the leading American universities: would the picture be lighter or darker if I had included the others — denominational institutions and state universities like Mississippi, where the Governor " discharges " president and professors without cause or ceremony?

[113] See, however, Dr. Henry S. Pritchett's *Preface* to *Bulletin Number Twenty-three* issued by the Carnegie Foundation for the Advancement of Teaching.

ern subjects — economics, psychology, government, and education. I have devoted more space, however, to what is silly, misdirected, and short-sighted. Why? Because we shall soundly develop the good, only if we get rid of the bad. A garden, three-fourths of which is lovely, one-fourth of which is burdock and nettles, would be a wretched affair. One would be ashamed to show it — there should be no weeds in a garden. Burdock and nettles are not only unsightly — they encroach and destroy the garden itself. Neither should there be any burdock and nettles in a university; they are not only ugly and inharmonious — they do harm. I have dealt with nonsense frankly, because it ought to be uprooted. Readers would not know what I am speaking of, or the extent to which nonsense has thriven, if I did not give abundant illustrations.[114] I am in no doubt as to the advancement of learning in America, even in American universities. Learning advances — do what we will: interest and devotion will not be daunted by confusion any more than by poverty. But it is assuredly the part of good sense to make conditions as favourable as possible — favourable to individuals, favourable to productive contacts, favourable to coöperation, favourable to the maintenance of intellectual standards. We are doing these things in America much less well than we might; and the truth must out.

XXIX

Administratively speaking, what is the outcome? A genuine university is, I have urged, an organism, characterized by highness and definiteness of aim,

[114] This manuscript has been read by several Americans prominent in academic life. They confessed themselves absolutely astonished as to the facts brought out.

unity of spirit and purpose. But it is quite obvious that
the institutions which we have used for purposes of
illustration — the best that we possess — are not organisms : they are merely administrative aggregations,
so varied, so manifold, so complex that administration
itself is reduced to budgeting, student accounting, advertising, etc. Such aggregations, even though called
universities, simply do not possess scientific or educational policy, embodied in some appropriate form.
In connection with them it is absurd to speak of
ideals. They are secondary schools, vocational schools,
teacher-training schools, research centres, " uplift "
agencies, businesses — these and other things simultaneously. In the reckless effort to expand, and thus
to cater to various demands, the university as an organic whole has disintegrated. Neither Columbia,
nor Harvard, nor Johns Hopkins, nor Chicago,
nor Wisconsin is really a university, for none of
them possesses unity of purpose or homogeneity
of constitution. Their centres are the treasurer's
office, into which income flows, out of which expenditures issue, and the office of the registrar who keeps
the roll.

How do we contrive to make the complicated machine go? By devices that are peculiarly American.
A board of trustees or regents holds funds and property, selects a president, and exercises some sort of
general oversight. Whatever may be said to the contrary and whatever exceptions may be cited, boards
of trustees do not as a rule bother either president
or faculty; but they do select the president — sometimes seeking expert advice, sometimes in ways that
pass understanding. Having selected the president,
they usually leave the current management of the institution to him and the faculty. Here and there indi-

vidual trustees give freely and generously of their time and energy; but these constitute a minority, though a very honourable minority. In so far as they are concerned, no words of commendation are too high. But, for the most part, the immediate and direct influence of the trustees, after they have chosen the president, is — whatever may be said to the contrary — rare and slight; their indirect and, I believe, largely unconscious influence may be and often is, however, considerable. In this respect there has been a change for the worse in the last half-century. The practical men — business men, lawyers, sometimes clergymen — were less sure of themselves fifty years ago; they had, I suspect, a higher respect for the poor professor than is common today. They led, moreover, simpler and quieter lives. Success and distraction at once preoccupy and mislead many — not all — American business men, for there continue, as I wish to repeat, to be trustees, successful men of affairs, who are conscientious, open-minded, modest, and whose experience and sound sense are invaluable. On the whole, however, boards of trustees are not composed of men of this type. The contention that they suppress freedom of speech cannot, I believe, be sustained, except in rare instances and in inconspicuous or inferior institutions. But in the social and economic realms they create an atmosphere of timidity which is not without effect in initial appointments and in promotions.

Following the choice of the president, almost anything may happen, good or bad, with or without the approbation of the scholars and scientists, who *are* the university. Diplomacy and earnestness may enable an intelligent and forceful president to attach trustees, alumni, and the general public to sound educational policies with which as individuals they might have had little sympathy. The academic miracles of the last fifty years are thus in part to be explained; and they are miracles: the sudden emergence of the Johns Hopkins, the best things at Harvard, Yale, Columbia, Princeton, Chicago, Pasadena, and the state universities are really little short of miraculous. I say " in part." For machinery cannot itself create. The American type of organization has not of itself created the best features of the American university; it has merely interposed fewer obstacles than tradition has created elsewhere and has enabled forceful individuals — Eliot, Gilman, and Harper — to make themselves felt. When a weak or mediocre president is in charge, the machinery remains the same, but nothing happens. I do not mean to imply that machinery is useless; on the contrary, I wish to show that it can make easier the doing of what is good or bad or of nothing at all; but it is not itself a motive, creative, or selective power. Other factors must also be taken into consideration. America is imitative, competitive, and has immense free resources; thus the Johns Hopkins was hardly under way when Harvard and Yale and other institutions endeavoured to get into its stride. I suspect that President Gilman did and planned little in 1876 that was not already part of President Eliot's intention; but the quick achievement in Baltimore enormously accelerated the pace at Cambridge. Momentum was increased by new creations at Clark University (Worcester, Massachusetts) and the University of Chicago. The pride, energy, and beneficence of alumni, trustees, and local communities did the rest. Soon the pace became so rapid that critical sense was dulled or the sense of direction was lost — put it as one will. Hence, the astonishing medley of excellence and triviality of the last thirty years which, thus far, has swept ahead without arousing effective protest. But the same imitativeness, competition, and abundance of money that made relatively easy the Mount Wilson Observatory, the Oriental Institute at Chicago, the Fogg Museum at Harvard, the new medical schools, made Harvard a prey to a poorly thought out and excessively rapid development in business education, and the Hopkins a prey to an unnecessary school of engineering. There is no brake or corrective in either tradition or ideals; nor can the best brains of the faculty have a direct influence on the trustees who " authorize " such measures as pass through the narrow neck of the presidential bottle. In occasional instances, there has been no gap between the president and faculty; the president has realized that the faculty, not the president, is the university. But such a relationship is nowadays unusual. An easy, informal relationship including social give-and-take has established itself in Chicago and Baltimore and still exists in both places; the president's house is modest, and members of the faculty are commonly present at all functions. But in the new presidential palaces of Columbia and Harvard, a professor living on his salary does not breathe freely. As Dr. Deller shrewdly observes, the president is *primus* but not *inter pares*. As long as circumstances drive him into the arms of influential trustees and important personages, it is not easy to see how he can avoid drifting away from a faculty, forced, as we shall see, to live on an entirely different social and economic basis.

The presidential salary ranges from $11,600 to $25,-000; allowances for entertainment, etc., from nothing to $20,000. The higher figures are so exceptional that they may be neglected. It may therefore be said that university presidents are not usually overpaid; the simple fact is, as we shall see,[115] that professors are underpaid. Academic dignity will not be restored until a professor is approximately as well paid as a president, lives as well, and is as highly regarded. If the presidential office were brought back to earth, a reasonable allowance would defray expenses to which ordinarily professors need not be put. The president would then be what he should be, *"primus inter pares";* America might perceive that learning is a finer product than executive talent and that democracy ought to begin on the university campus.

The duties of the president are various and exacting: he is the main agent in procuring funds or appropriations; he is a local magnate; he is pulled hither and yon to make speeches and to attend functions; he is made member of numerous committees and councils; he is a "good fellow" among the alumni; he participates more or less actively in choosing the faculty and in mapping out policies — policies for the college, policies for the service station, policies for the graduate and professional schools. He is the medium of communication between faculty and trustees; unless he approves, the faculty views may not even obtain a hearing. A heavy burden! One of the wisest of American philanthropists, head of a great business organization, long a trustee of a prominent university, once remarked to me: " A man may be president of a transcontinental railroad, an international banking corporation, a far-flung business; but the presidency of a great university is an impossible post." [116]

It is therefore important to understand how the

---

[115] See p. 205.

[116] For a fair and incisive analysis of the university president in the United States under generally good conditions see Edwin Deller, *loc. cit.,* pp. 20 ff. Dr. Deller's views on academic freedom (pp. 24–31) are also sound.

university presidency came about and what it has accomplished. Up to 1876, we had, as I have pointed out, only colleges. In that year under the wise and effective leadership of Mr. Gilman the Johns Hopkins University was established. Its influence was soon felt throughout the land; neither the trustees nor faculties would, had there been no university presidents, have quickly followed its example. President Harper at Chicago repeated the Baltimore experiment. Strong men here and there followed suit; they overcame inertia and opposition on the part of trustees, alumni, and faculty to a development in the university direction; they lifted the college out of ruts; they raised the necessary funds. I do not believe that we should today possess at their present stage of development the best things in the American university, if we had had no university presidents; I further believe that we should probably not be afflicted with the worst, if great scholars and scientists had during the last twenty years possessed more influence in determining university policies. In any event, the day of the excessively autocratic president is, in my opinion, over. He has done a great service — but henceforth his rôle should be different. To be sure, a permanent head insuring continuity of policy is necessary; an unwieldy faculty cannot, I believe, manage a university. The analogy often made between the American faculty and the fellows who manage an Oxford college or faculty government in Germany is faulty: for the Oxford colleges are small; the German faculties are in close touch with an influential ministry. Faculty government in America would, indeed, be democracy: the best minds would stick to the laboratory or the study; inferior persons, executively minded, would probably get control. The faculty should be represented; but it should not be overburdened. A president is a good device; but he should not alone come between the faculty and the trustees.

The president cannot, of course, do everything himself.[117] He acts therefore through an " organization " —deans, secretaries, filing-systems, punched cards, time-clocks, cost accounting sheets, and all the other paraphernalia requisite to the efficient conduct of a business. The spectrum is hard pressed to yield the number of differently coloured cards required to hold the data collected respecting every student. In thus adopting business apparatus fundamental differences between business and education have been overlooked. Business must pay a profit; business deals in standardized commodities. Steel ingots are steel ingots. Crude oil is crude oil, bricks are bricks, and silk is silk. Electric light is electric light, and bulbs are bulbs. Why should not business be organized? Why should its prosperity not depend upon the efficiency with which it is organized? But can one leap to the conclusion that there must also be organization in religion, in politics, in education, in which the real values are so largely the imponderables? To be sure, even in America it has happened that in a modest corner a group of men will somehow do a great work, but, alas, as soon as they attract attention, the business man, the expert, the man who can chart things, pounces upon them. Thereupon he " organizes " a university or " organizes " a philanthropic institution, and with the best intention maims both. He builds a nicely articulated machine; he distributes functions; he " correlates "; he does all the other terrible things that are odious to creative spirit. He thus gets to-

[117] The University of Chicago has created the office of vice-president, thereby greatly relieving the president of administrative duties.

gether a mass of mediocrity, but he can draw you a chart showing that there is no overlapping, no lost motion. He does not show that he has left " no place for the idea which no one has yet got." [118] Efficiency in administration and fertility in the realm of ideas have in fact nothing to do with each other — except, perhaps, to hamper and destroy each other. The rage for organization has invaded every phase of university life in the United States — clubs, seminars, research, athletics. Even " cheering " cannot be left to the spontaneous impulse of the spectator at a football game; that too must be " organized "; a university has its cheer leaders — automatons that shriek through megaphones and gesticulate like madmen — precisely as it has its deans and secretaries. And amidst the grinding and pounding of this huge machine, ideas are to be born and ideals are to acquire authority!

x x x

The tight organization of the American university has still other consequences. There is little student wandering. A boy who enters the freshman class at Yale, for example, remains for four years until he gets his bachelor's degree. During this period every possible effort is made to attach him to his Alma Mater; a fervent loyalty is cultivated, which has consequences, good and bad; he becomes a potential, often an important, benefactor, to the advantage of Yale — but, perhaps, to the disadvantage of other institutions that may require support, occasionally, for developments more important than anything under way at his own Alma Mater. Again, as an alumnus,

[118] For this sentence I am indebted to Dr. Beardsley Ruml of New York City.

he is a factor to be considered in planning university policies. On the whole, the influence of alumni in this direction has not been altogether happy; they are too deeply attached to inter-collegiate athletics and "the old college." [119]

The same habits that keep the undergraduate in his college for four years keep the graduate in his graduate or professional school for three or four years. A graduate student who begins to do Greek or mathematics or history at one of the great universities too often remains until he receives his higher degree. All influences conspire to make him believe that his opportunities and instructors are the best in the country. Gradually his loyalty is worked up to such a pitch that he is all but mad on the subject. If, therefore, a subject, like chemistry, declines, as it has so generally declined, the student does not usually find out the facts and go somewhere else. He simply gets his doctorate under inferior conditions. Once graduated, he frequently becomes an instructor in the same institution; and he must be poor indeed if he does not gradually rise. There is some shifting about subsequently, but much too little at any stage. Thus there are far too many Harvard men teaching at Harvard, too many Yale men teaching at Yale, too

[119] The following is quoted from a recent editorial in the New York World:

"Thus it is obvious that the situation which exists in our colleges is serious and that it does not get better. In order to stir up interest and also to obtain contributions to the endowments, presidents have bent all efforts to make alumni associations come to life, and they have succeeded. But having brought them to life, they find they have a lot of Frankenstein monsters on their hands. For these associations can think of little but football, and in their preoccupation with this they cause all sorts of trouble on the campus and interfere with scholastic work. What the eventual solution will be is by no means clear. But this much is clear: That the status of the alumni, particularly with reference to their assumption that the college somehow belongs to them, is one of the things that our colleges will have to clear up if they are going to enjoy continued usefulness."

many Hopkins men teaching at Hopkins, for the good of any one of them or for the good of the individuals concerned.

XXXI

We are now in position to understand a mystery. There were in 1927–28 over 900,000 students enrolled in 1,076 colleges, universities, and professional schools reporting to the Bureau of Education at Washington; there must be well-nigh a million today. In the same year, 83,065 baccalaureate degrees were granted. As the population of the country is approximately 120,-000,000, one person out of every 125 is today receiving a so-called higher education, and as this process, at approximately this rate, has been going on for some years, the number of " educated " persons in the United States must be enormous; the general level of intelligence and education should be high and should rapidly become higher. Such is not the case. Why not?

Quite clearly, because most of the 900,000 persons enumerated are not being educated at all; they are prematurely being trained in business, journalism, physical training, domestic science, or are registered in extension and other courses. Even if registered as college or graduate students, there is no certainty that they have been properly prepared or that they are pursuing a course that deserves to be called a liberal education. The fact that so enormous a number are interested in getting some sort of education is, from a social point of view, a novelty in the world's history and may ultimately have significance which today no one can foretell; but one cannot be really hopeful on this score, until universities and other educational institutions definitely discriminate between students on the basis of an intellectual standard. As ordinarily given, the figures are deceptive.

For example, the President of Columbia University reports a student enrolment of 48,722 for the year 1928–29. This huge total is reduced to 16,123, if summer session, university extension, and home study students are omitted, as they should be, for whether in earnest or not, they are not university students in any proper sense of the term. Of the 16,123 that remain, 3,730 are undergraduates, of whom I suspect that considerably more than half are doing mere secondary school work or are enrolled in some " ad hoc " department; 12,393 are classified as graduate and professional students, of whom almost 8,000 are registered in business, dentistry, oral hygiene, journalism, optometry, pharmacy, education, library service, and practical arts. Approximately 4,000 remain, of whom almost 3,000 belong in the graduate school, respecting whom Dean Woodbridge holds that only one-fourth need to be taken seriously. From the standpoint of a university none too rigorously conceived as devoted to higher education — the prosecution of learning or the mastery of a learned profession — Columbia University possesses not 48,000 students, but, on a generous estimate, perhaps 4,000. The teaching staff is reported as consisting of approximately 2,500 persons, of whom, however, 1,000 are merely extension or summer session instructors. The remaining 1,500 contain a large number of part-time professors and instructors in medicine and other branches and a considerable number giving elementary or secondary instruction. Obviously, it is impossible on the salaries offered to find 2,500 university instructors in the City of New York. A relatively small number are, to be sure, distinguished or rising scholars and scientists;

most of them are and must be persons of meagre background, training, and physique — unequal to a more strenuous life. Of the really able, a goodly percentage will gradually be drawn off into law, medicine, or business. Posts are therefore being created far more rapidly than they can be filled; and every new questionable venture — schools of business, of town-planning, of meat-packing — weakens the structure by drawing away economists, engineers, or bacteriologists from the central branches. We are thus forced to make professors of undertrained young men who would be assistants and docents abroad — sometimes not even that; and funds that might maintain a sound university are dispersed over an area so broad that adequate financial support can probably never be obtained.[120] None the less, for the time being, there they all are, teachers and students, thousands on the same campus, overlapping in their use of space, crowding into the same library — football, dances, prayers, teaching, degree hunting, research jostling all the time. "Scholarship and research," says Dean Woodbridge, " do not naturally thrive in an atmosphere of this kind." [121]

The University of Chicago handles — and, like other large universities, must adopt a form of organization capable of handling — almost 30,000 students; about 8,000 are home study students, 6,500 attend the summer school, 800 are registered in education,

---

[120] See pp. 196–208.

[121] *Loc. cit.*, p. 13. At the recent celebration of the 175th birthday of Columbia University, over 100 honorary degrees were conferred, 47 portraits were delivered to the institution, and the President of the Board of Trustees made the following statement with evident pride: " A quarter of a century ago, the university consisted of eleven faculties, 455 instructors and 4,709 students. Today, there are twelve faculties, five independent colleges, nine associate institutions, nearly 2,800 instructors and 50,000 students."

500 in commerce, 5,000 are undergraduates, over 4,000 are graduate students.[122] Suppose that extension, summer, and secondary school students were not counted; suppose that "*ad hoc*" departments of technical character were dropped; suppose that Dean Woodbridge's criterion were applied to the graduate school; how many university students would Chicago have? Assuredly less than 5,000. Is it not obvious that over-organization would no longer be requisite, that a different wind would blow on the campus, that the University of Chicago, thus stripped, might render the intellectual life and needs of the nation a far greater service than, panting for breath and money and buildings, it can now perform?

I have had frequent occasion to speak of the part played by the Johns Hopkins University in its early days. It had in my time (1884–86) a small undergraduate department (less than 150) and a graduate school of slightly over two hundred students. The Johns Hopkins of that day was influential beyond any institution the country has ever possessed. It was small, but size was irrelevant. Today it is twenty times as large; the *President's Report 1928–29* lists 5,446 students; whence do they come, and what are they doing? Four-fifths come from Maryland; and of the overwhelming Maryland contingent, all but 900 come from Baltimore. Baltimore ought therefore to be a cultural centre of rare intensity, which it isn't. The Johns Hopkins is thus, outside its enrolment in medicine, now almost as nearly a local institution as if it were attached to the public school system of the town. And what are these "students" — 5,446 in number — engaged in

[122] It is impossible to reconcile the figures given by the U. S. Education Office and those obtained from the universities, for the classification is different. But the figures in the text represent the situation as correctly as possible.

doing? There are 465 enrolled in night courses for technical workers, 1,171 follow evening courses in business economics, 1,107 are registered in the summer school, 1,526 comprise the College for Teachers, 72 are accounted for by the School of Business Economics — a total of 4,341, who are more or less usefully employed, but not in university pursuits. There remain slightly over a thousand students — 283 in the Medical School, still admirable, 144 in the School of Hygiene, also excellent. The undergraduate college contains 343, of whom less than half pursue studies above secondary grade; unless the graduate students in the philosophical faculty, 527 in number, are far better than Columbia's — which I see no reason to believe — perhaps 150 are worthy of their opportunities. The Hopkins' roll of more than 5,000 thus melts — excluding medicine and hygiene — to a few hundred. For this body, a competent group of teachers could have been found; and the Hopkins might today still be a beacon light on a hill top. Instead, it has a roster of over 5,000 and outside of medicine and hygiene has lost its significance — lost it, partly, of course, because other institutions have improved; largely and mainly because it has itself deteriorated through dilution and adulteration.

With these endowed institutions, free to go their own way, a state university like Wisconsin really compares very favourably. It registers over 28,000 students, of whom almost 8,000 are correspondence students, 6,500 in extension classes, 391 in the Milwaukee Day School, 4,000 in the summer session and short agricultural courses: the enrolment is thus reduced to less than 10,000. If the same process of discrimination above employed is used, it would turn out that the University of Wisconsin has an enrolment of university calibre that probably does not exceed 2,500. Harvard's 10,000 would be reduced by more than 50% — dentistry, business, extension, summer courses,[123] and the early college years being eliminated. Its graduate school numbers 1,326. Twenty years ago, according to President Lowell,[124] 70% of the graduate students devoted their whole time to study; now 44% — less than half. "The remainder are by no means always the weaker students, for the University itself is in part responsible by employing many graduate students in teaching. But it is by no means clear that this is good either for the graduate students or for those whom they teach." And again, " No one can suppose that all these thirteen hundred and more young men and women are capable of adding to human knowledge, or of attaining the higher grades in the field of education."

Who has forced Harvard into this false path? No one. It does as it pleases; and this sort of thing pleases![125] In the matter of enrolment Yale would lose less — its 5,000 being reduced to perhaps three or

[123] "Nearly all summer school courses are accepted, subject to the established regulations to count as half-courses for the degrees of A.B., A.A., S.B. A large number may be counted for the degrees of A.M. and Ed.M. at Harvard University." Thus patience and arithmetic combine to produce Harvard Bachelors and Masters of Art! (Preliminary Announcement, Summer School of 1930.) I do not object to summer schools; but the conditions under which they operate are largely non-academic. The faculties are collected from every available source; the students cannot possibly be properly selected. Academic " credit " in the American sense should not be "allowed."

[124] *President's Report 1928–29*, p. 11.

[125] It should in fairness be added that in the same report, President Lowell raises the question as to whether the size of the graduate school should not now be limited, as the enrolment in the College (3,233 students!), the Medical School (515 students), the Law School (1,589 students!), and the School of Business (868 students!) has been limited. (*Ibid.*, p. 10.) Indeed, in all the leading medical schools, the number of students annually admitted is limited; insistence upon intellectual and scholarly standards would effect a limitation in other departments.

four, mainly at the expense of the first two college years — Yale having developed none of the " service " features which loom so large in the other universities examined in this connection.

The combination of colleges and graduate schools which results in these gigantic enrolments is some-times defended on the ground that the college is stimu-lated by the graduate school, and sometimes on the ground that the graduate school is " fed " by the col-lege. As to the former, it would be quite as convincing to argue that the conglomerate university should also contain a high school, which would be stimulated by proximity to the college: indeed many colleges for-merly possessed preparatory departments, which were dropped as state high school systems were created. As to the latter, a strong graduate school needs no " feeder " of its own. The earnest student will seek the strong teacher, and " loyalty " is out of place. The figures show that the best graduate schools are more or less independent of their own colleges: thus, for the past four or five years, the Harvard Graduate School of Arts and Science derived 75% of its students from other colleges than Harvard; in the two-year period, 1928–30, the Harvard Law School derived over 80% of its students from outside colleges; in five years (1925–29, inclusive) the Johns Hopkins Medical School received slightly less than 85% of its students from other colleges than the College of Johns Hopkins itself. In so far as numbers go, the college therefore does not substantially help the graduate schools; the harm done to the graduate school by the combination I have already explained.

It is obviously impossible to make so accurate an analysis of the figures that one can estimate the num-ber of Americans now receiving a liberal or advanced education; but the number falls short — far short — of the number claimed. The figures are " padded." It is assuredly no error to assert that a relatively small body of American men and women are now so occupied in well staffed colleges and universities that they are likely to emerge cultivated, intelligent, or competent. This relatively small body might become a powerful force or ferment if it could be held together in a few intellectual centres; unfortunately its impact is reduced because the individuals involved are scattered, lose touch with one another, and thus tend themselves to be pulled down rather than to pull others up beyond the average level of taste and thought. The mediocrity of America is thus no mystery at all. Instead of a million students there are perhaps 100,000 — there may not be so many as that, most of these having had a defective high school education. *Ad hoc* training courses in great universities and in small and poor colleges in all sections — more in the South and West than in the East, courses that are technical or technological rather than scientific or liberal in aim and spirit, account for most so-called " students." And this conclusion is fully sustained by the cultural thinness of the supposedly educated classes — professors, teachers, lawyers, architects, journalists. The figures mislead, but Mr. and Mrs. Lynd in *Middletown*,[126] a study of a representative American community, tell the truth.[127]

[126] R. S. and H. Lynd, *Middletown* (New York, 1929).

[127] The inflation of college and university enrolment is partly due to an expanding system of prerequisites: nursing schools are urged to require for admission two years of college work; library schools are beginning to require for admission a bachelor's degree. Thus both college and university are burdened with unfit students and irrelevant graduate departments. Indeed, the entrance requirement for the School of Practical Arts at Columbia (a bachelor's degree) or for the School of Librarianship is actually higher than the minimum requirement for admission to the Columbia School of Medicine (two years of college work)!

XXXII

With generosity unparalleled in history, American citizens have in recent years devoted large sums to the endowment and support of colleges and universities, though the proportion of givers to those who are in position to give is commonly much overrated; but a considerable part of the giving goes to objects that are of secondary importance or no importance at all — buildings that are not required, departments and institutes that have no place in the university or that the university cannot afford. American generosity is therefore not controlled or directed by intelligent purpose. Whether in the long run, it will be so bounteous that waste and misdirection are negligible remains to be seen.

The resources are, as I shall point out, still far from adequate; but I wish, first, to inquire into their extent and the use made of them. In 1906, the United States Bureau of Education listed 622 universities, colleges, and schools of engineering,[128] in 1928, 1,076;[129] within this period, the assets in property rose from $554,000,-000 to over $2,400,000,000; the investments in library and apparatus from $45,000,000 to $245,000,000; the value of institutional grounds and buildings from $260,000,000 to $1,300,000,000; productive endowments from $250,000,000 to a little more than $1,150,-000,000, etc.[130]

As to the use to which these enormous sums, supplemented, of course, by income derived from fees are put, I shall employ approximate figures, since they will sufficiently illuminate the main point that

[128] Professional schools (law, medicine, and theology) are excluded.
[129] Including professional schools.
[130] I have given in the text the nearest round numbers.

I have been trying to establish. The heart of a university is the graduate school of arts and sciences, the solidly professional schools (mainly, in America, medicine and law) and certain research institutions. Harvard's annual expenditure is now approximately $10,000,000, of which only one-fifth goes to the undergraduate and graduate departments of arts and science. As well-nigh half of the undergraduate work belongs in secondary schools, it is clear that of Harvard's total expenditure not more than one-eighth is devoted to the *central* university disciplines at the level at which a university ought to be conducted. The expenditure on the library is relatively liberal and highly significant — a total of $300,000 yearly — a sum which would of course accomplish more if the university enrolment were restricted to competent university students. The School of Architecture, the Bussey Institution, the Law and Medical Schools, the Fogg Art Museum, the Observatory, and several Institutes are largely or wholly of university quality: perhaps $2,-000,000 more can be thus accounted for. Thus out of ten millions, four millions go to teaching and research at the university level. What becomes of the rest? The sum of $100,000 goes to the Summer School; almost a million goes to the School of Business; $600,000 to the dining halls; about a million to the Committee on Athletic Sports; more than half a million to dormitories; three quarters of a million to administration. Of these items, some, such as dining halls and dormitories, are balanced by income from the same sources; the enormous outlay on athletics is covered by gate receipts; the huge expenditures for administration and operation are due partly to the complexity and heterogeneousness of the institution, partly to the irrelevant invasion of business methods; but the one fact which stands out clearly is this — that Harvard spends a large portion of its present budget on things that do not belong to a university at all; that Harvard would today be a greater university, if, instead of expending ten millions annually on activities so largely alien to a university, it spent half the sum on a seat of learning, stripped of irrelevancies and absurdities; needless to add, that, if it spent its entire present income on a compact and high grade institution of learning, its significance would be much more than twice as great as it now is.

Columbia's total expenditure is likewise practically $10,000,000. But no such sum is devoted to teaching and research of university grade. Administration — costly, because complex and heterogeneous — absorbs over half a million a year; [131] buildings and grounds, extensive because of the number of students and the variety of activities to be accommodated, require almost a million a year; odds and ends of no university significance whatever call for more than $500,000; [132] university extension and home study swallow up over $1,500,000, though, be it noted, yielding the handsome profit to which attention has already been called.[133] The School of Business spends a little less than $160,000, of which $71.53 go for research! The Institute of Rumanian Culture expends $86.50! One must not forget, however, that the Institute of Distribution has not yet been established! The College, the Graduate School, publications, the Faculties of

[131] I omit certain items strangely classified under " General University Administration," as, for example, State Aid for Blind Pupils, Social Club for Kindergarten Class for Faculty Children, Research in the Humanities, Researches in Journalism, etc.

[132] Including " Commons," International Relations, *Maison Française, Casa Italiana, Deutsches Haus,* School of Dentistry, Summer Session, etc.

[133] See p. 144.

Law and Medicine, the Library, and a few research activities account for about $5,000,000. To speak of Columbia University as expending $10,000,000 is thus clearly misleading; in so far as it is actually a university, it spends perhaps four millions, not ten. It would possess infinitely greater momentum as an educational force if it spent the smaller sum legitimately, for it would be — what it is not at present — an institution of learning. It would be far greater and better still if it could devote its entire present expenditure to genuine university objects.

The financial operations of the Johns Hopkins University deserve careful notice. The University (exclusive of the Medical School and Hospital, both of which have been soundly conducted) was started with an endowment of $3,500,000 — a very large sum at the time. Financial disasters, for which the Trustees were in no wise responsible, largely dissipated this sum; but the endowment has been slowly built up until it now amounts to approximately $6,000,000, of which about $4,000,000 are free from restrictions, not including, however, about $1,500,000 of unrestricted endowment, which has been invested in a new plant.[134] The sum is, of course, entirely inadequate; its purchasing power is about one-fifth of the endowment given by Mr. Hopkins almost sixty years ago. The Faculty of Arts and Sciences — the very core — of the Johns Hopkins University is thus abjectly poor. Obviously, the Trustees should circumscribe their activities, avoid poorly financed adventures, and husband

[134] Whether a new plant should have been provided under the circumstances is in the highest degree questionable. The University could not afford it, and that should have settled the matter. But certain details border on the ridiculous; it was proposed to build "an alumni dormitory" to cost $500,000; the alumni provided $107,000; instead of dropping the project, the Trustees still further depleted the general fund by "borrowing" from it almost $400,000.

the institution's resources. The general academic situation in the country at large is, moreover, such that a small university of high grade might have accomplished in the university field at least part of what the Johns Hopkins Medical School and the Rockefeller Institute have been so largely responsible for achieving in the realm of medicine. Indeed, trustees, faculty, and alumni have recently all concurred in adopting precisely this policy. Funds would have been required, but the purpose was so sound, the need so clear, the sum so moderate that without doubt the scheme could have been carried through. Adopted with enthusiasm, it was within a few years through sheer inertia allowed to lapse. A new project — not without merit in itself, but badly launched — took its place. The funds available for university work had, as I have said, already been unwisely impaired. Nevertheless, though enmeshed in financial needs, the University has within the last two years started an Institute of Law, for the support of which during a three-year period $178,400 were raised. At the close of two years, expenditures exceed the sum pledged for three. No business, thus conducted, would long be solvent. The total annual budget of the academic faculty and the School of Engineering is less than $1,000,000 — of which the sum of $300,000 goes to administration, general expenses, extension courses, and various odds and ends. It is safe to say that not much more than a third of the expenditure is devoted to purposes in which President Gilman was primarily interested. More money is spent in maintaining the grounds than on the departments of botany, philosophy, plant physiology, or Greek. Meanwhile, exclusive of buildings, grounds and plant, the endowment of the School of Medicine alone is over four times as great as the unrestricted endowment of the Faculty of Arts and Sciences!

I have spoken of the unprecedented generosity with which the resources of American universities have been increased. It is a thousand pities that of this vast total so much has been applied to poor and unworthy purposes. Large sums have been wasted in useless or extravagant building schemes; " side-shows," as President Wilson called them, have been financed, while the central structure was still unsupported; costly adventures have been rashly undertaken; large sums have been tied up in special schemes, so that endowments have been spread out instead of built up; enormous sums are spent upon the complex administrative organization required to keep the unwieldy machine going; large amounts are annually wasted in " research " that does not fulfil the primary conditions of research. No American university president of recent years has fearlessly hewed to the line, accepting money for general and important purposes — the central disciplines, the accepted and necessary professions — and refusing to accept special gifts which almost invariably make the university poorer and weaker, rather than richer and better. For almost every activity once undertaken grows, and, as it grows, needs further support. The asset of today thus becomes a liability tomorrow. This consideration might make universities cautious about assuming obligations; such has not in practice proved to be the case. To the financial embarrassment of a large university, whose wealth, while steadily mounting, is so largely tied up in special projects, the new President of the University of Chicago, Dr. Robert M. Hutchins, has vigorously called attention; his predecessor, Dr. Mason, had already described the University as " gift-poor." The position of the university president is in this matter an extremely difficult one: the university needs additional funds to increase salaries — notably the salaries of the abler men — and to develop departments which are missing or defective. It is precisely such funds that are hardest to obtain. Instead, gifts are offered for special purposes — some worthy, some unworthy, some of which will surely in time win further support, some of which will probably prove a drain and an incubus. To refuse the gift may alienate the giver — a delicate business, fraught with unpleasant consequences. None the less, as policies depend to a degree on money, so to the extent that donors designate purposes, the university simply does not manage itself. Experience convinces me that universities have partly themselves to blame, for they have often been too timid to enlighten a giver. No endowed university has to do anything that it cannot afford to do. While, therefore, university assets occasionally look impressive, the unrestricted funds, available at the will of the authorities for the development of genuine university work, are amazingly meagre. Glorious buildings, Gothic, neo-Gothic, Colonial, concrete stadia accommodating fifty or sixty thousand enraptured spectators of a football contest, and student buildings of elaborate design, constructed while the college or university is pleading its inability to pay decent salaries — all these have sprung up on every hand; poor indeed is the institution which does not display buildings which it cannot afford to possess. Meanwhile, less than a dozen endowed American universities have as much as $20,000,000 in endowment — which is approximately the cost of a cruiser! Despite the schools in which they teach business, they have displayed a minimum of business sense, for they have embarked on enterprises that they cannot afford.

Dubious methods have in these latter years been adopted by some universities in order to raise funds requisite to an expansion that is in many particulars indefensible. Endowed universities depend for support on the intelligence and beneficence of the wealthy; on the growth of such intelligence and beneficence they ought to wait; towards its growth they should do nothing that impairs their dignity or decency. Unfortunately, in their hurry, they have made an opening for business corporations which undertake to assist them in raising funds by the methods employed by " realtors " in " developing " real estate projects. The Johns Hopkins, at the close of a " Half-Century Campaign " thus conducted admits that despite organized publicity carried on by such methods " the total amount (raised) which could be considered unrestricted was only $100,000." That it is beneath the dignity of a university to employ a group of advertisers who will for a fee undertake to " boost " almost anything that calls itself academic I shall not undertake to prove; so much I shall take for granted, even though it may be argued that, as Columbia and Harvard offer graduate courses in advertising, universities are entitled to practise what they teach.

A group of prominent citizens have just appealed to the New York public in behalf of Columbia University for the sum of $39,500,000; other institutions clamour for $75,000,000, $100,000,000, and 500 colleges for $500,000,000. Not one of them has made a critical study of its own doings. Not one of them knows whether to be a genuine university it needs either more or less than it now estimates. Until the university has a policy, which involves the firm establishment of intellectual standards, its financial requirements cannot be determined. Moreover, the totals asked for by en-

[203]

dowed institutions mount continuously and with dazzling rapidity. Can a department be dismantled and
started modestly afresh in a new direction? No one
asks. Yet nothing is clearer than the fact that forces
— including men, money, and equipment — should,
with the advance of knowledge, when their end is
reached, be demobilized and otherwise directed. Unless university authorities are constantly on the watch
for opportunities to readjust expenditure, the financing of higher education on a voluntary basis will shipwreck.

XXXIII

I have insisted that, in the last analysis, universities
depend on men. Spread, as it is, over a vast area and
with such sub-divisions of subject-matter as are recognized nowhere else in the world, the American university requires for its conduct a staff of maximum size.
The staff is needlessly large, because the university
tries to render absurdly meticulous service; it is so
large that it cannot be competently recruited, nor can
adequate funds be obtained. For all these reasons, the
staff of the American university is wretchedly underpaid. Huge sums have been expended upon building
and athletic projects that, if added to unrestricted endowment, might have substantially improved the
status of the professor; and further improvement
would take place, if the staff were reduced in size by
the ruthless abolition of trivial courses, trivial chairs,
trivial publications, and ridiculous " research." In its
best days, the Johns Hopkins University occupied two
converted lodging houses. A newspaper was reported
to have sneered at the new university on the ground
that it was undertaking to " conduct its classes under
a tent and to keep its books in soap boxes "; " That,"

President Gilman is said to have retorted, "is precisely what we propose to do."

America is an expensive country to live in: rent, service, food, clothing, amusements, travel, books, all are much more costly than anywhere else. The standard of living is high. Teaching and learning are not respected, so that social prestige does not compensate for diminished income, as it undoubtedly does abroad. There is no such thing as an academic status that is indifferent to the standards created by non-academic classes. Almost all the forces of social life, ponderable and imponderable, operate to drive young men and women into business, law, or the practice of medicine. Now no one would wish to see university posts so profitable that they would attract persons who have neither taste nor aptitude for teaching and research. But they are, as a matter of fact, so poorly remunerated that, with exceptions, to be sure, they largely attract persons who, having neither taste nor aptitude for anything in particular, can at least earn a livelihood by teaching, precisely as once — to some extent it is still the case — the same sort of person could earn a bare livelihood in the church. I say there are exceptions. There are gifted men, not a few, whom poverty and hardship do not deter; they are the salt of the academic profession of the United States; there are a small number, far too small for so rich a country, who, having means of their own, rejoice in the ability to lead quiet, productive, academic lives; there are others — not so very many, I presume — who have solved their problem by " marrying money." Finally, in recent years, salaries have been increased, though they are still far below the amount needed to enable a scholar or scientist to marry, have and educate a small family, live simply, buy books, and take a care-

free vacation. Many thorough studies tend to the conclusion that, comparatively speaking, a university
teacher is not so well off as he was thirty years ago.
"While the income of citizens on the average has increased about 200% that of professors has increased
less than 100% in gold values." [135] Mr. Trevor Arnett,
President of the General Education Board, on the
basis of a painstaking study of 302 colleges and universities, concludes that " despite all efforts " the real
average salary was only " slightly better" in 1926–27
than in 1914–15; [136] 66.5% of those furnishing information have to supplement their salaries by earnings
from additional work, and of these almost three-
fourths are driven to do so by sheer necessity. The
study of *American College Athletics* issued by the Carnegie Foundation shows clearly that athletic coaches
are more highly paid than professors. In over 100 colleges and universities the highest remuneration paid
to a professor was $12,000, the average $5,158; in approximately the same number of institutions, the highest salary paid to the athletic coach was $14,000, the
average $5,095; of 96 football coaches the most highly
paid received $14,000, the average $6,107. It pays better to be an athletic coach than to be a university
professor! [137]

Columbia, making a tremendous effort, has recently
announced a normal minimum professorial salary of
$7,500 — with special groups at $9,000, $10,000, and
$12,000 — an improvement, to be sure, but an im-

[135] Since 1900. Professor W. A. Noyes, *Are Equitable Salaries Paid to
Professors?*, a Report to the American Association for the Advancement of
Science.

[136] *Occasional Papers, No. 8* (Publications of the General Education
Board). For a detailed and admirable study of salary conditions at a representative university, see Henderson and Davie, *Incomes and Living Costs
of a University Faculty* (Yale University Press, 1928).

[137] *Loc. cit.*, pp. 171–75.

provement that still makes it impossible for the most highly favoured professor, dependent on his salary, to live comfortably in the City of New York, where, prices being what they now are, a professorial salary of $20,000 a year would assuredly not overpay a man of ability and culture. Harvard has just taken similar action, fixing the minimum professorial salary at $8000 and the maximum at $12,000. Unless a still higher scale can be soon reached, the severer disciplines — philosophy, ancient languages, mathematics — are bound to suffer from lack of recruits. A worse fate may, however, overtake other subjects. I began by urging the importance of modernizing universities — of bringing a sheer intellectual point of view to bear upon the problems of law, politics, industry, engineering, and education. But the men who are interested in these current problems are precisely the men whom industry, engineering, and business want; and they are more valuable to industry and business if their names carry the prestige of a university than as private individuals or as outright employees. The situation that led to the development of academic medicine has therefore developed in a far more acute form in some of the social sciences. An underpaid professor must thus either abandon the university or, perhaps unconsciously, subordinate his professorship to outside subvention or employment. There is no denying the suspicion that the latter has already happened. Faculties should be made as independent as courts, for, as Professor Seligman has urged, the robe of the professor must be as stainless as the ermine of the judge. It is not too much to say that the complete modernization of the university, the possibility of dealing fearlessly with the problems — legal, social, and economic — that now press upon society depends upon the ability of the university to make its staff absolutely independent of private remuneration or subvention. It is hard to see how otherwise the professor can retain an absolutely independent intellectual attitude; it is easy to see that, whether he retains it or not, the general public will have its doubts.[138]

The truth is that, with exceptions, of course, the American professoriate is a proletariat, lacking the amenities and dignities they are entitled to enjoy. Amenities are provided in plenty for the well-to-do students, who have club houses, fraternity houses, and at times luxurious dormitories; not, however, for the teaching staff. Thus a very small part of our unheard-of national wealth, even in the most cultivated and complacent section of the country, is devoted to the uses to which a civilized society would attach, and assuredly some day must attach, the highest importance. Meanwhile, the mental and physical vigour which should be attracted into universities is in unduly large proportion forced into activities which, if successfully pursued, will yield an adequate return. And this is happening at the very moment when the

[138] For a wise and temperate discussion of this problem, though without reference to salaries, on which, in my opinion, the solution turns, see *Academic Obligations* — a Report on Public Utility Propaganda by Edwin R. A. Seligman, published in the *Bulletin of the American Association of University Professors*, Vol. XVI, No. 5, May 1930. In this connection I may once more call attention to the unwisdom of the Harvard Business School Associates — men engaged in trade, in transportation, in the management of public utilities, who, however fine their intention, retain the management of the huge sum which they propose to devote to promoting research in the fields in which some of them have large financial interests.

Professor Paul H. Douglas of the University of Chicago in the preface to his volume on *Real Wages* (1830) exposes the difficulty involved in doing disinterested research: "Had I foreseen that, in order to complete the work, it would require the major part of six years and . . . the larger part of my income for most of that time, I might not have had the courage to undertake the task."

fortress of intelligence needs to be most strongly defended.

The professoriate is disadvantaged by one more consideration. Time was when it meant something to be a college or university professor, as it meant something to hold a college or university degree. And this legitimate distinction operated as a compensation for the plain living required. Now the situation is reversed. Professors of economics, physics, philosophy, or Sanskrit find themselves in the same boat with professors of business English, advertising, journalism, physical training, and extra-curricular activities. They bear, all alike, the same titles; the second group generally earn more, for they frequently do remunerative outside work. The universities, by sacrificing intellectual purpose, have thus sacrificed the intellectual distinction which counts for more than money. What with low salaries, enormous faculties, and diminished prestige, Professor Seligman is on safe ground when he calls the outlook for brains in American universities " an ominous one."

These facts and figures tell a story — and yet not the whole story. They tell of the well-nigh universal striving for education, the well-nigh universal, naïve faith in being taught, as though education were really a matter of taking courses, being instructed in person or otherwise, passing examinations and storing up " credits." There is some good in all this; yet almost the reverse is really true. Information can, perhaps, be measured by " credits "; not, however, education. Education is something for which the primary responsibility rests upon the individual, and a wise teacher will realize the narrow limits within which he can be helpful. Again, the figures and the rapidity with which they have mounted show the vigour with which the nation is at one and the same time undertaking to do almost everything — not only to fell trees and push back the frontier, but to lift the social, economic, industrial, and domestic level, to acquire art treasures, to combat disease, and to advance learning. Agencies had to be found or created to do all these varied and mostly disconnected things. The university happened to be the most capacious and flexible agency at hand, and it amiably allowed itself to be utilized to perform almost any function to which an " educational " twist can be given. While in the process good has been done, much humbug has been perpetrated, and the task of elevation and discrimination has been made tremendously more difficult.

XXXIV

In my opinion, the situation above described need not have come about, however great the pressure. No matter what the rest did, a few endowed institutions could have stood their ground, could and should have embodied thoroughly modern conceptions of learning, training, and inquiry, without opening their portals to practically every vagary. The very factors urged in extenuation or explanation of present conditions constitute the strongest possible reason for the maintenance of standards and ideals somewhere. The greater the energy and effort expended in lifting the ordinary level of comfort, health, happiness, and knowledge, the greater the importance of uncompromisingly maintaining somewhere sound and genuine intellectual values — first of all, for their own inherent value, then, because of the stimulus thus afforded to the general striving. The Johns Hopkins Medical School again furnishes an example in point. It began soundly and modestly; for twenty years its resources hardly grew at all. But it made no compromises. At last it was recognized as something different, something better, something excellent and unadulterated. Its influence was felt throughout the country. It became a recognized model. Others strove to reproduce it. Fortune turned its way. Endowments flowed in; new clinics and laboratories well supported were bestowed upon it. Would it have done better if, in its lonely and poverty-stricken days, it had come to terms with local proprietary schools, with osteopathy and homeopathy?

What the Johns Hopkins Medical School did, the Johns Hopkins University might have done; it could have remained " poor but honest." It is still poor. It has tried to be popular — has developed undergraduate work, has acquired a beautiful campus, has cultivated athletics, has made a wretched contract with the State of Maryland — and has lost the significance and importance which it once possessed and might have retained, infinitely to the good of the country.

Taking matters as they stand, it must be obvious that, in my judgment, no American university squares with the conception which I have outlined — because of irrelevancies, because of the spotty character of its really serious endeavours. " Put the blame where you will," writes President Angell of Yale, whom, by the way, no one could possibly regard as un-American, unsympathetic, or inappreciative, " put the blame where you will, we have not developed in this country any general respect for scholarship as such. . . . The great public that ultimately supports education has a good deal more appreciation of athletics, and especially of football and all that it symbolizes, than it has of distinguished Greek scholars. This may be a painful and disillusionizing fact, but a fact it is, nevertheless." [139]

What is to be done about it?

It is essential in the first instance to face the facts and to put a summary end to self-deception, practised in America on a hitherto unprecedented scale. The President of Columbia University, in a recent address,[140] seriously compares, in its relative significance to mankind, the slight elevation, called Morningside Heights, on which Columbia University is situated, " to the four most sacred and most inspiring spots in the world — to the summit of the Mount of Olives, to the Acropolis at Athens, to the Capitoline Hill at Rome, and to that gently sloping height in the City of Paris which bears the name of Sainte Geneviève." Such language lapped up by the uncritical millions is a serious obstacle in the way of real progress. There is another obstacle, hardly less serious. "We are a new people, we are passing through a phase." We have therefore only to get old, only to emerge from the phase, and all will be well with us. I find no comfort, however, in ignoring that spacious region, where, be conditions what they may, effort, intelligence, and resources can even now accomplish important results. "You have in your new American universities," wrote a great German anatomist to an American pupil thirty years ago, "a powerful ' *nervus rerum*,' and if abundant resources are directed into the proper channels, a great deal can be accomplished in a relatively brief period. But here is the main point — that the conduct of progressive movements should remain in the hands of persons who know what really

---

[139] *The Over-Population of the College* (*Harper's Magazine*, October 1927).

[140] Address entitled *Ave Mater Immortalis*, Oct. 31, 1929.

matters, when it is a question of creative intellectual activity." [141] The " phase " theory leaves unexplained Gilman's Johns Hopkins, Harper's Chicago, and the quick improvement of American medical schools, following the thorough exposure of their scandalous condition in 1910. I have said that almost anything can be accomplished in America if intelligence, effort, and resources are combined; that is just what we so rarely bring about. We have intelligence alone — and it is stalled; effort alone — and we are jumpy, feverish, aimless; resources alone — and we are wasteful. No sound or consistent philosophy, thesis, or principle lies beneath the American university today.

What with the pressure of numbers, the craving for knowledge, real or diluted, the lack of any general respect for intellectual standards, the intrusion of politics here and of religion somewhere else, the absurd notion that ideals are " aristocratic," while a free-for-all scramble which distresses the able and intelligent is " democratic," there is no possibility of a summary solution of the problem of higher education in America — or, for the matter of that, of education at any level; we lack teachers, facilities, standards, comprehension, and the willingness to accept differences. In the hurly-burly which exists, excellent work will go on, now here, now there; scholars and scientists, born to the purple, have never been defeated — not by war or poverty or persecution, and they will not be defeated in the future any more than they have been in the past.

It has, however, become a question whether the term " university " can be saved or is even worth saving. Why should it not continue to be used in order to in-

[141] Extract from a letter written by Professor Wilhelm His, April 22, 1899, to Professor Franklin P. Mall. For a copy of this letter I am indebted to Dr. Florence R. Sabin of the Rockefeller Institute for Medical Research.

dicate the formless and incongruous activities — good, bad, and indifferent — which I have described in this chapter? If indeed " university " is to mean, as Columbia announces, a " public service institution," then the university has become a different thing, a thing which may have its uses, but is assuredly no longer a university. In this event, in order to signify the idea of a real university, a new term may be requisite — perhaps a school or institute of higher learning — which would automatically shut out the low-grade activities with which institutions of learning have no concern.

It is, in any case, clear that no uniform, country-wide and thorough-going revolution is feasible. What may be practicable at Harvard, Columbia, or Chicago will, for a long time, be impracticable in Mississippi or Texas, subject as they are to political raids, or to Michigan, where a false conception of the university has been lodged in the minds of the voters. Nor can change be limited to universities. The high school is part of the problem. Secondary education includes the present high school and a large part of the college: we are dealing with two divisions (secondary education and university education), not with three (high school, college, and graduate school) a fact that is made clear by the sudden decrease of students at the end of the second college year.[142] The improvement of the university depends therefore upon the improvement of secondary schools, in which, as rapidly as possible, the system of credits must be abolished, practical or technical subjects must cease to be counted towards university matriculation, and far greater thoroughness

[142] See *Student " Mortality "* (Study issued by the University of Minnesota, March 17, 1924) and *Student Survival* (ditto, Feb. 10, 1925). These studies show that only ¼ of a given freshman class is graduated at the end of the regular four-year course.

and continuity (*i.e.*, higher standards) must be sought. I am, I know, asking for a great deal — not, however, for more than the universities which I have singled out might within a reasonable period obtain, if they cared more for quality than for quantity.

Within these universities — the others will follow in course of time — similar reforms could be carried out: majors, minors, units, credits might vanish without more ado. Some of the institutions might discard the first or second year; those that retained the college in whole or part could at least abandon the uniform four-year course, recognize differences of ability and industry, and segregate what is essentially teaching, the instructor's burden, from learning, which is the responsibility of the student. Uniformity is not feasible, perhaps not even desirable. The make-believe professions — journalism, business, library science, domestic science, and optometry — could be discarded: they would not be missed either by the university or society. What becomes of the things thus unloaded is, to be frank, not the university's concern; it is the concern of society to create appropriate organs to perform such of these functions as are really worth performing.

The most formidable " School " — the Harvard Graduate School of Business Administration — could be detached: it is fortunately situated in Boston: what more fitting than a Boston Graduate School of Business? That would leave the university free to attack the problem of professional training for business experimentally. Schools of education might be reformed and put on probation; schools of medicine, law, and engineering could be subjected to searching criticism and such reform as they may require. The entire teaching staff could be put on a full-time basis: no one would have to do " chores " to piece out a livelihood. On the other hand, and for that very reason, a closer and more helpful relation could be established between the university, on the one hand, and business, industry, government, education, and public health, on the other. For, lacking pecuniary interest in affairs, the faculty could treat the modern world as a great clinic. Only thus can the university be modernized in the sense of my opening chapter and at the same time preserve its intellectual integrity. Extension courses could be restricted, as they are in England, to subjects of university value and to students who are mature. The home study departments would evaporate. With these reforms, the American university would be enormously simplified; advertising would cease; administration would be slight and relatively inexpensive; further developments in the direction of faculty coöperation would in time take place; Harvard, Yale, Columbia, and Chicago would at once stand out as universities. They would need no buildings for years to come; their financial situation would become enormously easier. They would talk in terms of small groups of scholars and teachers. Far higher intellectual standards could be set up. I venture to believe that in less than a generation the influence of universities upon American life would be immensely greater than it is today.

The college is the graver problem. Years ago, I read in the Boston *Transcript* an indignant letter from a Harvard alumnus, complaining that the University was " suffocating the College," as with improvement in secondary schools it surely ought. In his *Harvard Memories*, President Eliot puts his finger on the spot:

"To this day there are many Harvard Bachelors of Arts who hold that graduates of Harvard professional schools cannot be considered to be genuine sons of Harvard, and do not yet see that the service Harvard University renders to the country through its graduate professional schools is greater than that it renders through Harvard College proper. A Harvard tradition that is still an obstacle to progress!"

Indeed, the obstacles are greater now than when President Eliot wrote, for under the present administration, though the graduate schools at Harvard have advanced, the distinctive policies pursued have concerned themselves largely with undergraduate Harvard.

Progress might be greatly assisted by the outright creation of a school or institute of higher learning, a university in the post-graduate sense of the word. It should be a free society of scholars — free, because mature persons, animated by intellectual purposes, must be left to pursue their own ends in their own way. Administration should be slight and inexpensive.[143] Scholars and scientists should participate in its government; the president should come down from his pedestal. The term "organization" should be banned. The institution should be open to persons, competent and cultivated, who do not need and would abhor spoon-feeding — be they college graduates or not. It should furnish simple surroundings — books, laboratories, and above all, tranquillity — absence of distraction either by worldly concerns or by parental

---

[143] A Harvard professor writes me as follows: "I think it is tremendously important at the present time to oppose the tendencies of administrative usurpation of certain academic functions which can only be properly performed by scholars. It has often seemed to me that we might profitably go back, at least in part, to the system which has long and successfully functioned in Germany — namely, to have the purely house-keeping and financial work of educational institutions carried out by business men and clerks, with deans and rectors appointed from the older men of the faculty for periods of one or two years, relieving them for the time from their purely teaching duties and having them concern themselves during their administrations with the guidance of educational policy in consultation with a committee of their colleagues."

responsibility for an immature student body. Provision should be made for the amenities of life in the institution and in the private life of the staff. It need not be complete or symmetrical: if a chair could not be admirably filled, it should be left vacant. There exists in America no university in this sense — no institution, no seat of learning devoted to higher teaching and research. Everywhere the pressure of undergraduate and vocational activities hampers the serious objects for which universities exist. Thus science and scholarship suffer; money is wasted; even undergraduate training is less efficient than it might be, if left to itself.

What could be expected, if a modern American university were thus established? The ablest scholars and scientists would be attracted to its faculty; the most earnest students would be attracted to its laboratories and seminars. It would be small, as Gilman's Johns Hopkins was small; but its propulsive power would be momentous out of all proportion to its size. It would, like a lens, focus rays that now scatter. The Rockefeller Institute for Medical Research is limited in scope; its hospital contains less than fifty beds. But its uncompromising standards of activity and publication have given it influence in America and Europe throughout the entire field of medical education and research. A university or a school of higher learning at the level I have indicated would do as much for other disciplines and might thus in time assist the general reorganization of secondary and higher education.

PART III

ENGLISH UNIVERSITIES

I

FOR the sake of contrast and comparison, let me, before discussing English universities, briefly summarize my conclusions respecting America. American universities are, as I have explained in the previous section, largely determined by local conditions and present pressure. Harvard and Yale have, to be sure, a history, but the thinness of the soil, in which they have grown, is evidenced by their close resemblance in spirit, effort, and organization to other American universities of recent origin. They think they are different from one another; but the differences are quite inconsequential, the resemblances, fundamental and far-reaching. Nor is this resemblance due to the fact that Chicago and the state universities imitated Harvard and Yale; on the contrary, Harvard, rightly zealous to be modern, has unfortunately become modern in the same fashion, more or less, as the midwestern universities; they are all alike in organization and activities, because the same forces operate upon them, and because there is not enough resistance in the shape of traditions or ideas or ideals within the older institutions to put up a fight. The result is plain: the American universities are open to innovation; that is excellent; but, alas, they have been invaded indiscriminately by things both good and bad. Nowhere else in the world has it been so easy to get a sound move made — witness the speed with which graduate schools have been created and medical schools reorganized. But, unfortunately, nowhere else, as new departures have been proposed, has critical sense been so feebly operative. On the one hand, a self-made American can become a professor on his own merit, as has recently happened at Johns Hopkins;[1] a new branch of learning can be quickly taken into the academic fold. On the other hand, the quack, the technician, the clever "salesman," and the practical man may obtain almost unhampered sway. He edges himself into a society to which he does not belong; and in consequence an alien type of government has had to be devised to keep the cumbrous mechanism going. Thus, a wild, uncontrolled, and uncritical expansion has taken place; the serious withdraw into their own shells; the quacks emit publications that travesty research and make a noise that drowns out the still small voice to which America should be listening. Thus a nation which "believes" in education permits its elementary and secondary schools to be demoralized by politicians and its universities to break beneath the incongruous load placed upon them.

II

I shall, as I proceed, qualify and explain what I am about to say in regard to the English. But a broad generalization, to be qualified later, will be helpful. The English believe in religion, in manners, in politics; throughout their history, education has been subordinated, now to one, now to another of the three.[2] This broad generalization is to be taken *cum*

[1] This happens in England too, as is shown by the careers of the late Professor Joseph Wright at Oxford, of Professor Okey at Cambridge, and of Professor Daniels at Manchester.

[2] On the continent also Protestantism has furnished an impetus to secondary education; but with the development of science and of a belief

grano salis; it is not so nearly correct today as it was a generation or several generations ago, when, politically and economically, things were running England's way; under force of sheer necessity, it will have to become still less true, if England is to pull out of its present difficulties. But even now, education as education — education disconnected from practice or church or poverty, education from the standpoint of principle or idea, as the privilege of unfettered human intelligence — does not, despite the efforts of the philosophic radicals and their successors, powerfully appeal to the English mind. Meanwhile, as far back as the record goes, within and without the English universities, even antedating them, scholarship and science in the most disinterested form have been patronized and encouraged in England. When the universities were very nearly dead, dead of religious, political, and social bigotry, great scholars found them quiet retreats in which to prosecute their studies; again, at all periods of English history, now and formerly, philosophers and scientists have gone their way without connection with institutions of learning at all. A banker was the author of the greatest history of Greece written up to his time; a gentleman of leisure made in the *Origin of Species* the most upsetting contribution to science and philosophy; neither Ricardo nor John Stuart Mill was a university professor. Thus the Englishman is, whatever else he is, an individualist; his pride in his illogicality is not without justification. Moreover, the ancient universities, whatever their defects — all, by the way, with characteristic English candour, acknowledged by some one or other — are as seats of higher learning incomparably superior to any-

---

in education as such its importance rapidly decreased. In England, as we shall see, it is still a living and controversial factor.

thing that has as yet been created in America. Of all countries, England is therefore the most difficult to describe and judge; yet not even in America has it become more important for men to judge and to act from the standpoint of principle, forgetful of expediency, history, or tradition.

The fundamental factor in determining the scope and quality of the university is secondary education. Despite the efforts of philosophers and reformers, the English universities and the endowed public schools formed a closed social and intellectual circle up to almost the last quarter of the nineteenth century. They were both organs of the Anglican Church; they were hostile to dissent; they were as institutions concerned with the production of a type — the English gentleman, a moral and social rather than an intellectual type. The revolution wrought by Dr. Arnold at Rugby made the formation of character the main object of a gentleman's education. That is still the centre about which the public schools and the Oxford and Cambridge Colleges revolve. One wonders, not whether character and manners are unimportant, but whether, like cleanliness or clear speech, they may not now be more or less taken for granted. Persistent emphasis on what has been so strongly established as to be an obvious, essential, and characteristic national trait tends to distract attention from something else — the increased need of intelligence in the affairs of life — personal, political, social, economic.

The circle I have described was easily maintained even after religious tests and other criteria were discarded because the public school is largely staffed by

Oxford and Cambridge men, and its students are afterwards sent to Oxford or Cambridge. A circle was thus established, *enclosing* certain definite influences, *excluding* certain contacts, some important, others, perhaps, deleterious. But one important point must not be overlooked: the public schools, whatever *their* defects, do articulate with the universities, whatever *theirs*. The boy who leaves Winchester or Rugby is at any rate competent to go forward at Oxford and Cambridge. Secondary education of the type provided by the public schools connects with the universities. The two have varied together; and now that intellectual achievement has risen in esteem at the universities, the public schools compete strenuously to obtain the largest list of distinctions. Meanwhile, both also continue to cultivate behaviour and sport in characteristic fashion; thus, along both lines, scholarship and sport, public schools and universities are harmoniously continuous.

Other factors, however, complicate this simple and one-sided situation. Radicals and utilitarians were never content with either Anglicanism or any other limitation of educational opportunity. Their position was not a happy one. Their philosophy of *laisser faire* was more and more plainly depriving the masses of educational and other opportunity: in letting things alone, the state was positively favouring the privileged classes. Aversion to state interference, not to say state control, is still powerful and effective in England. Hence, a state monopoly of education was and is unthinkable. Voluntary effort aided by a meagre state grant wrestled with the problem from 1800 to 1870. In the middle sixties Matthew Arnold urged with unsurpassed courage and intelligence the supreme national need of proper facilities for secondary education; his great report dealing with *Secondary Education on the Continent* is still a living document. In the elementary field, Mr. Gladstone's reform government made the local provision of elementary schools compulsory and even favoured dissenters and undenominational schools. Successive Acts of Parliament have proceeded further. The Act of 1899, largely the work of the late Sir Robert Morant, one of the outstanding figures of all time in the English Civil Service, smoothed the way for the legislation of 1902 and 1903, both of which, however, recognized the vested interests of the Anglican Church; quantitatively and qualitatively a transformation was thus wrought. With the education act of Mr. H. A. L. Fisher, passed in 1918, the structure was potentially rounded out. Local authorities continue to control the schools, elementary and secondary; but the central government supplies grants in aid. On what terms are grants in aid obtainable? The conditions are laid down at Whitehall; wise inspectors and directors, who know that influence is at once more agreeable and more effective than authority, roam the country, discussing programs and conditions with local authorities; they wield no " big stick "; they do not lay down the law; but they leave in their wake suggestions, queries, intimations as to what is doing elsewhere, on what terms state aid can be procured, and helpful syllabi prepared in London. Orderly and spirited progress has resulted; if carried to its logical conclusion, the Fisher Act will in course of time give England a highly flexible and adequate elementary and secondary school system, rooted in the soil, kept within bounds and up to a definite standard by the steering gear at Whitehall: a happy combination of voluntary and governmental coöperation, acceptable to the English temper. Voluntary (non-provided) schools still predominate in number though the number of pupils in council (provided) schools exceed the number in voluntary schools by about one-third; about 25% of the teachers in the elementary schools are still without certificates. But these facts count for less than one would think; for a liberal and elastic way of providing free places and scholarships to the more gifted pupils [3] opens the door of opportunity to those upon whom further progress depends. On the other hand, the English show no signs of being converted to the American theory that a college or university education is indiscriminately good for anyone who can make his way through a high school. Such is, quite clearly, not the case; hundreds of youths, 18 to 22 years of age, can be better employed than in attending a university; and the English, by increasing provision of technical and other schools, try to give this host — the majority — what they need and can assimilate. On the other hand, in England, as in America and the rest of the world, wealth may still triumph over reason: neither we nor they nor others have found effective means of putting the idle and stupid rich in their proper place.

In the maintenance of some sort of educational sanity, during a period characterized by the increase of educational opportunity and the rise of an equalitarian philosophy, the strongly intrenched and resistant ancient universities, enjoying great prestige, have exercised a powerful and beneficial influence. They have had to yield, as was right, to science and modern languages; but they have not yielded to physical exercise and cooking. Modernization has not in

[3] In England and Wales, there are 1,301 secondary schools on the grant list; they contained (1925–26) 360,503 pupils, of whom 36.5% had free places. Wilson, *The Schools of England* (London, 1928), p. 357.

England obliterated the distinction between intellectual and menial activities. Thus Oxford and Cambridge have been important agencies in maintaining sanity at a time when vocationalism and practicality endanger all sound educational conceptions.[4] This does not mean that England — primarily a commercial country — has not slowly awakened to the need of technical or industrial education. It means only that the English have not, like the Americans, lost sight of important cultural and educational distinctions. What trained capacity and intelligence in the education ministries of Germany did for Germany, to some extent at least the sheer recalcitrance of the public schools and the ancient universities, aided undoubtedly by a sense of real values, did for England.

Another limitation — for better and for worse: the public school serves largely a class; it produces a type — a type of mind, a type of manners; over a protracted period, it devotes itself assiduously to shaping its pupils in a definite way. Within its limits, it is an effective educational agency; but these limits are not coextensive with modern life — the life of a democratic society, involved in intellectual and industrial competition with all the rest of the world. As long as English society was aristocratic and stratified, the public schools could lead their own lives. But English life has

[4] On this point, one may quote with hearty approbation the words of Professor I. L. Kandel of Teachers College, Columbia University: "Foreign countries have well-defined notions of what constitutes secondary education and we (Americans) ought to take the trouble to understand why this type of education is separated from vocational and technical education. The attempt (in America) to include in one institution every type of educational activity for adolescent pupils accounts for the failure to attain thoroughness in any one of them. . . . Adjustment to special parochial interests will . . . become as disintegrating as the so-called aristocratic culture of Europe." *School and Society*, Vol. VIII, pp. 261, ff. The entire article merits careful attention; I have abbreviated the quotation without modifying its sense.

been rapidly democratized; it is, in certain aspects, more democratic than republican America — which is perhaps not saying so very much. To some extent, the public schools have recognized this profound social and economic change. They have, for example, developed modern sides. But they are still far too largely the preserve of aristocracy and of wealth that is ambitious to become aristocracy. For the time being, at least, their limitations have been curiously tightened by the very fact that secondary education is also otherwise increasingly provided for. Ranking just below the historic public schools, one must note the creation of perhaps a hundred newer schools, influenced greatly by the public schools, but making a wider social appeal — a middle group, which has adopted certain public school traditions, but serves rather the professional and commercial classes. The municipal school with its free places enjoys no social prestige; those who can afford the luxury of a public school tend therefore to be driven thither — and the spread of democracy thus curiously increases the breadth of the social rift. If they find no ways to check this tendency, the public schools seem to be doomed to gradual loss of relative importance.

The enrolment in English secondary schools has increased with great rapidity.[5] Nevertheless, the per capita enrolment as compared with population is far below that of the United States. But the statistics are misleading and meaningless. Most of the public high schools of the United States are high schools in name only. To some extent the same situation exists in England — especially in rural sections — though the indirect control of Whitehall through recognition and

[5] Between 1908–09 and 1925–26, enrolment increased 165% (Wilson, *loc. cit.*).

[229]

subsidies draws a line that is not drawn in the United States. Secondary education in England is therefore — despite enormous progress — neither as substantial nor as extensive as appears.

IV

We are proceeding on the assumption that a university is essentially a seat of learning, devoted to the conservation of knowledge, the increase of systematic knowledge, and the training of students well above the secondary level. This is, as we have discovered, not the current American idea of a university; it is not the English idea, either. Professor Wilson holds that " secondary and university education has and will always have a definite function to perform in the national economy, viz., to discover and train those minds best able to direct the ship of the state. Deny it this function, you check the flow of blood in the organism, you decree first decline and untimely death." [6] This description seems to me incorrect as a matter of history, and in any event inadequate from the standpoint of present and future needs. Hitherto, the English university has, like the American university, discharged three functions: part of it, much less than is the case in America, belongs to the secondary field; part of it has been devoted to "service," but service at a far higher level than obtains in America; part of it concerns itself with genuine university activities. I cannot, however, discuss English universities from these three points of view, as I discussed American universities; for while American universities, little inclined as they are to admit it, are generally alike, English universities belong to three distinct types;

[6] *Loc. cit.*, p. 10.

and it is more important to survey them from the standpoint of type than from the standpoint of function. It will be easy to consider the three functions in successive connection with each of the three types. There are advantages in this diversity — especially for a people that has felt its way along more or less blindly as have the English. For human society is infinitely complex, human capacity and aspiration infinitely varied. No single type of institution devoted to higher learning can hope to be completely representative, completely adequate. Difference may therefore be utilized to bring about something nearer to complete representation, something nearer to complete adequacy. Students and scholars may find conditions, environment, spirit, activities more congenial at one place than at another; indeed, the same student may be happier at one epoch here, at another, there. Such variation as exists by chance in England is favourable to the waywardness of the human spirit; and it is better that these differences should be incorporated in different bodies rather than that one institution should seek to include them all.

V

If a university is, whatever its type or form, a highly vitalized organism, vitalized, not by administrative means, but by ideas and ideals, with a corporate life, I confess myself unable to understand in what sense the University of London is a university at all. While avoiding the excesses and absurdities of Columbia and Chicago, it possesses even less organic unity than its nearest American relatives. It is not really a university, though it does possess central offices and an inclusive court and senate: it is a line drawn about an enormous number of different institutions of heterogeneous quality and purpose. Within this circle almost seventy institutions are included. Two of them are fairly complete colleges — King's and University — not so very different from American universities, though simpler, more solid, and less pretentious ; some are research institutes — for example, the Institute of Historical Research whose labours are gradually re-writing important epochs in English history, and the new Institute of Hygiene and Tropical Medicine; thirty-six of them — the so-called Schools of the University — are an indiscriminate medley, including, among others, the London School of Economics, a College of Household Science,[7] which, though far more substantial than the corresponding schools in America, is out of place in a university, a dozen or more Hospital Medical Schools, and the Imperial College of Science and Technology; twenty-three institutions possess recognized teachers — polytechnics, music schools, teachers training schools, research institutes, and special hospitals.[8] In essential respects every institution retains its autonomy, even though each of them surrenders something in order that

[7] " Almost unnoticed — on January 29, 1929 — . . . the Household and Social Science Department of King's College for Women became King's College of Household and Social Science, an independent School of the University in the Faculty of Science." *Annual Report 1928-29*, p. 5. It is thus on the same footing as the Imperial College of Science and Technology and the London School of Economics! Could anything be more absurd? The courses of study offered are more solid, for the most part, than the corresponding courses offered by an American School of household arts. Nevertheless they include lectures and practical work in " housewifery, laundry and cookery," " elementary book-keeping," " needlework," and " household electricity." Now, what does such a school gain by being a School of the University? And what does " University " mean when such a school is included?

[8] My difficulty in comprehending is shared by the Department Committee on the University of London (H. M. Stationery Office, 1926), p. 30, § 50.

there may be a combination at all. Thirty-six of
these institutions are "schools" and constitute the
core of the University; while they are still entities, the
University appoints their professors and readers —
not, however, their junior teachers — and allocates to
them such public funds as they receive. They continue,
however, to manage their own finances, though the
University sets the standard for and confers degrees.
The University "inspects" and thus tactfully influences and, where necessary, gradually elevates, the
quality of the work carried on. The remaining twenty-
three are merely institutions with recognized teachers
competent, however, to offer courses leading to the University's degrees at far lower rates than the "schools."
Some of their students may, however, be University
students, ultimately going up for the University degree; thus at the Battersea Polytechnic, out of 2,940
students, 226 (less than one-tenth) were University
students. Among the teachers who carry on the sixty-
odd schools and institutions, there are four distinct
classes: professors and readers, appointed by the University; juniors appointed by the several schools, on
their own responsibility; recognized teachers, appointed by the schools, but stamped with approval by
the University; unrecognized teachers, with whom
the University has no direct concern. There are now
1,140 appointed and recognized teachers in the University, as against 2,306 who are unrecognized. Recognition is a matter of grave importance: for the teacher,
because it is a certificate of approbation issued by the
central authority; for the student also, because in the
case of institutions which are not "schools," only students taught by recognized teachers may be candidates
for the internal degree. Yet recognition is itself governed by no clear principle: it is more or less capricious

and episodic. This description makes it clear that London University fails to qualify as a university not because it lacks the amenities of Oxford and Cambridge, but because it lacks unity of spirit and design. I do not deny that the constituent members of the University in their respective ways serve purposes; they may even serve their respective purposes in some instances somewhat better for being included in a University which discharges certain more or less effective police functions. But it still does not follow that this is a sufficient reason for including them in a university or that the University of London is a university in a proper sense of the term. I grant that in general the Hospital Schools have been helped by the " standardization " and contacts which they owe to London University. But are they really standardized? And at what level? And are the contacts, while stimulating to them, uplifting to the University? The University has forced this level up to some extent; but it has not made and, in my opinion, cannot make university clinics of them.

The University of London began soundly when a group of enlightened liberals and radicals established University College, for the purpose of giving a university education, as it was then understood, to all qualified students " irrespective of class or creed "; the new College has had a remarkable career — it is even the parent of the great Cambridge school of physiology. Shortly afterwards, the Anglican interest created in the metropolis a corresponding institution, King's College, to compete with the " godless university." The University of London was a step towards the association of the two: each retained its autonomy, while the University gave the degree examinations. Meanwhile, independent teaching bodies were springing up all over the country. To check chaos, the

University of London was in 1858 authorized to examine for a degree any students who presented
themselves, regardless of how or where they had
studied. Good was, of course, accomplished; education
was in a manner stabilized; opportunity for procuring
direction and stimulus was immensely increased. But
even so, harm was done. The significance of written
examinations was — and is — greatly exaggerated, and
the possibilities of a genuine university development
were seriously hampered. The haphazard ways of dealing with the problems of growth, current in English-
speaking lands, thus create difficulties; gaps cannot be
bridged in such hit-or-miss fashion.

The University of London is defended because like
the British Empire it is a federation, within which
large liberty is allowed to constituent units. The British Commonwealth of Nations is an illogical, but
operative concern, holding together lightly but firmly
England, Ireland, Scotland, Wales, South Africa, Australia, and Canada. It may well prove the most beneficent way of bringing peace and good will among scattered peoples who might otherwise be troublesome to
one another and to the rest of the world. Analogically,
the University of London is justified as an easy-going
federation of all sorts of enterprises that get along better that way than they would separately. The analogy
does not carry conviction — analogies rarely do. London is, to be sure, a large city; but it is, after all, not
the world. The vast distances between Canada, Cape
Colony, and Australia eliminate most causes of fric-
tion; the proximity of King's, University, the Polytechnics, and the external students makes for increased
complexity. There is no federal governing body on
which the dominions and dependencies are represented; they obtain their unity through the Crown.

But there is in London a University Senate, in which the constituent parts of the University seek unification; that creates a situation very different from the situation of the British Empire. But even if the analogy were perfect, it would not make a university out of the University of London. It would at best prove that, things being what they are, a numerous group of different institutions and activities can be carried on in this fashion. It would still remain to be proved that the highest tasks of a university are not slighted or abandoned under such conditions.

The University is governed through Committees by a Court, which holds the purse-strings, and a Senate of approximately sixty persons, representative of institutions or subjects and responsible for educational policies. But the central machinery, whatever its powers and authority, has, as I have said, but limited and indirect control of policies. The Medical Schools have — with the exception of University College Hospital — recently excluded women students. They have their own reasons for so doing. A Committee of the University is " unable to see any valid argument on the merits against the provision for coeducation in medicine." But what is the most that the Committee can suggest? That its " report be forwarded to the Schools which should be invited to consider the possibility of admitting a quota of women students as a means of giving effects to the policy of the University " ! The Court is an innovation, which may encroach on the educational preserve of the Senate, since it is endowed with " power to determine finally any question of finance arising out of the administration of the University," though, " before determining any question of finance which directly affects the educational policy of the University, the Court shall take into consideration any recommendation or report made by the Senate." [9] But the Court, while containing certain institutional heads, contains no professors. The teaching body lacks direct and immediate contact with it. It stands accordingly in reference to the institutions composing the University precisely where the trustees of an American university stand in reference to the faculty. The Court cannot thoroughly know the merits of the specific propositions on which it is to pass; a hostile head can thus snuff out any proposition that his faculty might like to present and urge. The Senate is obviously a cumbrous body; but that is the least of the objections to be urged against it. It is representative — as no central educational body trusted with responsibility for dealing with problems on their merits should ever be. In consequence, the Senate may at any time split on lines that a unified organism would never know — which the attempt to secure financial impartiality through the creation of the Court would appear to admit; the external side, of which more hereafter, has stood up for itself and may again do so; it is likely to be more concerned for its own dignity and prestige than for the common interest, if any one could ever make out what in so diverse a situation the common interest actually is; and of course, by the same token, the medical schools, of which there are a dozen, have their interests and ideas to represent and protect. University politics are inevitable; and politics and ideals are impossible bed fellows.

The Boards of Studies cut across institutional lines; but the Boards, though drastically reduced by the new statutes, are still heterogeneous. They are probably

[9] *The Statutes made for the University of London under the University of London Act, 1926*, p. 7, No. 36.

effective against too low a minimum, against which there exists in huge American institutions no effective protection whatsoever; they and the Senate are only partially effective against absurdities, since somehow journalism, pharmacy, household work, and various merely technical schools have not been shown the door. The contacts brought about by the Boards are educative and stimulating; but their work is time-consuming and energy-consuming; I should think it doubtful whether they help the best men — and, from the standpoint of the University, that is the point of supreme and dominating importance. And a similar statement may be made from the point of view of the student. The undergraduate and the professional student easily finds his proper nook; but, in London, as in Oxford and Cambridge, the graduate student, unless directed by suggestion from his teacher before he reaches his destination, may readily be lost. There is, in most departments, no organization or publication that assists him in finding what he wants.

In a very real sense the University of London is not actually made up of or identical with even its constituent schools. It is external to them all. It is a remote body constituted of persons chosen from the constituent institutions and from other sources regulating and governing to a limited degree the constituent institutions from the outside. University College, Westfield College, the London School of Economics, and the Hospital Medical Schools send representatives concerned to look out for their interests to a central body, whatever it be called, and this central body operates through an executive staff. Thus the governing body is with respect to any one institution made up of persons almost entirely external to that institution. For example, when the governing body deals with a matter that pertains to the School of Economics, most of the persons who vote have nothing to do with the School of Economics, know little about it, and have no particular interest in it. On the contrary, they have an interest, each in his or her own institution. I do not say that they do not make honest attempts to do justice to the London School, but they would be more than human if they cared as much about the London School as they do about their particular institutions; and the same would be true of any other constituent institution in its relations to the governing bodies of the institution. It is not easy to get a faculty which takes broad views; but, after all, within a unified university the faculty is made up of scholars of the same general texture; a much nearer approach can be made to broad, impartial, far-sighted action, though difficulties enough arise. The fact that such difficulties arise within unified universities constitutes the best of reasons for not needlessly multiplying them by including in the governing bodies and on committees representatives of all sorts of institutions, many of whom have no conception of university work whatsoever.

The secondary and the service schools, institutions, and teachers are, then, entirely out of place in a genuine university. The research institutions and two or three colleges constitute the backbone of the structure. The latter I have compared — not unfairly, I think — with American universities. They are mainly secondary institutions dealing with young men and women, starting at eighteen or nineteen years of age. Graduate work is less organized than in America; it is more a matter of individuals — and more, rather than less, effective for that reason. Some of the greatest of English scholars and scientists have been and are found in the faculties of University and King's — witness, among others, Pearson, Starling, Hill, Pollard, and Richardson. But it is not and cannot be the primary function of either the University itself or of the colleges, as things now stand, to create conditions favourable to the teaching and research of men of this type. Such conditions do indeed exist in the Institute of Historical Research; but where else? In general, advanced teaching and research are usually, though not wholly, carried on in hours snatched from undergraduate routine.

The London School of Economics may once have been a university faculty of economics and political science. It still retains among its faculty distinguished teachers and investigators: Bowley, Laski, Toynbee, Malinowski, and Westermarck, among others; like a corresponding American faculty, it still makes a point of research or advanced work; a few men have organized seminars for mature students; in subjects like economic history or political theory, subjects fit for university cultivation, it is the most important centre for graduate work in its field in the United Kingdom. Nevertheless, the School is mainly undergraduate. It does not enjoy a monopoly in its own field; and it offers instruction in English, French, and German. A professor lectures to a mixed class, as he would in America, though the level is above the American level, and his attention oscillates in consequence. In the new building a few rooms for research students have been provided. It is, however, mainly a place where an advanced student may take a book under his arm, sit down, and read quietly. Moreover, the centre of gravity seems to be shifting towards " service " and undergraduate teaching. The night students are frequently tired, and it is often, though again not always, a

drudgery to the professor to repeat his lectures. They
are not, for the most part students in the university
sense. The School enrolled (1928–29) 2,577 students,
of whom 678 were candidates for a diploma or undergraduate degree, 1,720 were part-time students, and
179 were engaged in research: quite plainly, then, in
so far as enrolment means anything, the School is
mainly undergraduate, and the students a miscellaneous collection.

I have said that there are a dozen medical schools in
the University of London: eleven of them belong to
an obsolete type, one — that of University College
— approaches the university level. And they are obsolete for three reasons, involving their faculties, their
student body, and their facilities. In the pre-clinical
sciences, full-time men, some of them excellent, predominate; but their budgets, staff, facilities, and preoccupation with teaching make independent work
difficult and scarce. Conditions are most favourable
at University College, where the medical sciences are
cultivated in proximity to other sciences, and where
the resources and facilities of the laboratory subjects
are more nearly satisfactory than in other London
schools. But the London hospitals are not really clinics. The laboratories connected with them are scarcely
adequate to anything more than routine work, though,
of course, a man with ideas will somehow find a way to
work. The hospitals have, to be sure, usually beds
enough; but the beds are not so distributed as to constitute clinics in the scientific sense of the term. The
hospital staff is made up of busy practitioners and
struggling youngsters, destined to succeed them; they
are mainly practical men — experienced physicians
and surgeons with little time, resources, or interest for
clinical science. A " firm " consisting of a senior and

his associate look after a small number of beds —
precisely as practising physicians have to handle a
variety of complaints. The strong feature of English
medical training is its contact with objects; there is
little, perhaps too little, that is theoretical and discursive; the student dissects, studies specimens, examines
patients in the dispensary and in the wards. But the
instruction is practical without being at bottom scientific; it is good hospital training rather than university
training — university training being conceived as hov-
ering on the borders of the unknown, conducted, even in
the realm of the already ascertained, in the spirit of
doubt and inquiry. Medicine may be practised in this
way; but it does not follow that it is best taught in this
way; and even more certainly experience shows that,
when medicine is taught in this way, knowledge is not
best advanced in this way. The fact is that the London
hospitals are amateurish — and so, with individual exceptions like Sir Thomas Lewis, are the clinicians.

In medicine more than in any other branch, the
English fare badly when compared with German faculties or the best American faculties. Indeed, a university hospital in the German or American sense — a
hospital staffed and financed with an eye to education
and research, conducted like a university, not like a
charity, and under the management of the university,
in organic contact with the scientific work of a university — exists nowhere in England today. It is idle to
argue that England does as well with things as they
are. Such is not the case. Occasionally a Lister,
Horsley, or Head persists despite untoward conditions; but these men are rare. A germ has been planted
in the form of full-time clinical units; though they are
understaffed and underfinanced, they may in time
succeed in convincing the University that a man may

be good enough to belong to a hospital staff without being good enough to be a University teacher of medicine. The University appoints the full-time clinical and other professors; the schools themselves make other appointments. Boards composed of teachers of the several subjects in the various schools reach certain general decisions; but these formal and occasional contacts do not create university departments nor can the various boards ever be so completely integrated as to constitute a medical faculty. The influence and power of the University and of University ideals as against the preference or prejudices of the schools is slight. It has not reduced the number of medical schools, though some of them are moribund; it cannot confine a medical school to the instruction of students who are candidates for a London degree. It cannot finance a single school properly. Finally, as I have already pointed out, it pleads to deaf ears in the matter of admitting women, not on equal, but on any terms. Many of the students in the London Hospital Schools are indeed not University students at all and do not go up for the University of London degree; they aim at some other degree or the qualification of the Conjoint Board. In 1927–28, there were altogether 3,425 medical students in London, of whom slightly more than half (1,814) were candidates for the University of London degree. The teaching is distinctly " *ad hoc* " — the goal being the particular examination chosen by the student. Special courses are offered, according as the student aims at this goal or that. The best of the students are, as a rule, those who have been trained in the pre-clinical sciences at Oxford and Cambridge; but they get nothing in the way of clinical or laboratory opportunity that is not also offered to students with inferior previous education beside whom they sit.

The loss to medical science in general and to medical science and practice in England due to adherence to a type of school that is fifty or seventy-five years in arrears is simply incalculable.

The external side of the University of London has long been the subject of acute controversy. There is no question that the external side renders a valuable service; it guides students who cannot attend the University; and in a country where colleges and universities have so tardily developed, some kind of central examining body had a part to play. Perhaps, too, it had to have an imposing name, if it was to play any part at all. Able men have thus been discovered and developed. This is, however, the " Abraham Lincoln " argument so often heard in America. Whatever may have once been the case, arrangements of this sort may, if persisted in too long, hamper rather than help university development. At any rate, they confuse things that are different: a former Vice-Chancellor with whom I discussed this question remarked: " We keep on calling ourselves the same thing — constituent schools of the University of London, Bachelors of Arts of the University of London — when we know perpectly well that we are not the same thing and not even the same sort of thing." The external standard always endangers the internal standard; it copies the internal procedure, instead of facing its own problems independently.

I grant, however, that the external side has made the external degree [10] more definite than the American degree. Yet I was authoritatively told that in making appointments inquiry is always made as to whether the

[10] On the other hand, the University also has " associate students," candidates for other than the University degree. So confusion is still further confounded.

degree is the one or the other — a difference in quality is therefore assumed. However, the external side has in London respected the dignity of subject-matter. Its opportunities are confined to serious subjects of genuine intellectual interest and importance; [11] it serves often as the degree examination of those who have been internal students elsewhere; in these respects it puts to shame the wretched " offerings " of the home study departments of certain American universities. It may well be that there are external students who surpass internal students in all essential points. None the less, if there is anything vitally important in the relationship of teacher and student or if there is some subtle element in education — as there is — which the written examination does not test at all, external study and external examination based on a syllabus form an entity that should do business on its own account. A syllabus and an examination are not substitutes for the personal contact of teacher and worker; they may be excellent of their kind — but they are something different. They do not test, they may even kill, what is most precious in culture. The post office is not the same as a professor in the flesh. Democracy needs many types of opportunity and training; they do not necessarily all or mostly belong to universities. Indeed, universities are likely to fail in their highest obligations precisely to the extent that they assume irrelevant and distracted activities. And the external side of the University of London is no exception. The very existence of the issue, " internal *v.* external," proves that they are incompatible. The service should be rendered, but by some other agency, and should pretend to be what it is, not something else or something more. In England as

---

[11] The same is practically true of its extension courses.

in America, there is a growing movement in the field of adult education. There is every reason why it should be conducted by a flexible and capacious organization, concerned to render to persons who cannot attend schools and universities the particular service that they require for training or enjoyment. But these functions cannot be discharged on a large scale by universities except by a diversion of energy and an increased complexity of machinery that cost the university too dearly. English experience shows clearly the feasibility of a detached examining board for those who do not aspire to a university degree under university conditions. The Conjoint Board is an external examining body that has set up in medicine a good external standard: an adult education examining board without connection with the University of London could do the same in any other field. This would merely involve acceptance of a distinction in fact that is now overlooked. No examining board, even though called a University, can possibly hold University College, Westfield, East London, and the external students to one standard; why pretend to do so? and what difference does it make? There are millions of Englishmen without degrees at all. What of it? The University of London has, of course, improved as the secondary schools have improved; research has increased in quantity, quality, and range; but it will not become a great or a real university, worthy of London and of the Empire and in harmony with the modern spirit, until it has been reorganized as a teaching and investigating seat of learning, leaving outside its orbit most of the schools — technical, medical, and other — which it will never be able to assimilate, because they live at other and lower levels. To be sure, great scholars, scientists, and economists have been and now are professors in one or another of the constituent schools of the University of London. But, as I have repeatedly urged, great scholars and scientists have always flourished in England and sometimes in other countries, even outside universities altogether. When one is speaking of institutions, one's criticism cannot be met by citing men who overcome obstacles; institutions exist to minimize obstacles, not to aggravate them. If it be the purpose of a modern university to promote the search for truth and the training of men competent to advance and interpret knowledge, would one regard the University of London as well designed for this purpose? Whatever else one may say as to its usefulness, this question I venture to answer in the negative. Can the present University of London ever be made to answer this purpose? Perhaps. But its resistance to innovation does not warrant a sanguine opinion as to the near future, say, the next generation.[12]

V I

The provincial universities like the American universities, especially the American state universities, constitute an amazing achievement within a brief period. Owens College, Manchester, began its teaching career in 1851; but it did not become a degree-conferring institution in its own right until 1880 — just half a century ago. From 1880 to 1903, Victoria University with its seat at Owens College included the colleges at Liverpool and Leeds. Liverpool which began its career as a constituent college of Victoria University in 1881 has but recently celebrated its twenty-fifth anniversary as an independent univer-

[12] On this point, see Viscount Haldane's *Autobiography* (London, 1929), pp. 124–25.

sity. Yorkshire College became the University of Leeds within the present century. Other colleges and universities are passing through a similar evolution; there are now eleven degree-granting universities and five non-degree-granting university colleges in England. Beside these institutions, Harvard and Yale are already hoary with age.

It is obvious why the provincial universities could not have been born earlier; they had to wait upon the provision of secondary schools and the dissolution of the Anglican monopoly at Oxford, Cambridge, and in the sphere of politics. The late start of the newer universities was not wholly unfortunate. They began as colleges, the work of which was passed on by the old University of London. The results were inevitable: in America too little depends on mastery of subject-matter; in England too much. The subtleties by which culture is in the last resort determined counted for too little. This was bad and, despite a general recognition of its evil influence, continues. But if the provincial colleges had to be good in London's way, there were great countervailing advantages. They had, at least, to be as good as London, and in its way London did really mean something; and if they had also to be good in London's way, rubbish was certainly excluded. The beneficent influence of an intellectual and cultural tradition traceable to Oxford and Cambridge was and is still felt. The provincial secondary school student may obtain a certificate for an examination that includes a limited amount of cooking and needlework, but he will not be helped thereby towards matriculation in a provincial university. The subjects which he must present are, however, sufficiently broad and varied to give all legitimate kinds of intellectual ability and training their proper chance. And action through

a joint board enables the northern universities to preserve a relatively high scholarly level.

But London and the provincial universities have not
as yet impaired the tremendous prestige of the ancient
universities except in the newer subjects, such as economics. The abler boys who can financially afford to
do so almost invariably go to Oxford or Cambridge.
A scientist of international distinction, long a professor in a provincial university, once told me that he had
never found an acceptable assistant among his own
students. This is of course not equally true in all subjects, and with the passage of time it is rapidly becoming less and less the case. Circumstances are, therefore, forcing a change. Oxford and Cambridge can no
longer accept even all those who would go in for honours; the professional classes, whose income has been
seriously reduced by taxation, can no longer so generally afford to send their sons and daughters away from
home. Meanwhile, with the improvement of secondary education, another factor tending to improve the
provincial universities has come into play. The quality
of the student body is, however, kept down by the
great preponderance of students expecting to teach;
and honours courses in arts are swelled by the increased salary held out by recent legislation to those
who win distinction in a given subject.

The organization of the provincial universities has
been greatly influenced by American experience, modified, however, to advantage by English university tradition. The head — a principal or vice-chancellor —
is, like the American university president, appointed
for life; he participates in the work of faculties and
committees, wasteful of time and energy in England
as everywhere else. Time was when he might even keep
up certain scientific activities; but that day is past.

Administration is time-consuming; funds are needed. The English scorn — and very properly — the " advertiser " and " money-raiser " who have latterly emerged in America. Moreover, the new universities are developing upward: a trained scholar with executive talent must, in the absence of a central ministry, guide that development. But by no chance could the principal or vice-chancellor possibly exert the enormous power sometimes exercised by the university president in the United States. In practice, the faculties govern their own affairs; the burden of attending committees is therefore onerous. The teaching staff is organized on American, itself largely influenced by German, practice; every one of the universities possesses faculties of arts, science, and medicine; faculties of engineering, applied science, and commerce exist variously. The faculties consist of the higher members of the teaching staff; grouped together, they form the Senate, not, as a rule, a very active body. More influential is the Council, meeting twice a month and consisting, at a representative institution like Manchester, of the Vice-Chancellor, four professors, certain members of the non-professorial staff, and a considerable representation of the Court. This is the effective body, and it is, as will be observed, representative of the lay interest, the professorial interest, and the executive interest — a better device, in my opinion, than the American faculty and the American board of trustees with the president alone as the connecting link. In the provincial university, the teaching staff thus weighs out of all proportions to its numbers. As to finance alone does the Court decide. On the whole, in view of their origin in provincial industrial communities, the record is highly creditable. Donors and local authorities have represented trade and industry, and trade and industry give each of the provincial universities a distinctive flavour. But, despite an occasional untoward incident, the universities have led independent lives at a respectable level without serious interference from capitalistic or political influences. In my judgment, the independence of the ancient universities has in this matter once more been a steadying and helpful factor.

In respect to facilities and support, the provincial universities are unpretentious affairs. Their income, derived from local sources and from exchequer subventions, is modest compared with the income of American institutions; Manchester, oldest and one of the most solid of the provincial universities, has a total budget of $1,000,000 annually,[13] derived partly from fees, partly from income from endowment, partly from local subventions (too small in the total to endanger the independence of the University) and, last and most important, from the central government through the University Grants Committee. This Committee, headed since its inception in 1919 by Sir William S. McCormick,[14] a Scot, who knew at first hand the universities of Scotland, England, Germany, and the United States, has been a gentle, but powerful influence for good. In the absence of control by an education ministry, it has assisted what is good and quietly ignored all else. Its counsel and its funds have been almost equally acceptable.

In the matter of recruiting a staff, the provincial universities are at a disadvantage: their salaries are low, though professorial salaries are rising and are rela-

[13] Liverpool makes practically the same showing. Its income from all sources was in 1913–14, £83,720; in 1928–29, £213,150. Its assets were at these two periods £1,004,109 and £1,967,772. Local appropriations amounted in 1928–29 to £25,233. The need of money is urgent, but it is amazing how much is accomplished with small expenditure and resources.
[14] Deceased March 23, 1930.

tively higher, distinctly so, than professorial salaries in the United States; the posts few; their prestige as academic institutions is inferior to that of Oxford and Cambridge, and from the standpoint of the attractions of the metropolis, to that of London. They do, however, obtain promising appointees from the older universities, even if they do not usually keep the best of them. Two recent Regius professors of history at Oxford where they had begun their careers were later recalled from the provincial universities at which they first reached professorships; Professor A. V. Hill went from Cambridge to Manchester and thence to a research professorship at University College, London. It is better for the provincial universities to hold brilliant men like Rutherford and Sherrington for a brief period than a mediocre man permanently; their presence shows that the institutions are by no means wholly at the undergraduate level; and some of the brilliant remain, witness, for instance, Manchester with Roscoe, Tout, and Alexander. Indeed able scholars have been known to flee the insidious serenity of Oxford and Cambridge for the simpler environment of the provinces in order, as one of them said, " to save their souls." Of the present heads of houses at Oxford, two were at one time provincial vice-chancellors, the present Warden of New College, at Sheffield, the present Master of University, at Leeds. Outwardly — in respect to buildings and facilities — there have been great improvements, notably at Birmingham, Leeds, and Bristol. But the financial burden of the War will long operate to retard the increase of endowment and the development of the physical plant.

In scope, the provincial universities are, even more than the best of the American universities, undergraduate affairs. The undergraduate is undeniably more mature, better trained, more highly selected, and even so a year younger than his American counterpart. But between the secondary school and a genuine university there remains a gap which for the time being the universities must bridge. "The foundations of knowledge and training," writes one who has long been in close touch with the educational situation, " are not firm enough and not broad enough to sustain the attempt at original or exploratory work at the university without a further period of instruction and training." Most of the undergraduates, having attained a bachelor's degree, thereupon leave the university. I say that the bachelor's degree is more significant than the usual bachelor's degree in the United States, partly because it is based on sounder subjects and on more difficult examinations, and partly because external examiners participate in the degree examinations, as happens systematically nowhere in America except at Swarthmore College. Honour students carry three subjects for three or four years — a far more concentrated course of study than is pursued by the American undergraduate. The bachelor's degree therefore signifies greater depth and further progress; but the universities, free though they are from the absurdities so common in America, do, nevertheless, as a caustic English critic once remarked to me, " have goods in the show window somewhat in excess of what is to be found on the shelves."

While the provincial universities are therefore primarily engaged in teaching undergraduates, advanced work nevertheless goes on. The undergraduate honours work undoubtedly covers the first year — perhaps more — of the American graduate school. At Manchester, distinguished schools of mediaeval history, of philosophy and physics have been developed. Professor

Bragg has, at his disposal, a dozen research rooms in physics. On the scientific side, the Committee on Industrial and Scientific Research now dispenses grants amounting to £31,000, largely devoted to the maintenance of advanced workers in the universities, provincial and other. The English are, however, curiously averse to recognition of graduate students as a group. They are excessively conscientious teachers: " It is our first business to teach," one hears again and again. They labour under the conviction that, having passed with honours, the student thenceforth needs only occasional contact with the professor. This is undoubtedly better for him than the American procedure which so frequently keeps him in leading strings in the graduate school, just as he was kept in the college. But it loses sight, I think, of the unique value of the seminar, in which students are brought into contact with one another, as well as with the professor; the clash of student minds with one another and with their teachers, which should take place in a graduate school, is in England almost an accident. I am, I hope, not likely to be accused of being too fond of organization. In America, it has played havoc. Yet it has its place. Something akin to the German seminar is needed in order that the ablest, best-trained, and most mature workers may be kept in contact with one another and with their leaders. No English universities, least of all London and the provincial universities, have developed to the point of fully realizing this important truth. Take Manchester, once more, as an example. Between 1882 and 1928, it conferred 2,932 B.A. degrees, 1,019 M.A.'s, 3,543 B.Sc. degrees, 1,227 M.Sc. degrees, 143 D.Sc.'s, and 74 Ph.D.'s. These figures are significant, not because the number of advanced degrees is small, but because the disproportion shows that the teaching staff is too largely engaged in instruction. Of these students, an excessive proportion become teachers. To be sure, teachers need to be educated. But a point is soon reached, where a university is saturated with prospective teachers; beyond that point, leisure and inclination for research suffer, and the university tends to deteriorate into a teacher-training establishment, though, of course, the right man will win through.

The provincial universities sprang from the soil; they obtain part of their support by heeding local needs. Thus technological activities, varying with the locality, are highly, in places, too highly developed, and, for a university, too highly specialized. Here and there they have the *ad hoc* character which is wholly indefensible. Degrees are fairly well protected, but diplomas and certificates can be obtained for work that is largely technical in character. Thus Manchester gives certificates (not degrees) in Higher Commercial Studies (two years), in Photographic Technology (two years), in Industrial Administration (one year); Birmingham grants certificates or diplomas in Brewing (two or three years), in Social Study (two years); Bristol a degree (B.Sc. in Domestic Science) (four years) and a testamur in Education or Biology (one year); Leeds, diplomas in Dyeing, Gas Engineering, Colour Chemistry; Sheffield, a diploma in Glass Technology (two to three years). Equally short-sighted and absurd are such excrescences as the School of Librarianship and course in Journalism at University College, London (for which the University grants diplomas, not degrees), the Department of Civic Design at Liverpool, and the work in Automobile Engineering at Bristol. This technical development is slight, as compared with that in America, but is none the less deplorable and, we may hope, the defect of youth, for it is of neither liberal nor university quality.

Local factors have, however, been balanced against other factors. Though created by local sentiment, the provincial universities were, as I have already stated, originally staffed and to a very large extent are still staffed by Oxford and Cambridge men; their governing bodies contain, as I have pointed out, scholars as well as laymen. The older and more solid disciplines are therefore represented not only in the curriculum, but in the management. The universities have therefore not run wild, as have our American institutions. No university head that I met fears that English universities will indulge in the capers that are making American universities ridiculous; they have too much sense and too little money! A legitimate response to environment is exemplified by the Mining Research Laboratory, conducted by Professor John S. Haldane, at the University of Birmingham. In the early days, it was supposed by some persons that the Institute would do the chores of industry — make analyses, etc. Professor Haldane " put his foot down on all that." In the spirit of Pasteur, Professor Haldane has worked fundamentally on the problem of heat and respiration. " The practical things are brim full of scientific interest and stimulus, if one only studies them properly," Professor Haldane once wrote me. These " practical things " correspond to the patients in the medical clinics of a university. So much from the standpoint of research. From the standpoint of training, the sound theory is equally clear. A university abdicates its function if it undertakes a course in the salesmanship of coal; it is within its sphere in dealing with the sciences involved in mining — physics, chemistry, and metallurgy. So brewing should, from the university point of view, be a department of bio-chemistry and bacteriology. The undergraduate degree is simply a degree in the bio-chemistry of fermentation. The honours degree, with a diploma in malting and brewing, connotes in addition two years of " interneship " in a brewery, a dubious device. This is not a university or post-graduate degree in the sense in which I have employed those terms. And a similar statement may be made as respects teaching and research in a few other industries at other institutions.

As respects commerce: when the University of Birmingham was founded, Mr. Joseph Chamberlain secured local interest by offering a School of Commerce without a clear idea as to what it was to be. The Birmingham School undertakes little or nothing that could not without propriety be done in the same fashion by the faculty of arts; perhaps it gains something in intensity, just as it loses something in cultural outlook by integration. Some research in the economic history of the area is carried out; for the rest, the work falls into economics, economic history, transportation, and modern languages, and would in America lead to an ordinary degree. Practical courses in salesmanship and advertising are conspicuous by their absence. The teaching staff are not unfamiliar with American developments, but they are out of sympathy with them. They do not pretend to be practical men capable of advising business concerns; no member of the business or commerce faculty at Manchester has any remunerative connection with industry; advice is sought, but fees are not accepted by the professors. They have also found that successful business men have nothing to tell their students. The Schools are essentially advanced undergraduate schools of economics, modern languages, etc., with a more definite outlook on the local situation than an ordinary academic department would possess. On the whole, then, the provincial universities represent a conservative deviation from the policy of the ancient universities in respect to industry, mainly keeping, however, on the undergraduate plane.

A word, at this point, as to education. The provincial universities have schools or departments of education; Oxford and Cambridge have readers in education. But the subject is nowhere seriously taken — perhaps not seriously enough. The provincial course is for three years identical with the ordinary academic course; the fourth year is spent on the " principles," " methods," " psychology," and " history " of education — " potted " stuff, as I was told in one university. It is deficient on the practical side; but leaving, as it does, something to intelligence and insisting on knowledge of subject-matter, it is, in so far, preferable to American absurdities. Cambridge and the provincial universities grant degrees — but clearly, the basis is mainly academic performance; Oxford grants only a diploma.

The extension, extra-mural, and tutorial courses, offered by the provincial as well as the ancient universities, similarly avoid the narrow, practical, *ad hoc* character of much of this work in America. The courses are educational; they deal with subjects of intellectual and cultural importance — economics, mediaeval and modern history, political science, literature, industrial history, and sociology, like the external side of the University of London. The students do not appeal to the universities for help in their trades or vocations; nor do the English universities traffic in the trivial. The English worker wants to use his leisure to get away from the limitations of his daily grind. Of profound significance is the program of Coleg Harlech, a small and independent Welsh institution, whose students have been shop-assistants, miners, steel-workers, quarrymen, lodging-housekeepers, weavers, and clerks. What did they study in 1928–29? History, philosophy, psychology, economics, political science, Welsh and English literature. This is, as I have urged, likely to be secondary school work; but it is reputable and in subjects like ethics and economics, in which experience counts, may well go deep and add much to the academic view.

As the universities under discussion develop on the university side, these service activities will perhaps be otherwise cared for; they will obtain their own congenial type of organization and administration; but for the time being they do not lower the dignity or pervert the object of the institution. University extension tutorial classes are in a sense temporary devices; they cannot permanently take the place of a sound national educational system. Neither England nor America possesses such a system; the English universities, unlike the American universities, have tried to bridge the gap honestly, soundly, and without regard to pecuniary profit. A keen and trenchant foreign critic writes: "There is hardly a town where it (university extension, etc.) has not played its part in educational development. In many the movement has grown into a college (Nottingham, Exeter), in others (Sheffield, Reading) it has developed into a university. Everywhere university extension has become a powerful antidote against that dreary matter-of-factness and bleak materialism which crop up in English life, not least among English workers." [15]

[15] Wilhelm Dibelius, *England* (translated by Mary Agnes Hamilton, London and New York, 1930), p. 426.

Of the several professional faculties, I shall limit myself to medicine. The provincial medical faculties differ from the London schools in respect to the situation of the laboratory sciences. In London, they are, as I have pointed out — except at University and King's Colleges — developed under heavy handicaps in the several hospital schools. In the provincial schools the professors of anatomy, physiology, and pathology have the status and facilities of the rest of the scientific faculty — the professor of chemistry or physics, for example. Their budgets are modest; their facilities usually cramped; their libraries are limited; their teaching routine is far from light; none the less they are professors, freely chosen by the university and with a future before them. The conditions as respects research are therefore as favourable as in other fields. Sherrington, A. V. Hill, and Dean — now occupying three of the most attractive chairs in England in their respective subjects — at Oxford, University College (London), and Cambridge — were formerly professors at Liverpool and Manchester, where they had distinguished themselves as medical scientists.

The clinical side is in the provincial universities quite unorganized and undeveloped, lacking even the few full-time clinical units that relieve the London situation. The hospitals are philanthropic institutions, not clinics: their staff is the local profession, as a rule not sympathetic with or active in strictly scientific re-

---

Very enlightening also is a small pamphlet issued by H. M. Stationery Office, 1929, entitled *Adult Education in Lancashire and Cheshire*. The subjects are large and solid (p. 6), the students are workers (p. 23), and the following comment involves a stinging criticism of the attitude of American university home study and extension courses: " The academic point of view is more readily grasped and there is less difference in outlook between extra-mural and intra-mural classes than there was in the earlier days." (p. 18.)

The same is true of the extra-mural courses of Oxford and Cambridge.

search; laboratory facilities for research are insufficient; the wards are fortunately open to students who come close to the patient, but further modernization has not yet taken place. The university is powerless to procure more effective internal organization or to open a career in clinical teaching and research by calling promising young men from elsewhere to fill vacancies on the staff. The rule of seniority generally prevails; radical steps have not been taken as in America to reorganize existing hospitals or to create new university hospitals in which the university may have a free hand. An opportunity presents itself in Birmingham, where the two existing hospitals have a site on the University grounds for the construction of a new and ample hospital. If now the present organization could be discarded, the clinical material properly redistributed, laboratories provided, and a staff equipped to teach and investigate assembled, utilizing the local profession as far as may be sound, England would possess a modern medical faculty; but the opportunity will, I fear, be allowed to pass. The one mitigating factor of importance is the Medical Research Council, which maintains the National Institute for Medical Research at Hampstead and also makes grants to individuals or to groups for the prosecution of their individual work. It has mobilized those interested in scientific medicine; it has provided the salaries, maintenance, and equipment required for particular investigations throughout the field of medical science. Unfortunately, however, the young men thus trained still have no exit. This or that task may get itself done; this or that person may thus be trained; but on the clinical side there is still lacking the assurance of continuous opportunity or support. What England needs is a modern medical school — one at first, others in course of time. The universities with the coöperation of the Medical Research Council are engaged in training the men; but the Council, being a governmental organization, cannot concentrate its funds so as to establish somewhere a university faculty of medicine. At Oxford, at Cambridge, at Manchester or Birmingham, the thing could be done; and it would probably in time affect the general situation as the Johns Hopkins Medical School affected medical education in the United States. The need is not unappreciated; but thus far the funds and the opportunity have not been forthcoming.

VII

The development of the provincial universities may be said in a general way to resemble the American development. They incline towards science and are by no means free from the danger of becoming too amenable to local and practical considerations. But, for reasons already emphasized, the danger is far less serious than in America. On the other hand, at the moment, in the English provinces as in the United States, humanism cannot be said to get its due. Whether, for many years to come, sufficient funds to support an adequate university development will be obtained is a serious question: that depends on national prosperity and a redirection of national expenditure. In any case it will be years before the English secondary schools grow into institutions as solid and extensive as the continental *lycée* or *Gymnasium*. Nor is the separate creation of the advanced secondary school, known in America as a college, apt to take place. The English university will therefore, like the American university, long discharge secondary as well as service functions. Meanwhile, under the stimulus of research boards, research ideals, practical needs, and other influences, there will be a marked and better organized provision for higher training and research. The splendid English amateur has had his day in industry and in politics; graduate schools must convert him into a professional. In the British Commonwealth of Nations, more than in any of the more compact states, trained men are needed — not merely subordinates, but men of wide, disinterested cultural and scientific training who can conduct organized attacks upon the problems, practical and philosophic, of modern life. I see no reason to fear that the best qualities of the English amateur will be sacrificed or impaired; they are indeed as striking in the savants of Oxford and Cambridge as in the master of a public school or the governor general of a dominion. There is no sounder or saner type than this unique combination of scholar, scientist, and man of the world that England produces, without possessing the organization needed to produce the type in large numbers. Need the development which I have called organization impair the type? Only if it carries with it the machinery that has been set up in America. But this machinery is unnecessary in America and would revolt England. Perhaps a radical reform in America would be hastened, if the English universities showed that a graduate school, the heart of the university, can be created on the basis of freedom in an atmosphere favourable to the development of ideas.

VIII

In the field of higher education, the ancient universities dominate and, as far as one can guess will

long, perhaps permanently, continue to dominate.
Their peculiar situation carries with it enormous responsibilities — not, in my opinion, and for reasons
that I shall disclose, just now fully discharged. As
compared with the provincial universities, they are
national in scope; and prestige and resources enable
them to bring together in democratic fashion a student
body that, on the whole, represents those who have
inherited wealth and opportunity as well as those who
have inherited only brains. Whatever their defects —
and they are neither few nor slight — the concentration at these two seats of learning of able students,
accomplished scholars, and brilliant scientists furnishes England, and indeed the Empire, with that
from the lack of which America chiefly suffers — two
real centres, sufficiently large, varied, strong, and independent to set up and to maintain intellectual standards. I have shown how Harvard, Columbia, and Johns
Hopkins have been carried into the vortex and thereby
lost the authority which, in a cultured nation, must
be lodged somewhere; in England, this authority is
lodged in the ancient universities; [16] and for this reason among others, England, however democratic it
becomes, will be spared the academic orgy in which at
this moment for the lack of a few steadying influences
the American university and American life flounder.
There is, to be sure, something on the other side:
" authority " is apt to be conservative; Oxford has
been and is so, more so than Cambridge. But one does
not cure the defects of " authority " by throwing distinctions to the wind. Some other and better way must,
and I think can, be found.

[16] Were I writing of Scotland, I should undoubtedly include in this
statement the Scottish universities which have also upheld high ideals of
genuine scholarship.

How do Oxford and Cambridge happen to be great institutions of learning? The question is not easy to answer. They are, as we shall see, largely advanced secondary schools; they still abound in prejudices and customs apparently calculated to interfere with their being institutions of learning; Oxford was up to recent times dominated by Anglicanism and still cherishes Anglican forms; progressive efforts are likely to encounter an impalpable, resistant tradition as difficult to penetrate as a London fog; both universities, while freely open to poor students, who have won scholarships, and to the middle class, are frequented by the scions of wealth and aristocracy, expecting to enter a profession or public life [17] — strange material, one might suppose, from which to recruit disinterested scholars and scientists in numbers sufficient to create and maintain an ideal; Oxford's greatest leaders in recent times, men of the Jowett type, scholars themselves, have been less concerned with the training of philosophers and scholars and scientists than of men who are primarily interested in Parliament, the Civil Service, or the Dominions. At Cambridge, during approximately the same period, a differently minded group, Whewell, Henry Sidgwick, Alfred Marshall, the late Master of Caius (Sir Hugh Anderson) and the great group of scientists connected with Trinity College over a period of years stood out prominently. The Universities have had a strange and chequered history, the recital of which would naturally create grave apprehension; off and on, for centuries, they were partisans of this cause or that, or all but went

[17] "We viewed Oxford as sharing with Cambridge the special function of completing the education of young men, coming from cultivated homes, trained for the most part in our Public Schools, and destined for political life or the learned professions." H. A. L. Fisher, *The Place of the University in National Life* (Oxford University Press, 1919), p. 4.

to sleep; small rebellious groups still chafe at their inertia; yet there they are — institutions of learning, nevertheless, in the finest and highest sense of the term, national bulwarks against all that is frothy, shoddy, and paltry in academic life. I have not penetrated their secret; but I shall endeavour to reach as nearly as I can the heart of the mystery.

Cambridge and Oxford are different, different in their main and characteristic cultural interests, and different, too, in subtle ways that no foreigner is likely to appreciate at their full value. A brilliant Cambridge man to whom I put the question wrestled with the problem as he rode homewards on the bus: "There are, perhaps" — he wrote me before breakfast next morning — "two kinds of knowledge — exact knowledge and the knowledge of values. Cambridge stands mainly for the former, Oxford mainly for the latter — though of course you may sometimes find real values in a laboratory, but that is only after a bout, if it is nothing more material than a debate on dogma." But as science and the scientific cast of thought develop at Oxford, the two institutions will be less and less unlike in this respect. Again, within each of the universities, the colleges have their idiosyncrasies, very real, but almost lost upon the outsider. Nevertheless, even the outsider is aware of a real distinction between Balliol and Magdalen at Oxford, between Trinity or Caius and Corpus at Cambridge. Varying, competing, and stimulating centres, now of one subject, now of another, are thus maintained. Perhaps, it is precisely the quiet competition of subtly different entities beneath the surface that has provoked the higher intellectual activity which has created an institution of learning out of aggregations of colleges so largely concerned with training young men. "I spent my life at Cambridge paid to do one thing and doing another " — it is that " other " that goes so far to make the university. Quite clearly — and I have noted this point before — the same conditions that permit idleness, neglect, or perfunctory performance of duty are necessary to the highest exertions of human intelligence. Oxford and Cambridge are fortunate enough to supply all sorts of conditions — conditions that permit the idle to be idle, or nearly so, the conscientious to be conscientious, the creative to be creative; and to the idlers a certain value is attached on the basis of the possibility of their subsequent service to the Empire, though opinions vary greatly on this point. Anyway, the English colleges do not try to force all into one Procrustean bed; they do not try to do every sort of thing. We try this in America; we fail, and the best suffer; Germany in its universities is, as we shall see, wiser; so, for all their regulations and formalities and conventions, are Oxford and Cambridge.

IX

Historically, the universities preceded the colleges: they were places to which poor scholars resorted for teaching and study. The colleges were dormitories; the fellowships were " research," not teaching posts. As the colleges became teaching centres, the university shrank in importance; it came to be in course of time hardly more than a name for an aggregation of colleges. Even university professors and lecturers became simply a convenient way of instructing in this or that subject undergraduates from the different colleges, as is still very largely the case. To get into the university a student must enter a college; and the colleges wish mainly undergraduates. Graduates from overseas are usually advised to take the Oxford B.A. degree — for most of them doubtless an advisable step, but a policy not conducive to the upbuilding of graduate work. Graduate instruction carried on by men who are mainly college tutors becomes thus the secondary interest of a first-rate instructor: his distinction depends on the training of " firsts," not on productive scholarship. The main preoccupation of Oxford and Cambridge has therefore for centuries been undergraduate and still is, if numbers mean anything; though I surely am not disposed to overemphasize their importance, this is the story they tell. According to the report of the University Grants Committee, there were in 1928–29, 8,900 full-time men students and 1,312 full-time women students at the two universities — a total of 10,212; 482 men and 81 women, a total of 563 were doing advanced work. Cambridge with approximately 5,000 students registered at the close of the Easter term 1929, 308 advanced students; during the year 1928–29, 58 higher degrees were awarded (49 Ph.D., 7 M.Sc., 2 M. Litt.). At Oxford, on the first day of Trinity Term 1930, there were registered with the Committee for Advanced Studies 79 candidates for the degree of Bachelor of Letters, 49 for the Bachelor of Science, 84 for the Doctor of Philosophy — 212 in all — surely a disproportionately small number, scattered through all the faculties, as they are.

The government and organization of the Oxford and Cambridge Colleges and of the University are extremely complex; nor would much be gained were it possible to describe them, for the way in which statutes and regulations actually function cannot be inferred from the language in which they are couched. In order to describe the organization as clearly as I can hope to do, I shall for the moment consider Oxford alone, and I shall artificially separate the inseparable. Thus viewed, the University of Oxford can be broken up into three parts, none of which really is by itself an entity: (1) it is a collection of about thirty colleges [18] that happen to be located in the same small city; the Colleges are, as I have said, autonomous and self-governing; as far as feasible the fellows of the College, who are sometimes, as at All Souls, advanced workers and sometimes are, or would elsewhere be, professors, do the College teaching; but as the Colleges cannot each have fellows enough to teach every subject, the Colleges coöperate in certain subjects; and largely in modern languages and science they leave teaching and research to the University or University institutes, the demonstrators in which may or may not have been appointed to College fellowships. Thus separate and autonomous and independent institutions are curiously intertwined with one another and with the University which they constitute and which is also something more than the Colleges form, when they thus come together.

(2) The University is in the next place an agency for supplementing the Colleges by maintaining professors, institutes, and institutions utilized by the Colleges and by persons without College connections. At Oxford, for example, the Bodleian Library, the Examination Schools, the Institutes of Agriculture and Forestry, the Taylor Institution for Modern Languages, the Scientific Laboratories, the Museum, and the Ashmolean are University Institutes which furnish the Colleges with facilities; at Cambridge, the University Library, the Fitzwilliam Museum, the Mu-

[18] This figure includes 21 colleges and 9 additional institutions (women's colleges, etc.).

seum of Classical Archaeology, the Cavendish Laboratory, the Molteno Institute for Research in Parasitology, and the laboratories for other sciences pure and applied belong to the University. There are ten University faculties, made up of professors, readers, and lecturers, nearly all associated by courtesy or right with the Colleges, paid either by the University itself or by a College or by the University assisted by College subvention and offering lectures and courses to which College students have access at their pleasure; there is also a general Board of the Faculties and a Committee for Advanced Studies of which more, hereafter.

(3) Finally, the University is in itself an autonomous, self-governing entity that confers all degrees and decides matters of general policy, such as matriculation requirements, the status of women, etc. And yet, here again, it is intertwined with the Colleges: for in all its activities the University is governed by a body that is mostly Collegiate. At Oxford, the Hebdomadal Council, elected by Congregation, happens at present to consist of the Chancellor, practically an honorary official, the Vice-Chancellor, who is head of a College, serving for three years as head of the University, two fellows who are annually chosen as proctors, seven College heads, and eleven fellows (or students), of whom several are either University lecturers or University professors, some of whom may be College-minded rather than University-minded. In addition, almost innumerable committees are to be found in all English as also in American and German universities. Thus from the standpoint of government, the University is really the creature of the Colleges — a point of extreme importance when innovations or expenditures come into question. For the Colleges, though

varying in financial strength, are on the whole well-to-do and in any case manage their own funds; the University has little; it obtains funds from the Colleges and latterly from the national exchequer, without which the remuneration paid by the University to its professors would often be but nominal. This is from the standpoint of a post-graduate development a serious matter: the Colleges are mainly undergraduate; a graduate development would be a University matter; but the University lacks the requisite funds and a governing body interested in graduate work and capable of inaugurating and pursuing a far-sighted and continuous policy.

At the risk of repetition, let me review and try to bring together the three aspects which I have described more or less separately: the thirty self-governing Colleges are governed by their teaching corps, *i.e.*, the fellows, who fill vacancies in their own ranks as they occur. The administrative head, variously called warden, master, principal, or president, has more or less influence according to his natural ability and eminence: the fellows are in theory and fact the governing body. The Colleges are relatively autonomous — hold endowments, make rules, elect officers, admit undergraduates, etc., precisely as if there were no University at all, though one can enter a College only by meeting the matriculation requirements set by the University. On the other hand, the Colleges, voluntarily or in consequence of legislative enactment, yield some authority and power to the University which is a corporation including the personnel of the Colleges as such and the College students. The Colleges appoint their own tutors; but the University appoints professors, demonstrators, and readers, whose lectures are freely open. As long as the body of instruction was mainly confined to language, history, and philosophy, a College could be fairly sufficient unto itself. But with the progress of knowledge in general and the development of science in particular, the several Colleges became increasingly uneven and inadequate. Inter-Collegiate teaching grew up; in certain fields, notably science and medicine, University institutes for the teaching of students of all Colleges were created. But apart from certain endowed University posts, the University lacked funds with which to finance this development; they have been obtained partly by taxing the Colleges and partly, as need became very acute, from the national exchequer. No one has planned a University development, towards which College appropriations might be applied; unless the English people contract the habit of giving unrestrictedly and more freely to institutions of learning, the contribution, and ultimately the influence, of the central government will have to grow.

The government of the University of Oxford is lodged in a hierarchy — Convocation, consisting of all University masters and doctors, resident and non-resident and now numbering almost 10,000; Congregation, consisting of resident masters and doctors chiefly concerned with teaching or administration; and the Hebdomadal Council, the composition of which I have already described. Convocation has become a shadowy body; legislation originates with the Hebdomadal Council and is subject to ratification by Congregation.[19] From the standpoint of university de-

[19] At Cambridge, the corresponding bodies are called The Senate (consisting of all Masters, Doctors, and Bachelors of Divinity), the Council of the Senate, chosen by the resident members of the Senate, and the Vice-Chancellor, holding office usually for two years. The two Universities are not well informed about each other; at times one has in the several Colleges a strange feeling of their unawareness of one another.

velopment, the government is weak. A College has a permanent head, whose hands are full; the University has a changing head, who is simultaneously a College head; his College and the Colleges generally almost inevitably come first with him. Finally, on the Hebdomadal Council, University professors are pitted against persons whose natural interests are, as a rule, Collegiate, and against Congregation, which is overwhelmingly Collegiate in composition and attitude. Moreover, inbreeding has gone on for years. Fellows fill vacancies in their own ranks by election; the Oxford Colleges elect freely men from other Oxford Colleges but rarely Cambridge men, hardly ever, if at all, provincials. The Colleges are so numerous and different as to escape stagnation; but they know far too little of the rest of the educational world. Under such conditions that general and higher interest which I call the "University" does not get adequate representation, efficient government, or continuous policy. Three successive Royal Commissions have during the last seventy-five years wrestled with Oxford and Cambridge problems; they have accomplished much in bringing the Universities into the main stream of modern life; but they have in my opinion hardly touched the fundamental problems of University activity and organization — largely because, being composed mainly of Oxford and Cambridge men, their natural loyalties have interfered with incisive and objective analysis; with the best intentions, they tend to become representatives of their respective Universities as they are representatives of their respective Colleges.

On paper, policy appears to be determined by the University through faculties, each of which acts through a Board, every advanced student being assigned to a supervisor. But the Boards of Studies are heavily loaded in favour of the Colleges as against the University. Thus, though apparently, successive enactments have nominally increased the power of the University, the actual gain in the strength of the central government has been considerably less than appears. The Colleges, concerned [20] with the teaching of young men and women, are still dominant. There are, in the proper sense of the word, no faculties; for a faculty would, under existing conditions, be likely to be disturbed by Collegiate considerations and would have to run the gauntlet of Council and Congregation, the latter too largely controlled by the older subjects. Moreover, the choice of professors by specially constituted electoral boards increases the difficulty of enforcing a single point of view — that, for example, of a University bent upon increasing opportunities and organization adapted to post-graduate study.

In so far as undergraduate teaching is concerned, I have been searching for a term that will describe what the ancient universities accomplish. I have not found the word in English. I wonder, however, whether the German word, *Bildung,* does not roughly answer my purpose. What is *Bildung?* Knowledge, culture, the power of expression, character, manners, a rare balancing and maturing of qualities calculated to equip men to meet with dignity and competency the responsibilities of life. The Oxford Colleges as individual institutions are — as the large number of honours students indicates — interested in ability. Yet the life of the College is so organized that brain power cannot be said to be its besetting passion. It makes far more of examinations than is wholesome, of examinations as testing knowledge and the ability to

[20] Excepting All Souls, where there are no undergraduates.

handle it, rather than examinations as a means of discovering unusual talent. Its pride is in able gentlemen rather than in original men and women; the selection of students is often prompted by suggestions emanating from secondary teachers, Oxford or Cambridge men themselves, who are on the lookout for the peculiar abilities that the Universities esteem. Manners are the product of the public schools, of the country houses, of the communal life of the Colleges themselves, of the clubs that periodically form and disappear. The ultimate product is admirable — cultivated gentlemen, who can think and write and act, and who have thus far been singularly adequate to the practical situations in which the Englishman with his far-flung interests sooner or later finds himself. Thus they have made the men who have created the provincial universities, who have governed England and the Dominions honestly, efficiently, and like gentlemen. And these men are distinguished by the possession of a certain sanity, which, to be sure, may in part be the product of social and political experience, but is assuredly in part due to the type of education that the English receive in school and college. We talk in America endlessly of educational technique; there is, I grant, something in it. But Oxford and Cambridge establish a personal relationship between the undergraduate and his tutor, that is, despite possible personal limitations, the most effective pedagogical relationship in the world. The absence of class instruction, the weekly meeting of tutor and pupil, the informal relationships, that sometimes extend into the long vacations, throw the student on his own and expose him directly to the influence of his teacher. Unquestionably, the simplicity of the arrangement involves dangers for both students and tutors. A student may get a poor tutor. If so, the University lectures may help him out or the man may himself object. The tutor lacking the stimulation of a class may fall into a rut: now and then a promising man has, as I have said, fled the University for no other reason.

Thus strangely are the defects and the virtues of the ancient colleges involved with one another. As separate bodies they lead their own social, intellectual, and educational lives, not entirely detached from, and yet by no means merged with the life of the others. The undergraduate usually comes from a public school where he has been taught by Oxford and Cambridge men; he enters an Oxford College; he is mainly influenced by his tutor, an Oxford or Cambridge man, to whom he submits a weekly essay, which is more or less severely criticized. Nobody knows whether tutors pursue the same or different methods or use the same or other standards. There is no way of comparing or transferring or pooling teaching experience. If a tutor is good, he is good, and if he is poor, he is poor, and only the examinations at the end tell the tale. These test mainly a student's acquisition of knowledge just as a trial in court tests a barrister's cleverness. No one would say that a barrister's mastery of the facts of the case or his skill in cross examination or argument or presentation to the jury is in the proper sense a creative intellectual performance. The best proof that it isn't is the small contribution successful lawyers make to the world's thought. Undoubtedly, many tutors do inspire their students; but if they do, there is no organized way of giving other tutors the benefit of their experience. Tutorial instruction may, as I have stated, be supplemented by attendance on University lectures, though students are not usually lecture addicts.[21] They

[21] President Gilman (writing, it is true, twenty-five years ago) quotes

are sent to lectures likely to help in the examinations, for rank in the examinations is exaggerated in importance, not only at the University, but through life: it is never forgotten. Do these conditions perhaps combine to produce rather too conventional a type to deal in the broadest fashion not with the world which is passing away but with that which is obviously being born?

At any rate, so much for the undergraduate who spends three or four years at Oxford or Cambridge and passes on, a charming and intelligent young person, but essentially an amateur, into parliament, the civil service, business, or a profession. Thus far, Oxford and Cambridge have just passed the fringe of the modern university, as I have conceived it. But they *have* passed it. The Cambridge or Oxford undergraduate working for honours is undoubtedly doing some work that in America would belong to the graduate school, and in Germany to the university. Indeed, the type of instruction employed, the extent to which the honours student is thrown upon his own resources, his close relation to a superior mind, the avoidance of the spoon-feeding so prevalent in America — this type of instruction has, I say, much more in common with genuine university spirit than much of the work of the American graduate school. And the honours schools easily dominate, for at present there are at Oxford a small number of pass men and women, as against several thousand reading for honours, though some of the latter might better be reading for a pass degree. It is, in any event, no exaggeration to say that a fair

Professor Freeman as follows: " It is all so disappointing and disheartening; I have tried every kind of lecture I can think of and put my best strength into all, but nobody comes! " *The Launching of a University* (New York, 1906), p. 84.

share of undergraduate Oxford would, in America and Germany, be found in a graduate classification.

Let us pass now to tutors who stay behind, the University professors, and the advanced students; how favourable is the University to them?

In reference to the tutor: it is precisely at the moment when the selected student becomes a college tutor that one's most serious misgivings arise. The recent undergraduate becomes, I say, a tutor. He is, if unmarried, at once financially and socially at ease. He is a member of the most charming society in the world, the peer of his elders. He has space, quiet, isolation, good food and drink, and long vacations. In America, we would say that he has " arrived." He may, of course, work on. Equipped with the capacity and desire, assuredly he will and does, especially if a professorship here or elsewhere is his goal. But he is under no great competitive pressure to do so. He is already " hallmarked " as a " first-class " or " senior wrangler." It is almost assumed that he will continue to be what he was when he won his fellowship — a dangerous assumption. Most men need incentive continuously; is stimulating incentive inherent in the organization that I have described? Indeed, is not the reverse likely to happen? For the tutorial fellow takes on a heavy teaching burden which he usually carries most conscientiously — carries, as a tutor remarked, till he is " used up." He has, therefore, won his great social and material reward at the very outset; he is heavily burdened with routine at the same moment. I am, of course, not speaking of individuals, but of tendencies and conditions. Do these conditions make for university ideals?

There are other drawbacks from the university point of view. The heavy teaching burden would seem likely to keep the tutor in a critical attitude towards under-graduates rather than in a competitive attitude to-wards scholars and scientists at large. He looks down rather than up. If he marries, his opportunities for creative work are again limited; yet "the fellowship system originated in a desire to promote study and not to promote teaching." [22] Unless he becomes a pro-fessor, he finds that he began with the maximum of opportunity and remuneration. If there are children to be educated, more routine is involved; for income can usually be increased only by taking on additional burdens — writing, examining, etc., though there are roundabout ways, especially in the wealthier colleges, of helping men out, and a simple, unexacting, and democratic way of living that is infinitely valuable. One wonders, however, whether somehow the thing is not upside down. Hardship is wholesome for young men; it stiffens their backbone, makes them achieve. Oxford and Cambridge remove hardship, just when it might be intellectually stimulating. But hardship at forty or fifty is depressing. That would seem to be the period at which it is most likely to be encountered by the Oxford or Cambridge tutor.

As distinguished from the College tutors, of whom I have been speaking, the two Universities possess, as I have said, professors, readers, lecturers, and ad-vanced students. The University routine is light. The professor gives thirty-six lectures a year; what else he does is his own affair. For the benefit of tutors who also hold University appointments, the College bur-dens are lightened, though the combined burden may even then be a heavy one. The difficulty of piecemeal reform is clear from the fate of certain of the recom-

[22] *Endowment of Research, loc. cit.,* p. 51.

mendations of the recent Royal Commission. In order to promote a University development, lectureships were set up; but instead of filling them with research workers, the Universities bestowed them upon tutors who had merited promotion, even if not precisely the kind of opportunity that the lectureships were designed to create. At Cambridge the new lectureships were largely given to the old lecturers as compensation for loss of fees. The Commission's scheme cannot therefore be regarded as a success. Professors, sometimes readers, are called from all parts of the Empire; sometimes from outside the Empire. The University as such has grown and is steadily growing both independently and at the expense of the Colleges; the library facilities are, in many subjects, excellent. Laboratories have greatly improved in recent years. In some branches — physics, bio-chemistry, physiology, and pathology, for example — they are excellent, genuine university institutes in the continental sense. They are effectually protected against unfit students, because the student is individually scrutinized before he is admitted to the privileges of advanced work. This appears admirable as far as it goes, but as one surveys the world's and England's needs, one asks, " Is it adequate? " One would not wish to lessen the opportunities in classics, palaeography, philosophy; one would rather wish to extend them to fields not yet covered. But emphasis is not well distributed; the social sciences and perhaps modern languages do not command the facilities which they require. For economists and political scientists there is no adequate outlet.

As to the advanced student: I have already pointed to the English notion that, having achieved a degree with honours, the advanced student can be safely left more or less to his own devices; I have suggested, too, the inadequacy of this conception. On the other hand, "spoon-feeding" and "over-organization" would be worse. To be sure, there is a central Board, which passes on topics of study which it is proposed to undertake with a view to a higher degree; but this is hardly the organization needed to bring about the steady forward pressure and the intimate internal association that the complexities of modern knowledge, in the humanities as in the sciences, require. If, as I believe, a post-graduate development is England's most urgent educational need, then somehow graduate faculties devoted to advanced teaching and research must be organized. For the moment, the Colleges need not be considered; the superstructure, now irregular, accidental, incidental, requires to be built out and built up. The memoir of Vinogradoff by the present Warden of New College shows that and how the thing can be done — shows also how immensely more fruitful it will make the scholarship that Oxford now contains — not to mention the science and scholarship that must in time be added:

" Less accordant with Oxford tradition was the institution of a seminar: but Vinogradoff made his seminar thoroughly successful, a feat of some difficulty in a University in which success in very difficult examinations of a general character carries with it far more prestige than the patient work of the discovering specialist. No Professor of Law in Oxford, possibly no Professor of History, set so many young men and young women on fruitful lines of historical inquiry. His method, his thoroughness, his grasp of law and history, his rare combination of a gift for minutiae with a wide knowledge of comparative law and history made him a very impressive teacher for the elect. If he could be encouraging, he could also be severe. When a somewhat casual member of his seminar wrote to him for a testimonial, he thundered out at the next meeting of the class: ' I will give you nothing, nothing, nothing!' As he did not spare himself so he expected a like effort from his pupils.

[281]

'The Seminar,' writes Miss Levett, 'was a somewhat strenuous discipline.' 'The young men in Oxford do not love the higher education,' he would say in moments of disappointment. Yet he had always a small keen band of students prepared to follow his lead through Celtic manorial custom, or the Year Book manuscripts, or the Salic Law, or the economic statistics of Domesday Book. Some of them had learnt from his friend Charles Bémont in Paris the meaning of the 'higher education' in Vinogradoff's sense, and many welcomed the extension of the Seminar method to Oxford. Among the Rhodes Scholars he found congenial additions to his little band. More than one came from the remoter regions of Cambridge and London.

He cared nothing for preliminary ignorance, if only the student had some fixity of purpose, some capacity for work. Pretentious work was the only thing on which he was severe. He could hand back a paper with the curt comment, 'This is all to do again,' but it was never the beginner or the diffident who was thus treated. He had a not altogether unjust contempt for certain types of reviewing in this country. After a particularly inept attempt of a reviewer to deal facetiously with a piece of serious scholarship, he remarked, 'You will think me very rude, but I call it an example of the stupidity which you *cultivate* in England.' Inadequate published work provoked his ire. 'It is a mistake, it is a failure, it is a sin' was his summary in one case and, finally, with a lapse into the colloquialism which he never quite mastered, 'He is a bad gent.' Nevertheless his appreciation, when it came, was generous and genial. 'If Maitland were alive, he would be very glad' was a sufficient reward in itself." [23]

One of Vinogradoff's students wrote as follows:

"About four weeks were spent with this preliminary matter and we then made our contributions in turn. This consisted in reading an Essay on the subject agreed upon — for instance, mine was 'Selden's Criticism of Bracton,' and each of us had some subject related to both Bracton and the particular branch of history in which we were specializing. The Essay would be read aloud to the Seminar: then Vinogradoff took it away in order to read it at leisure and at the following meeting would give his suggestions and criticisms. He was always sparing in

[23] *Economic Journal*, June 1908.

praise, but on the other hand his criticisms were never conveyed in such a way as to give any cause for offence and his suggestions were always extremely practical and helpful. After the conclusion of the Seminar he kept in touch with its members, and one never left him without feeling that he had stimulated one to one's very best efforts.

My experience of this Seminar confirmed my view that Vinogradoff was a great teacher. He had the power of diagnosing his pupils: stirring up their enthusiasm, and directing and sustaining it by encouragement and guidance. But he could never have been a popular teacher because his work was not so much to convey information as to create the zeal and the equipment for seeking knowledge. His Seminar was thus specially valuable as a training in method and, in my own case, this was specially valuable because at the time I had a very large amount of routine College teaching and was in danger of coming to think of myself as fitted only to be a mere drudge. Vinogradoff restored and amplified my old ideals, and I have never met one of his pupils who did not share some of this personal enthusiasm." [24]

It is impossible to put the case for a graduate development more fairly or more convincingly: every one profits — the scholar himself, his group of advanced students, the College tutor, learning. Suppose that, in place of one Vinogradoff, there were a post-graduate organization in each faculty: what would not Oxford, Cambridge, and the world gain? And Vinogradoff is not a solitary example. He himself mentions Maitland; the whole line of Cambridge physiologists, great classicists, mathematicians, and philosophers might also be cited. But each is an individual phenomenon; each individual has to hew out his own path, though the succession of Cambridge physiologists — Foster, Langley, Sherrington, Hopkins, Barcroft, Hardy, Lucas, and Adrian — shows that it can somehow be done. But the system does not help them. And system

[24] Collected works, Introduction by H. A. L. Fisher, (Clarendon Press), pp. 32, 34, 35.

[283]

there nowadays needs to be — not system in the sense of a machine, but system in the sense of flexible opportunities provided by the University for the various types of individuals who, in their own way, will be best circumstanced to advance knowledge and to train recruits; how many and under what conditions, will vary with the subject and the teacher.

I wish, however, to be careful not to overstate my case. The dynamic force in an American university is usually the president. Without an energetic president, an individual professor may do his work, but the institution as a whole will not move forward. In Germany, as we shall later see, omitting the part played by the Ministry of Education at Berlin or some other capital, the faculty made up of *Ordinarii* manages things while the *Extraordinarii,* assistants, *Privatdozenten* have less to say.[25] Now as against these centralized systems, the one centralized in an individual, the other in a relatively small group, stands the Oxford and Cambridge system, where a body of Colleges, each an entity with its own history, peculiarities, usages, traditions, constitute a University, to which they are loosely and more or less variously related. On its face, it would seem difficult to devise a type of organization less calculated to make progress, and in fact there have been epochs in the history of the Universities when things were at a standstill. As machinery it is poor, cumbrous, unwieldy, wasteful, and thus trying to those who are right and know they are right. Yet if we compare the progress made by an institution like Harvard under the leadership of one great man over a period of half a century with the progress made by Cambridge during the same period, the former having no traditions to struggle against,

[25] See p. 326.

[284]

but only a barrier to break through, the latter loaded down with traditions, restrictions, and prejudices incorporated either in custom or in law, it is startling to find how far within the last sixty years the ancient universities have advanced from what they were in 1870. To be sure, they hold tenaciously to the graces, amenities, and customs of previous generations. More than that, in framework, constitution, and customs, Oxford and Cambridge in respect to the relations of the separate Colleges and the University somewhat resemble the United States in that unhappy period between the close of the Revolutionary War in 1783 and the adoption of the Federal Constitution in 1789. And yet there is a difference, for the Confederation made up of sensitive colonies could get nothing at all done. Oxford, moving, as Matthew Arnold says, " tho' in its own slow way " [26] has somehow done much. Though muddling along, it has none the less established institutes in the sciences and is now shyly approaching the question of organizing facilities for higher degrees and the project of a more adequate University Library. What was the cause? A few able individuals hewing out their own path and enabled by the loosely jointed College system to be just as individual as they pleased; the competition between Colleges when one of them, like Balliol, Trinity, or Caius, forged ahead; the occasional intervention of a Royal Commission which swept away restrictions and cobwebs; the internal pressure of developing subjects free to expand in their own way just because the structure was a loose one; the possibility of making any kind of special arrangement for the benefit of a special tutor, professor, or subject.

From the point of view of research and respect for

[26] Written in 1865. *Letters*, Vol. I, p. 341.

research, Cambridge is, on the whole, the more modern and weighty of the two institutions. To be sure, Oxford has to its credit the great dictionary and is developing its scientific laboratories; Cambridge achieved its modern history and has in general outstripped Oxford in science and economics. It is not easy to explain the difference. But one suspects that the result is not unconnected with the tradition of Newton, the founding of the Cavendish Laboratory, Michael Foster's unique genius,[27] and the earlier abandonment of the separate College laboratories. In recent years, four Nobel prizes have gone to the Cavendish Laboratory. Strange and casual is the history of University mathematics at Cambridge. Originally, of course, each College taught its own mathematics; later four smaller Colleges pooled and differentiated their teaching of the subject; Trinity was large and rich enough to continue its own independence. The present Bishop of Birmingham, a tutor in mathematics at Trinity some twenty-five years ago, induced Trinity to enter the pool; the next step — the creation of a University Board of Mathematical Studies — followed naturally. On the other hand, there are curious inadequacies. In the new and splendid laboratory of pathology, only animal material is dealt with. The department has no standing in Addenbrooke's Hospital, where a small amount of clinical teaching is done and where autopsies are rare.

Elasticity has in America led to the strange results on which I have dwelt at length. It has led to absurdities in London. Oxford and Cambridge are practically free of them. One does, however, raise one's eyebrows

---

[27] Foster was called to Cambridge not by the University, but by Trinity College, to be pre-lector in physiology. The Master of Trinity at the time chanced to be interested in the subject.

when one finds at each institution a School of Agriculture and a School of Forestry, established by the government and meagrely provided for. Of course, agriculture and forestry deserve schools. But why divided between Oxford, Cambridge, and Rothamstead? Even English sanity cannot quite maintain itself under such conditions. Among much that is admirable, the Oxford School has issued " The Butcher's Shop," [28] a research publication, in which the country butcher is told that " in slaughtering a bullock, a team of four men is usually considered necessary. It is possible to do with less," but in that event, " the bullock may have time to struggle and injure itself." [29] Are we in England or in America, when we are told "that there is a subtle art in the exhibition of meat "? In England, surely, when, in enumerating consumers, the author includes in the " professional class " " doctors, barristers, stud-owners, parsons, school teachers, etc." [30] Of this text, 120 copies had been circulated at the time of my inquiry.[31] The futility of this sort of thing could not be more plainly shown. I venture to raise the question whether the subjects of forestry and agriculture have in the creation of these scattered schools been dealt with absolutely on their merits.[32]

X

I have tried to hold the scales fairly in describing and estimating the ancient universities. It must be

[28] Clarendon Press, 1928.   [30] Ibid., p. 26.
[29] Ibid., p. 11.   [31] May, 1929.
[32] To the University of Oxford belong (1) a School of Rural Economy, (2) the Agricultural Economics Research Institute, (3) the Agricultural Engineering Research Institute. All three are governed by the University through a Committee for Rural Economy. The Ministry has established five institutes of research at Cambridge: Animal Nutrition, Animal Pathology, Horticulture, Plant Breeding, and Small Animal Breeding.

clear that, while aware of what appear to me to be curable defects, I, as an American, profoundly envy them. Only the foreigner who has grown up in the glare and newness of a new world, be it America or Australia, can do full justice to the charm and educative value of the quiet quadrangles, the College libraries, the Bodleian, rich in treasures and associations, the fellows' gardens — the strange intermingling of democracy and tradition, of asceticism and dignified luxury. No American or German institution of any kind enjoys, as do Oxford and Cambridge, the inestimable advantage of possessing ample means of associating in worthy, scholarly fashion with men of learning and distinction — not only an amenity, but a source of profound spiritual stimulus. However modest the means of the Oxford or Cambridge scholar, he can without effort or sacrifice be host to a minister of state, a great scientist, or philosopher. Finally, among the tremendous assets of Oxford and Cambridge one must reckon the Clarendon Press and the Cambridge University Press. Publication and research are inseparable; what is accomplished if the work of a lifetime grows mouldy in the drawer of a desk? American scholars are constantly worried by this depressing fear. Since the War, continental scholars have also encountered serious difficulties. With wisdom and unselfishness the managers of the University Presses have splendidly served not only the scholars of Oxford and Cambridge, but the scholars of the entire English-speaking and English-reading world.

So far I have discussed Oxford and Cambridge — Colleges and University — in general terms. I can perhaps make my feeling clearer, if in concluding, I consider a few specific problems. The industrial revolution transformed England from an agricultural into an industrial nation; a political and social revolution has been simultaneously going on. I have criticized severely the short-sighted *ad hoc* American university schools of business and commerce. But that does not mean that the phenomena of industry, commerce, transportation, and government do not require the same type of study that is conceded to disease and to crime. Britain is an industrial nation wrestling with the most serious economic problems of its whole history; it is a democracy whose actual government is still too largely Victorian in theory, while its problems are the problems created by the industrial revolution and the rapid spread of democracy. How boldly do Oxford and Cambridge attack them? Cambridge seems, curiously enough, more distinctly aware of them than Oxford. For Oxford, the training ground of statesmen, diplomatists, and journalists, was up to the outbreak of the War only dimly conscious of economics as a legitimate and important subject of undergraduate training and post-graduate effort. No degree — a mere diploma — was obtainable; there was no college tutor in the subject; only a struggling unofficial group represented in Barnet House a subject in which English thinkers had for over a century blazed a trail for the whole world. Following the war, "Modern Greats" was established. It consists of philosophy, politics, and economics, a pretty heavy load. The new "Greats" was not permitted to get too far away from the old. In economics adequate library facilities and a sufficient staff of assistants are still lacking. The research worker finds far greater opportunities at the London School of Economics. Yet think what Oxford offers in history, law, and other subjects that would enrich the worker in economics, deepen his insight, and broaden his vision! All this is lost to economics, unless economics is itself made adequate.

Economics is, however, only one of the political or social sciences. If it be among the primary functions of universities to study problems, assuredly, the English nation, beset by financial and governmental problems, needs to devote some of its ablest and coolest minds to their objective consideration. There are two obvious avenues of approach: Oxford and Cambridge train the men who rule the Empire — proconsuls, diplomats, soldiers, and civil servants. The Universities, through their graduates, are thus in contact with the problems of government, finance, industry, political experimentation all over the world. What do the sons of Oxford and Cambridge bring back to their respective Universities from this rich practical experience? What do the Universities do to garner experience for the better training of the next generation? Oxford and Cambridge are in position to make a unique contribution to government and politics if only they will utilize the experience and deal with the problems of their own graduates.

But this is after all an empirical approach, fraught with danger, if pursued alone. The problems of colonization, raw material, contacts of nations, the breakdown of ancient forms of government, the construction and creation of new forms of government, which will satisfy the aspirations of native races and the insatiable longings of the old races not so much for power as for space and for raw materials — all these are now being handled in a hand-to-mouth fashion by well-intentioned and capable administrators, who, however, do not and cannot know the experience of other places and who have no adequate time for thought. It ought to be the function of faculties of law and government not only to teach what is known, but to study, not what is going to be done tomorrow but what can be done ten years hence, precisely as it is the function of a first-rate medical school to look out that its students should not only know what we know today, but should be able to understand what someone is going to be discovering and propounding a decade hence. The economists and publicists are not so organized as to do this. Those who are thinking in Oxford are thinking mainly in terms of the present British Empire, and with a view to being helpful to the anxious administrators in India and Africa. I feel quite sure that they are thus too near to actual responsibility for policies and that it is their business, as it is the business of the physiologist and the pharmacologist, to study phenomena, to report upon them, to think about them, and to leave to the administrator, as the physiologist and pharmacologist leave to the clinician or some middleman, the process of converting this material into available form. This cannot be done wholly in libraries; workers must have the time and the detachment to study problems in the field, gathering the experience of practical administrators, listening to them, but never feeling bound to be guided by them. The administrator may be trusted to modify the more academic or theoretic conclusions of the investigator. The investigator must not be hampered by the everyday necessities of the administrator or the colonist. He needs more vision than either can possibly use or either is likely to have.

An interesting and perilous possibility thus arises in connection with the new Rhodes House at Oxford, constructed by the Rhodes Trust. Characteristically, it was designed and constructed without a clear conception of the use to which it was to be put. Now that it has been built, a tangible affair around which things may cluster, it is suggested that it become the home of a faculty of political science or some portion thereof. The Professors of American History and Colonial History already have seminar rooms and departmental libraries in it. It would be easy to expand the building, in order to give similar facilities to other scholars needed to create a faculty of government — practical and theoretical — with quarters for clerical assistance. The danger lies in the association of the Rhodes name with a particular school of statesmanship. The scholars who would create a school of government, forgetting nothing in the way of history and experience, must rise to a height from which their vision would transcend this association. They must study politics without reference to policies. To theoretical studies in these fields, the Englishman does not take kindly, despite the fundamentally important contributions made by Englishmen to both. But even the practical problems of today and tomorrow are apt to be short-sightedly managed, unless influential and detached schools of thinking can be developed in the Universities. Something is lost when Hobbes, Ricardo, Bentham, Mill, Hobhouse, and Wallas lack successive groups of trained disciples in great universities.

Dangerous as I realize it is to leave the fairly safe ground of generalization, I venture even to touch the prickly subject of the Bodleian. The Library situation at Oxford is not only unsatisfactory — it actually hinders a University development. Some of the fellows use their college rooms for books and work; some of them use their homes. No general catalogue is in existence anywhere: there exist therefore uncoördinated College libraries, the library of the Taylor Institution, the Bodleian, Barnet House,

Rhodes House. Meanwhile, work in the intellectual sciences depends for its vitality and cross-fertilization on the close association of groups of advanced students with the literature of the various subjects. Quite obviously, the Bodleian is too lovely to be touched; just as obviously it has been outgrown, not only in size, but functionally. As far back as 1880, its practical inadequacy for the mere storage of books required the annexation of the adjoining " schools " and subsequently the construction of capacious vaults. To no avail: long in advance of the calculated time, the tide of incoming volumes has flooded every nook and cranny. Where is the Bodleian to find additional space? Over this question an acute controversy rages. Meanwhile, eminent scholars lecture in the bare halls of the Examination Schools, meet their few advanced students in their college rooms, and do their own work, partly in the Bodleian, partly in their college rooms, partly at home. The inadequacy of the present Bodleian even as a storehouse for books thus opens the question as to the future of the University and offers an opportunity to encourage and facilitate advanced work. The question is not a new one. Mark Pattison raised it in vigorous terms over half a century ago. The recent Royal Commission had something to say on the question. But a great opportunity to deal effectively with the problem — to develop graduate work through the University, while letting the undergraduate Colleges alone — arises out of the need of doing something about the Bodleian, something about storing books, something about filling out existing gaps in the collection, something about providing wholesome and easy conditions for post-graduate study, teaching, and research.

Now, I venture to suggest that, while storage is a

real problem, the battle is just now being too largely fought over a secondary issue, not over the decisive point. The real question is not: How shall we house Oxford's books, but is Oxford to develop on the University side? If the latter question is affirmatively answered, as, in my judgment, under the pressure of the age it is bound to be, then storage is an incident to the fundamental consideration of function. Conceive the University not only as an aggregation of Colleges, with a fringe of research workers, but as a well-developed upper storey, providing facilities and opportunity for the prosecution of systematic research and the training of a much larger body of the intellectual élite. The new Library will be the University in all bookish subjects — in philosophy, in history, in language, in literature. It will be a library readily accessible for reading, study, and teaching. Its books will therefore be partially reclassified; they will be open to the use of qualified students, without the restrictions now due to an obsolete catalogue, lack of staff, lack of order; and in close contact with each subject there will be rooms in which the professor and individual students may separately be at home, and in which small groups of advanced workers may meet. The notion that a " first " or " second " class brings the student far enough to be independent of the stimulus and direction of an advanced group will have been abandoned. A half dozen students, each of them prosecuting his own work, can be immensely helpful to one another by being brought together to discuss with a professor something different from what any one is just then pursuing. And this can best be accomplished in easy reach of the literature of the general subject. To be sure, there must be adequate space for the storage of books; to be sure, there will still be departmental libraries in the various laboratories and at Rhodes House. But storage will no longer be the primary consideration; other questions will displace that. What functions should be served by the library of a modern university? What kind of building is suited to their easy discharge? What kind of library staff is requisite? Where and how can the Radcliffe, the Taylor Institution, and Barnet House be fitted into this capacious scheme? How large must it be (the storage problem) to answer the needs of generations to come? If these be the vital questions, the Bodleian will remain, used I know not how, but a new Library, harmonizing with Oxford architecture at its best, will arise as close as possible to the Colleges, representing not a mere spatial addition to the University, but the addition of a developed idea which has burst its present shell. Why not? The University has proved its vitality by assimilating new ideas as times have changed. College after College has been founded, each with something novel in its conception; tests have been abolished; women's Colleges have been constructed; a string of laboratories has spread along South Parks Road; Schools of Research in Oriental Studies, in Agriculture, and in Forestry have been added. At every step the University has increased in strength; and the Colleges are more highly vitalized than ever: no need for concern as to them. The development of the University ideal hinges thus on the solution of the problem of Bodley's Library: if the solution is sound, Oxford will be a more powerful force in the life of the Empire, it will mean more to the civilized world than ever before. And a no less radical solution will appease the forces that in Oxford itself are seeking an outlet.

Medicine shall furnish the final example. It is a subject in which physics, chemistry, biology, even mathematics play a part; but medicine is not physics, chemistry, or biology, any more than it is merely anatomy, physiology, or pathology. Disease is an entity; the physiologist is not concerned with it; neither is the chemist nor the pathologist. For the scientific study of disease — and our hope lies in the extension of the scientific at the cost of the empirical — one needs a unified group — anatomists, physiologists, pathologists, chemists, physicists, and of course clinicians themselves scientifically trained. There are unified schools of medicine answering these specifications in Denmark, in Holland, in Austria, in Germany, and in the United States. There is not a single one in Great Britain. The London Hospital schools are fair places in which to train practical doctors; but they are not organized, equipped, or supported to promote scientific medicine. At University College, London, a great group has been assembled in the underlying medical sciences, but the clinical situation, though improved, is as yet far from satisfactory. At Cambridge and at Oxford the underlying sciences are again strong; by singular good fortune, the medical laboratories lie together in South Parks Road. But up to the present time, neither at Oxford nor at Cambridge, has the medical group, even on the pre-clinical side, functioned as a faculty. The Oxford or Cambridge medical student, after an inspiring course in physiology and pathology, drops down to a lower level when he goes to London for his clinical work. In the provinces, once more, there are no clinics in the university sense. Both Oxford and Cambridge as centres for the scientific study of disease — a real imperial need — could be completed; the smallness of the two towns is no obstacle, for patients in sufficient number and variety will go wherever they learn that they will be most intelligently treated; as they go to the Mayo Clinic and Greifswald, so they would go to Oxford and Cambridge.[33] Meanwhile, the English physician may be an excellent practical doctor; and individuals like Hughlings Jackson, Henry Head, James Mackenzie, and Thomas Lewis do in our day what Harvey and Addison and Bright did in their day — make epoch-making contributions to the elucidation of disease. But they do so, unaided by organization, equipment, and support; they are less and less likely to train successors, or successors in adequate numbers. America has in recent years done better in medicine than in any other field. Why? It has had leaders like Welch and Osler, as England too has had. But the American leaders have led. We have in several universities brought together in close contiguity the natural sciences, the medical sciences, and one by one the requisite clinics, equipped with trained men and adequate equipment. England cannot, in my judgment, achieve the same result unless it makes similar provision; and Oxford and Cambridge Universities, the universities upon which the rest of the national university structure leans heavily, must therefore take the requisite steps.

One perceives in many places the beginnings of a modern university, superposed upon the solid collegiate structure; one perceives, too, in certain persons and in certain subjects something very far beyond beginnings, indeed some of the finest work in the world in scholarship, mathematics, and science. But where are the architect, the bricks, and mortar of a modern university? Where is the conception that will complete

[33] Despite its great schools of physiology, bio-chemistry, etc., the Cambridge school is less a faculty than the Oxford group: there is no dean, and there is a distinct aversion to organization, however loose, of a medical faculty.

the foundation? Numerically " Classical Greats " has lost; but, *as a state of mind*, it still prevails.

The creation of the University Grants Committee, the Medical Research Council, the Department of Industrial and Scientific Research indicates recognition of the fact that England lacks modern universities. The organizations just named give temporary relief — a block grant, support for a promising investigator or an important investigation. Such agencies are not superfluous; under all circumstances they have their uses; but they are no substitute for universities, amply endowed, amply equipped, and amply attended by a sufficient group of men and women dedicated to the search for truth. They seem to say: " We lack developed universities. While we are waiting for them or in preparation for them, let us train this or that promising man, let us get this or that thing done." It is all very well, but it does not answer.

To be frank, despite their great scholars and scientists and ours, this sort of thing does not come easy to either Great Britain or America. Both nations pride themselves on being men of action; have the British not conquered an empire? Have not the Americans in a few decades subdued a continent? They are both doers, not thinkers or dreamers. That was all very well when Great Britain's fiat was law upon the ocean, when India poured its wealth into English coffers, when coal and iron and steam gave England an overwhelming predominance in foreign trade, and when a nation was sufficient unto itself. Under such circumstances one could live by rule of thumb. So, in the United States, all was well so long as its forests were barely touched, as long as any energetic emigrant could in a decade become a capitalist, and as long as the nation could ignore the rest of the world. But this order has, in both countries and in all countries, passed away. Rule of thumb no longer suffices; amateurs can no longer do the world's thinking or governing. Internal problems — social and industrial, external problems — colonial, diplomatic, have got to be understood; intelligence based upon sympathy and understanding must somehow be put in control. Not only in science and industry, but in politics, in philosophy, in literature, and in art, nations will henceforth be significant not in proportion to their numbers or wealth, but rather in proportion to their development in the sphere of ideas.

Though the word " research " occurs more and more frequently in the literature dealing with Oxford and Cambridge from 1850 on — in the successive reports of the Royal Commissions, in Pattison's writings, in Curzon's Memorandum, one has the feeling that the critics are almost always hampered by timidity. Lord Curzon perceived that research and advanced teaching, on the one hand, and undergraduate instruction, on the other, belong in general to different categories; there is as much objection to jumbling them together as there would be to jumbling together Winchester and New College. The hesitant attitude will therefore sooner or later have to be discarded; graduate faculties with continuous direction, modelled perhaps on the principalship of the English provincial university will have to be set up; the present machinery, capable, perhaps, of simplification, will care for the undergraduate work; the Colleges may be left free to pursue their own way; the best and most promising of the scientists and scholars must receive a more or less separate organization, must be free to adopt such methods of teaching and research as are inherently suitable to person and subject, and must be equipped with the facilities needed by scholars and scientists to train disciples. In the effort to accomplish this great step forward, all minor matters affecting the Colleges and undergraduate education may well for the present be ignored.

XI

The sums available for the support and development of university education in England are pitifully small. The Oxford and Cambridge Colleges vary — some are well-to-do, others possess relatively little. Their output seems to bear little relation to their wealth. The total sums at the disposal of the University for advanced work are far from adequate. For graduate work, the provincial universities provide only incidentally. Even with the aid of the University Grants Committee great projects like the building of a university library at Oxford or the completion of the medical schools by the construction, equipment, and support of even small university clinics cannot be undertaken. Funds are lacking: the total annual expenditure for higher education is approximately £5,000,000 — a meagre sum. Notable and praiseworthy, however, is the relatively small amount expended on administration.

Salaries are relatively better than they are in America; the average professorial salary in 1928–29 was £1,082; but at the next level, readerships and lectureships, there is a drop of almost 50%. As professorships in so small a country are not numerous, the inducement to enter academic life is not powerful. But there is fortunately an academic way of living — simple, dignified, unworldly, so that, especially in the professorial grade, the amenities of life are not lacking and reliance on industry for additional income is dis-

tinctly "bad form" — and, in consequence, very unusual. On the other hand, the

"competition of other professions and lines of life has been
constantly on the increase. The situation is, indeed, very different from what it was at the time of the previous Royal Commissions. Fellows are now allowed to marry, and in most cases
wish to avail themselves of the privilege; and the usual type
of 'don' is now a person who could command a high salary
in many different walks of life. His choice no longer usually
lies between the Church and the teaching profession. Well-paid
professorships, all over the English-speaking world, are frequently offered to Oxford and Cambridge men. Excellent business openings are now available to successful students, particularly in science, sometimes with enormous salaries attached.

It is not, indeed, possible or desirable for the Universities
to compete pound for pound with offers of this last description;
but a living wage is necessary. People are ready to sacrifice
higher salaries and even posts of greater power and influence
in order to enjoy the amenities and the intellectual privileges
and ideals of life at Oxford and Cambridge. But however
anxious they may be to stay, few can do so except on terms
enabling them to provide for a family and to educate their
children. If this could be done before the War on an income of
£500 or £600 a year in middle and later life, it cannot be done
on those terms today. Each University must be placed in a
position to offer to all those who do its work a salary and
pension prospects enabling a man to marry and bring up a
family, with amenities and advantages of education like those
of other professional families. On that condition Oxford and
Cambridge will be able in the coming era to keep enough of
their best students to do their teaching and research — but not
otherwise." [34]

[34] *Report of Royal Commission on Oxford and Cambridge Universities*
(H. M. Stationery Office, London, 1922), p. 49. See also *Report, University
Grants Committee, 1928–29*, pp. 22–30.
To the same effect, though with especial reference to medicine, see Sir
Walter M. Fletcher's Norman Lockyer Lecture on *Medical Research* (*British
Medical Journal*, Nov. 30, 1929). "I am very often reminded," he says, "of
what was heard during the war from a wounded man in a hospital in
France. A gallant fellow, well over 50, and the chauffeur of a millionaire,
was asked why he had left a secure and useful job at home to fight; he
smiled through his bandages and said modestly, 'I suppose my curiosity

From the standpoint of ability to finance universities and research, it is, however, well to remember that as a matter of fact the British debt at the close of the Napoleonic Wars bore the same relation to the national wealth as is now borne by the present debt. The previous debt was not extinguished, but it was virtually reduced to insignificance by the expansion of English industry, by steam, coal, iron. Is it not conceivable that, if England similarly developed physics and chemistry, a comparable phenomenon would occur?

One thing, however, seems clear. Nations have recently been led to borrow billions for war; no nation has ever borrowed largely for education. Probably, no nation is rich enough to pay for both war and civilization. We must make our choice; we cannot have both. The new naval treaty permits the United States to spend a billion dollars on warships — a sum greater than has been accumulated by all our endowed institutions of learning in their entire history. Unintelligence could go no further! In Great Britain, the national budget devotes a huge sum to war — present, past, or future — as against an inconsiderable sum to education. Until the figures are reversed, the two nations deceive themselves as to what they care about most.

---

got the better of my intelligence.' Very many research workers I know are entitled to make the same kind of whimsical but heroic explanation of their motives."

PART IV

GERMAN UNIVERSITIES

I

OF the countries dealt with in this volume, Germany has in theory and practice come nearest to giving higher education its due position. America, I have said, places a naïve trust in education; but its lack of comprehension is indicated by the miscellaneous character of curricula, by its aversion to discipline, by its over-emphasis on social activities as against intellectual effort. To be sure, curricula were long too barren and monotonous; to be sure, the school is a social agency; to be sure, social attitudes are profoundly significant. But, important and essential as all these are, education has at its heart a tough and indispensable intellectual core. Losing sight of this factor, we have in America heedlessly and recklessly jumbled together in secondary schools, colleges, or universities all sorts of persons, all sorts of activities, all sorts of purposes, all sorts of subjects. Exceptions, brilliant and solid, may be noted, but they can also be counted.

In England, the situation described was different. Society and the Church needed and obtained specific types of education, which, whatever their defects, did at any rate establish a sane, solid, and authoritative, though far too limited, concept of educational ideals. A genuine or disinterested concern for education awaited the rise of the labouring class; only in our time have the public authorities endeavoured, by bringing together disjointed pieces and inserting some of the missing links, to take steps towards the creation of a national system of education conducted by different coöperating agencies. The system, as it will one day become, will be a striking illustration of English ability to combine official and private agencies in the achievement of a large public purpose; the rapidity of its development is almost wholly dependent upon the redirection of English financial expenditure.

II

In Germany, as in other countries, the university level depends on the level of secondary education. Prior to the War, secondary education in Germany was practically covered by three gymnasial types; the universities knew therefore precisely what they were dealing with in respect to the training and equipment of the incoming student. Since the Revolution, this can no longer be claimed. Changes were, as we shall see, needed to correct social inequalities; but the changes made were not limited to the changes needed, with the result that the educational edges are more or less frayed.

Pre-War Germany possessed, as I have just said, three types of secondary schools — *Gymnasien, Realgymnasien,* and *Oberrealschulen* — each adapted to a different type of mind and purpose, each selective, and all severe.[1] The *Gymnasium* was a stern humanistic discipline; the *Oberrealschule* an equally severe discipline for those scientifically minded; the *Realgymnasium* took a medium line. Differentiation on the basis of ability and taste was thus provided; but

---

[1] The dividing lines between these types were softened by so-called " Reform " schools embodying curricula that departed from the strict type. The *Oberrealschule zum Dom* at Lübeck includes several. Unquestionably too many different types can be — indeed have already been — created and at too great expense.

all three types ensured continuous intellectual training under competent masters over a long period and
aimed at an understandable result. Nor was this goal
technical or vocational: the school type was varied to
meet the cultural possibilities of the pupil — *not the
needs of the vocation* which he might subsequently
enter. A cultural ideal, *i.e.,* education, not training
ad hoc, controlled educational organization. Criticism
was, to be sure, never silenced; but one could make no
greater mistake than to suppose that German criticism, often severe, meant what the same words would
mean in English, if applied to English, and still more,
to American secondary education.[2] Here and there
concessions have been made to organized vocational
interests. But the greater the pressure from this side,
the more strenuous the opposition from those who
are unwilling to undermine the main structure.

I have said that the curricula represented coherent,
solid training over a protracted period — nine years at
least. Unfortunately, it represented also too nearly the
same kind of training throughout. Between the subject-matter of the gymnasial curricula there were
marked differences. But there was a striking similar-
ity in instruction and management. The defects lay
largely on the physical and social sides: far too little
provision was made for open-air exercise or sport,
which, in moderation, is an indispensable element in
the moral, civic, and physical training of youth; far
too little scope was given to individual initiative and
to social activity. And in these respects there was little
to choose between the plight of the child who entered
the *Gymnasium* at nine or ten and the young man who

[2] It is hardly possible to over-praise the memorandum issued in 1924
by the Prussian Education Ministry, entitled *Die Neuordnung des preus-
sischen höheren Schulwesens.* It is a frank review of the current situation in
secondary education in Prussia, fearlessly critical and suggestive.

at eighteen or nineteen left for the university, where his personal freedom suddenly became complete. He had entered a child; he left a young man, having in the mean while passed through the period of adolescence. But throughout the entire course he had been severely regimented. He had worked hard, he had had to toe the mark; but he had tasted little freedom; little had been left to his own choice, though in recent years the cultivation of sport had been coming to his relief. In the end, it was perhaps at times more difficult for him to recover from the virtues of his admirable education than for a clever American to recover from the defects of his superficial education: which is, however, not to be interpreted as an argument for poor schools.

The students came mainly from the middle and lower middle classes: they were the sons of merchants, officials, lawyers, doctors, and village clergymen — often quite humble people. But the children of the working class were rarely to be found in a *Gymnasium*, or, as we shall later see, in a university. The rise of the working class introduced into German life a new factor, of which, prior to the War, higher education was unconscious. I know a scholar who attended three different *Gymnasien* without ever meeting the son of a worker (*Arbeiter*) in any of them. The obstacle was partly economic; the worker could not pay his son's way; but it was by no means solely economic. The children of the workers had therefore usually to be content with the *Volksschule* from which, following their fathers, they entered agriculture or a trade — a distinction that bred a smouldering resentment, which is one of the main sources of Germany's present woes.

Here then in brief were the bright and the seamy sides of secondary education in pre-War Germany:

its great virtue was its completeness and solidity; its weaknesses were inelasticity, overloading, and class-consciousness. German reformers, always vocal, and especially so during the last decade preceding the War had already pointed out these defects. Occasionally one heard even a suggestion that the long gymnasial period should be broken and something like the American college should be set up. But the American college is far too unsatisfactory an article in its own country to be recommended for export.

The Constitution of 1919 broke down distinctions; it enlarged the powers of the federal government; it provided that the training of teachers should be uniform. Thus a general and uniform level will, it is hoped, be secured. The program itself was not really new. The idea of a common elementary school as the basis of a system of national education had been broached in the great period of educational fertility, the time of Süvern and Humboldt; laid aside, it was revived in '48; but with the collapse of liberalism, it was forgotten until the World War reminded the defeated country of the essential unity of a nation's culture. With such resources as it can now devote to the task, Prussia and other states are endeavouring to develop their educational systems on the basis of a common elementary school. Thus the social gap that formerly existed between the common school (*Volksschule*) and the *Gymnasium*, cleaving the nation in twain, is in process of being closed. Can it ultimately be closed without lowering the plane of the secondary school and therewith that of the university? That is the question that democracy faces not only in Germany, but even more clearly, as we have seen, in America and also in England.

Other changes, designed to introduce equality of

opportunity and elasticity have been made. Young men and women who have not followed the official schemes may apply for a special examination, and a small number of students have thus entered the universities — a small number, because the applicant must prove himself worthy of being made an exception.[3] In Prussia and certain other states a fourth gymnasial type has been created, the *Deutsche Oberschule*, originally conceived as a modern school, emphasizing modern languages and science, but already hardly distinguishable from the *Oberrealschule*. In addition, the universities have been opened to the graduates of a large number and variety of so-called "*Aufbauschulen.*" Simultaneously and with characteristic thoroughness sport is emphasized — a development that is sure to react upon the schools.

But while the Revolution opened the doors of opportunity far more widely to those who might wish to seek a university education, it did not try to legislate distinctions as such out of existence. Special branches of training are in Prussia lodged, not in the Ministry of Education, but in the Ministry of Commerce, the Ministry of Agriculture, and the Ministry of Public Welfare.[4] The smaller states do not carry administrative differentiation to this extent; and even in Prussia, it has not passed unchallenged. There is overlapping; there is additional expense. But an American can perhaps best appreciate the importance of recognizing distinctions of this kind. At the close of the elementary school, various paths open out; they lead in different directions; they invite different kinds of persons. In America all are shepherded on one broad

---

[3] See official circulars regarding "*Studium ohne Reifezeugnis.*"

[4] As for the arrangements made for adult education and university extension, see pp. 339–344.

highway — the high school, the college, the university — each trying, and of course failing — to act as a comprehensive institution. Germany accepts diversity of capacity and aim and is trying to provide for it appropriately. Of the soundness of German theory there is no stronger proof than American practice.

III

The German universities originated in the Middle Ages; but for our purposes, they began with the nineteenth century. They have maintained their outer form, precisely as have Oxford and Cambridge; even the new universities at Cologne, Hamburg, and Frankfurt have assumed the same form as the others. But on the founding of the University of Berlin new wine was poured into the old bottles; and the old bottles burst. Never before or since have ancient institutions been so completely remodelled to accord with an idea. The process had of course been long in fermenting; in the result, looking back, one discerns the influence of Leibnitz, Kant, Goethe, and others — all of those who participated in the creation of the national culture. But the new era is concretely associated with a later group — Hegel, Fichte, Schleiermacher, and Humboldt; and the occasion was the protest of spirit against the domination of brute force.

The helplessness of a Germany, splintered into small states and lying prostrate beneath the armies of Napoleon, was defiantly answered by the Hegelian philosophy of the unified state as the embodiment of reason. Paradoxically enough, this conception was embraced by the divided nation, despite its continuing division; and, if I may anticipate, the theory is still accepted, though particularism continues to make itself felt. Within the ideally unified state, Hegel and his successors saw the university as offering unhampered opportunity for the complete development of the individual. A state constituted of developed personalities — this was Hegel's conceptual contribution to the renascence of Germany.

The creation of the University of Berlin, heralded by preliminary steps at Halle, Göttingen, and Jena, was a deliberate break with academic tradition. Freedom in the modern sense could not have characterized the mediaeval university; it emerged only with the development of rationalism in the late eighteenth century. The new University was intended primarily to develop knowledge, secondarily and perhaps as a concession, to train the professional and the official classes, at the level at which knowledge may be promoted. Humboldt conceived the salvation of the German nation as coming from the combination of teaching and research, and time has proved him right. To be sure, the philosophers of previous centuries had laid the foundation; to be sure, the soldiers and statesmen of the nineteenth century made an indispensable contribution to German intellectual unity. Though Bismarck and the first William appear not to have been particularly intimate with the universities, the second William gloried in them, precisely as he gloried in the German army and in German commerce: he knew and aided scholars and scientists; they were evidences of success in the empire of thought, as the army and commerce were evidences of success in the arena of action. It would, however, be a serious misinterpretation to represent the professor as seeking imperial favour though as wholes the universities were gradually permeated by the monarchical spirit. The monarchy affected the universities in some such way as business now affects them in the United States. Social Democrats were excluded from the highest academic posts; honours, decorations, and attentions were freely showered upon professors, though always a few like Paulsen, preserving to the last their democracy and simplicity, refused to crook their knee to the court.

"Blood and iron" were then only partly the makers of United Germany. The real Germany was not only the Germany of Bismarck and his generals and his emperors, but the Germany of Goethe, Schiller, Fichte, Schleiermacher, Carl Schurz, Paulsen, and Virchow — a Germany in the making of which originally philosophy, literature, science, and war all coöperated. After a detour, brilliant, dazzling, but of relatively short duration, in which the warlike element was greatly exaggerated, Germany has now returned to the main road: returned — but with a difference. For without entirely eliminating German particularism, Bismarck welded Germany into a unified, though fortunately not uniform, political entity. His ruthlessness persuaded the German states that they must hang together; so much good at any rate came from their military career; but German education — the *Gymnasium* and the universities, despite profound social, philosophical, and political differences — welded Germany into the intellectual unity that was originally signified by the word "*Kultur*"[5] to which the War attached such sinister and inappropriate significance.

The Hegelian philosophy, with its rounded personalities, seems to conflict with the development of science, requiring, as it does, ever increasing specialization. But, as Rathenau maintained, experience

---

[5] Becker maintains that German unity came, in consequence of Bismarck's policy, to be too largely a military, too little a cultural achievement. C. H. Becker, *Kulturpolitische Aufgaben des Reiches* (Leipzig, 1919), p. 3.

may be regarded as a circle, from any point on the circumference of which an educated man can make his way towards the centre. The individual is intellectually saved in Germany, as he is often saved in England and rarely in America, by his excellent secondary education and the rich cultural tradition into which he is born. That is why English and German scholars and scientists so frequently strike one as better educated or more highly cultivated than their American colleagues; that is certainly why neither English nor German universities tolerate the weeds that grow so rankly in American institutions.

Changes have followed in the wake of the Revolution, to some of which I have already alluded. The partial demoralization of secondary education, due to the sudden collapse of the Empire and the sudden rise to power of the working classes, has, for the moment, by lowering the standard and excessively varying the types of the secondary school, lowered to the same extent the plane of the university. The overcrowding of the university, due partly to the lack of employment and partly to the naïve desire of the heretofore repressed to " taste the fleshpots of Egypt," has operated to the same end. Here and there, vocationalism or quasi-professionalism has won a precarious foothold. The increase in the number of students who must " work their way" has damaged the non-profitable subjects in favour of subjects that promise a return in the shape of a ready livelihood. The professors, whose savings have been destroyed, have been compelled to take on extra burdens for no other purpose than the earning of paltry sums. Rehabilitation and improvement of building and equipment have been gravely hindered. The wonder is not, however, that temporarily the university has slipped: the wonder is the clearness with which its original function is still on the whole perceived, the steps that have been taken to bring it into closer touch with present-day realities, and the high quality of the permanent administrative staff, who, frankly admitting past errors and present shortcomings, are endeavouring to adhere to the historic idea.

The German university has for almost a century and a half fruitfully engaged in teaching and research. As long as those two tasks combine in fertile union, the German university, whatever its defects of detail, will retain its importance. It has stimulated university development in Great Britain; from it has sprung the graduate school of the new world; to it industry and health and every conceivable practical activity are infinitely indebted. Neither utility nor even practical professional training is of its essence. Indeed, from time to time, it has been more open to criticism on the ground of indifference than to criticism on the ground of worldliness.

IV

There are, including the *Technische Hochschulen,* thirty universities in Germany,[6] externally the same, and within limits kept fairly well to the same general standard, partly by the influence of the Reich through various *Staatsexamen,* partly by competition, partly by constant migration of students and teachers, partly through the interchange of views at the annual[7] *Hochschule* Conference. Yet there are subtle differences, due to historical or geographical factors. We

[6] In their classical form, best described by Friedrich Paulsen in *The German Universities* (translated by Frank Thilly and William W. Elwang, New York, 1906), and by W. Lexis in Vol. I of *Die Universitäten im Deutschen Reich* (Berlin, 1904).

[7] The Weimar Constitution established an Imperial Committee for this purpose, but it is ineffective.

have seen how the founding of Berlin in the early years of the nineteenth century shook the entire system, with the result that essentially mediaeval universities made all possible haste, one after another, to modernize themselves in accordance with the Berlin idea. Prussia took the lead at that time; its size and the number of its universities have given it a kind of hegemony ever since. But it would be incorrect to assume that the other federal states have subordinated themselves. The larger states, such as Saxony and Bavaria, not to mention the smaller, have, within the same general framework, preserved and exercised liberty of action. Thus with all its tremendous influence, at no time has Prussia been slavishly copied; other states have experimented, and since the Revolution, even more independently than formerly, on lines quite remote from Prussian example. German culture is thus fruitfully individualized as one passes from Vienna to Munich, Freiburg, or Hamburg. Bonn and Cologne feel a peculiar responsibility for maintaining the cultural flavour of the Rhineland; the new University of Hamburg casts its eyes overseas. Breslau is distinctly conscious of East-Europe; Königsberg of East-Germany. The new universities, staffed mainly from the old, cannot, however, wander too far afield; and fundamental ideals are too deeply imbedded to be uprooted.

The German university is ultimately governed by a central authority, the education ministry of each of the eight federated states. The ministry, whatever its precise title, is charged with oversight of education, art, the theatre, and the opera — the state thus assuming a direct responsibility for the upholding of the cultural level; but our present concern is with education only.

The minister of education is a member of parliament — occasionally, like Becker, a scholar in his own right. The several divisions of the ministry are usually headed by men trained in the universities and are usually forced by the competition of other states to go forward. Administration causes much less distraction than in the United States: the business affairs of the university are looked after by the local *Kurator* both through subordinates on the ground and through his own immediate contact with the ministry; the confidential representative of the government, he likewise is the trusted representative of the university in its dealings with the administration. The revolving *Rectorat,* lasting only a single year, neither spoils a scientist nor makes continuity of policy impossible: for faculties and ministry follow well-worn paths, sometimes, indeed, too well worn; and the *Kuratorium* acts as a " shock-absorber " in respect to minor matters of detail. The faculties — philosophy (equivalent to arts and sciences), medicine, jurisprudence, theology — are distinct, autonomous, and, as a rule, equally prominent and equally developed. Business is transacted by committees of the faculty, who through their deans negotiate with the proper division of the ministry. Progress is sometimes slow, committees and conferences abound, and talk prolific; and yet, though local dissatisfaction is at times great, no other country made equal advances in respect to equipment, finance, and expansion during the seventy-five years preceding the War.

I select as of outstanding importance four features of university life. I begin with *Lehr-* and *Lernfreiheit.* The German teacher, whether *Privatdozent* or professor, selected in the way I shall shortly describe, pursues his own course, unhindered. He is perfectly free in the choice of topics, in the manner of presentation, in the formation of his seminar, in his way of life. Neither the faculty nor the ministry supervises him: he has the dignity that surrounds a man who, holding an intellectual post, is under no one's orders. His function is the double one that I began by ascribing to the university — that of conserving and of advancing knowledge: teaching and research. There is a common notion that the German professor is from the very nature of the university interested only in research — that he takes teaching lightly. The error arises doubtless from the fact that in teaching he avoids spoon-feeding. His students do not require any such method; he himself is above it. From Humboldt's conception that the university should combine teaching and research the university has never departed. The recently published partial bibliography of the more important publications of Wilamowitz covers almost eight closely printed pages;[8] to foreigners he is the typical German " *Gelehrter* " — the productive scholar at his best. Yet, looking back upon his career, Wilamowitz speaks of his books as " the cast off slough of my (his) development. . . . In Germany one is only a scholar in a subsidiary sense: the chief duty is the professorship, and I have always treated it as of paramount importance."[9] Three forms of instruction and work are commonly employed: the lecture to large groups (*Vorlesungen*); practical exercises (*Übungen*), in which assistants coöperate; the seminar, reserved for the elect — nowadays, alas, not quite elect enough, inasmuch as " *Zwang* " (compul-

[8] The bibliography is printed not in the original German edition, but in the English translation (London, 1930), pp. 391–99.

[9] Ulrich von Wilamowitz-Moellendorf: *Erinnerungen, 1814–1914* (Leipzig), *Vorwort*. My subsequent references are to the German edition, not to the English translation.

sory) seminars are at times employed, and a super-seminar privately arranged for the really able. The necessity of presenting to his students his subject in its entirety requires that the professor's scholarship be broad in scope; the necessity of conducting a seminar for advanced students requires that he be active in production. Of course, the balance is not always perfectly struck. But it is surprising how often great investigators are reputed to be conscientious and inspiring teachers. From recent times, one may mention Virchow, Mommsen, Cohnheim, Ludwig, Erich Schmidt, Harnack, Friedrich Müller, Wilamowitz; they attached to themselves groups of devoted students; they formed schools of disciples, who, one by one, carried new ideas into old chairs; and in the general lectures covering their respective subjects in broad outlines they inspired large masses, the scientist often attracting humanistic students, the humanist often attracting students of science and philosophy. Poor teachers exist; trivial and pedantic essays and theses are of course not unknown. Heine's ridicule has not even yet lost its point entirely. Carlyle's gerund grinder may still be found. But even so, German pedantry rests upon scholarship: the philologian or philosopher who spends a lifetime on a trifle after all knows his Plato and Aristotle. And the pedantries which may attach themselves to the Early Fathers are assuredly different from the trivialities that attach themselves to the making of ice cream or the duties of a school janitor. One of the ablest of the younger German administrators writes officially: [10]

"The university is a seat of research, but also the training ground of those who govern. Just as a people is interested in theoretical problems, so at present especially it must train

[10] Unpublished memorandum.

men competent to apply learning at the university level —
quite aside from the stimulus that science can procure from
the realities of life." [11]

And again:

"Specialization that looks to a vocation simply dazes the
German student. This is a point that concerns all faculties
equally: for it is not the business of the university to introduce
the student to all future and possible details, but to train him
in fundamentals so that he can later solve his own problems."

Theoretically the student is equally free. His cre-
dentials being recognized at face value, he can go
where he pleases — thus, if he will, overcrowding
Berlin, while Tübingen might do better by him. He
selects his own teachers; he wanders from one university to another; he may waste his time in fencing or
drinking; he may forego vacations in order to work
as "*Famulus*" in a laboratory or clinic. In the professions where a logical order of studies prevails, he
may take advice or neglect it at his peril. He is treated
like a man from the day he matriculates.

In practice, however, the student who contemplates
passing an examination is less free than theory would
indicate. There are two distinct examinations, that of
the state, which is the gateway to a calling, that of the
university, which leads to the doctorate. While professors figure in the former or are consulted regarding
them, the university itself conducts and regulates the
latter, which is, as a matter of fact, taken by only a
minority of the students. Prescription and compulsion
thus creep in. Sometimes prescription lies in the very
nature of the subject: for example, one cannot pursue
physiology in ignorance of anatomy, or physics in
ignorance of mathematics. In such matters, the sub-

[11] See what I have previously said regarding Pasteur, Haldane, etc.,
pp. 131–32, 256.

ject itself abridges *Lernfreiheit*. But *Lernfreiheit* is further and harmfully abridged by the examinations. Strong efforts, too often successful, are made to increase the number of separate subjects in which students, especially professional students must be examined,[12] either by the state or the university or both. Fortunately attendance is not, as a rule, rigidly " controlled." The student may be industrious or idle; may accomplish his purpose in the minimum number of semesters or may consume more; may stay in one place or go elsewhere. Neither dean nor professor has him on his conscience. He is regarded as competent to care for himself and he takes the full consequences. Finally, he has, when he himself thinks the moment has come, to submit to an examination. No calendar tells him when or precisely on what. As to the number of examinations, one hears it said that there is observable a tendency to divide Germans into two classes: those who examine and those who are examined. Unquestionably, the more the student is examined, the more restricted become his opportunities to pursue his own thoughts and work out his own salvation — the very essence of university work. But it must not be forgotten that neither the German nor the English student can obtain a degree or qualify for examination by arithmetical accumulation of points or hours or credits: he is examined, when he himself thinks he is ready, and he is exposed to any line of questioning that his examiners regard as germane.

I place second the selection of the full professors, which starts with the suggestion to the faculty of three candidates by a committee of the faculty. This list the faculty is free to modify before it is submitted to the

[12] The moment a branch is included in the examinations, the student must register and pay a special fee.

minister. Here is a strong bulwark in the university against the danger of encroachment on the part of the state. And it works both ways — holding both university and ministry up to high standards. The faculty, keen to preserve its prerogatives, must beware of giving the ministry a pretext for appointing an outsider: its list will therefore as a rule be good; and good suggestions having emanated from the faculty, the minister cannot easily justify himself in ignoring them. He is free to appoint one of the three, or, if he so please, an outsider. It happens occasionally that the minister disregards suggestions emanating from the faculty, or refers its nominees back for further considerations, but his power to do so discourages, without of course entirely preventing, internal cliques. Almost invariably the three persons named by the faculty have attained prominence in some other university. Writing, however, of his Greifswald days, half a century or more ago, Wilamowitz in his recent memoirs objects that important personages at Berlin at times prevailed upon the minister to dictate to the faculties of the less conspicuous universities. "Virchow," he writes, "had assistants to find places for, and Mommsen, when I complained, openly said, 'We had no use for him.' So he was good enough for Greifswald." Thus the young and brilliant Erich Schmidt was once passed over for someone who enjoyed the favour of Minister Falk. "That in a small university youth preponderates gives it a special stamp; but it is deplorable when a man remains permanently, just because he should never have been appointed at all." [13]

In Saxony, since the advent of the present government, the ministry has more than once overridden the

[13] *Loc. cit.*, p. 187.

suggestions of a conservative university. In Jena, more recently, an appointment, widely regarded as unfit, was forced upon the university by the ministry. But it has never been impossible for strong individuals to be passed over or to find themselves uncomfortable. "The unity of teaching and research," writes the present *Ministerialdirektor* of the Prussian Education Ministry, "signified during the last century that a scholar could usually reach his goal, if he became a member of a university faculty. But the fate of Schopenhauer, Nietzsche, Dühring, Hartman, Robert Mayer, Freytag, and others, who either knocked in vain at the portals of the universities, or profoundly disillusioned turned from them—that, alas, is still possible. Science must not fail to recognize what it might gain from such spirits." [14] Personal, political, and racial considerations thus mar the ideal working of the German scheme.

Since the War, the more progressive states have had to press more strenuously, on account of the generally conservative attitude of the faculties. At the present moment, a conflict between the ministries and the faculty of law, which is widely criticized, is in prospect. Generally speaking, the German arrangement works best when a strong *Ministerialdirektor* or ministry negotiates with a strong faculty: both being strong, deliberation takes place, and out of deliberation between equals, a sound result usually emerges. If, on the one hand, the ministry is weak, a university clique may prevail; if, on the other hand, the faculty is weak, the ministry may get an unfair advantage. Althoff, the ablest personality in the Education Ministry of Prussia during the last fifty years, undoubt-

[14] Werner Richter, *Die Organisation der Wissenschaft in Deutschland*, p. 4.

edly antagonized the universities at times; but to his judgment of men and his vigour in action the promotion of men like Ranke, Harnack, and Helmholtz, who had already shown their quality, the creation of research institutions, and the amazing development of medicine were largely due. Undoubtedly, so strong and self-willed an individual may make trouble and evoke resistance. Wilamowitz tells us that Althoff preferred to find things out for himself and liked best curators who resembled "messenger boys"; on the other hand, he freely admits Althoff's great reverence for the universities and the immense efforts which he made to raise them to a high level. "His work remains; one who visits his grave in the Botanical Garden should know that there rests an honest and loyal man." [15] On the whole, one may infer from results that the strength of the universities and their great prestige are sufficient proof that, generally speaking, legitimate considerations have prevailed as frequently as is humanly possible.

The third point I have in mind is the "wandering" of the university instructor. Though there is a family likeness throughout the German, Swiss, and Austrian universities, they are not locally inbred; a man will get his degree and become *Privatdozent* in Munich after having studied previously at two or three other universities; he will be called as *Extraordinarius* (reader or lecturer, as the English would say, associate professor, as one would say in America) to Tübingen or Graz; he will next be called as professor to Bonn; thereafter, if he continues productive, to Leipzig, and perhaps finally to Berlin or Vienna, though some of

[15] *Loc. cit.*, pp. 199, 251. He remarks, further, that during his $13\frac{1}{2}$ years at Göttingen only once did the ministry appoint a professor not proposed by the university, viz., a case in which the faculty had no expert; the choice was universally accepted as admirable. (*Ibid.*, p. 250.)

the ablest men, despite calls to the metropolis, cling to
the smaller universities, on account of their "*Ge-
mütlichkeit*." The progress and the financial welfare
of the university depend on a severe nation-wide competition, in the winning of which the main factors are
two — fame as a teacher, distinction as an investigator; the lack of either element is likely to be fatal
to promotion.

A still more effective guarantee of both freedom and
scholarship is to be found in the "*Privatdozentur.*"
The docents are the recruits from among whom the professors are ultimately obtained. The ministry has a
veto, even the possibility of initiative, in the choice of
the professor; it has no voice whatsoever in granting
" the licence to teach" which is wholly the prerogative
of the faculty. But the "*Privatdozentur*" is more than
a bulwark of academic freedom and security. In its
pre-War form it was a large group of persons who
entered a severe and unpaid novitiate in the hope
of making an academic career. There could be no
better proof of the esteem in which the universities
were held. The German student had won his doctorate
on the basis of a thesis, presumably showing some
capacity to do original work, and an examination,
presumably showing a competent knowledge of the
literature of his subject. He wanted to make a career
in scholarship or science. Did he get a university appointment which at the crucial moment of his development made him comfortable and overloaded him with
teaching routine? Not at all. He got an unsalaried
licence to teach, became, as they say, *Privatdozent,*
offered a lecture course or two, and in any one of a
variety of ways attached himself to a laboratory, a
clinic, or a library, in order that he might continue his
productive work. The *Privatdozenten* formed the

nursery from which, as I have said, the German university selected its *Extraordinarii* on the basis of teaching ability and scholarly productivity; from the *Extraordinarii* of all Germany and German-speaking countries in the fashion above described, the *Ordinarii* were selected; at every stage the two factors counted; the candidate must have been able to expound his subject, he must have produced. It was a severe system: often the *Privatdozent* had for years hard sledding, especially if the *Ordinarius* was indifferent or hostile to him, as might happen. Thus it resulted in a learned proletariat, sometimes unhappy; but in every field — in science, in the humanities, in law, in medicine, and in theology — it developed a host of workers, a supply for the universities, for the secondary schools, for the governmental services, and for industry. As a well thought-out institution for the doing of certain definite and difficult things, the German university — the essential features of which I have just described — was a better piece of mechanism than any other nation has as yet created.

Finally, the German student is, like the professor, a wanderer, though, for financial reasons, less so nowadays than formerly. The loyalty which marks the Harvard man in the United States, the Oxford man in England, is unknown in Germany, except perhaps to the extent of a sentimental attachment to the university in which the student spent his first semester. There is no such thing as a Berlin man, a Greifswald man, a Vienna man. Unquestionably, this indifference is costly: it costs some of the personal and institutional attachments that add to the amenities of life in English-speaking countries. It costs something from the standpoint of the student as human being. None the less, whatever the personal or social loss, intellectually the German gains far more than he loses through wandering. It has its disadvantages: for example, it enables an indifferent student to seek his degree wherever it is most easily attained. But what is more important, it enables the able student to go where his subject is most vigorously prosecuted, and it stimulates the professor to do his best in order to attract the most competent students; for on the quality of his students depend the fame of seminar and laboratory and to some extent the professor's income.

v

The traditional faculties are the faculties of philosophy, theology, medicine, and law, each headed by a dean, who is, however, less heavily burdened than his American colleague, partly, I suppose, because he deals with more homogeneous tasks. The faculty of philosophy is the backbone of the structure. Theology has had its day; medicine and law are too near to practical life: they are constantly in danger of drifting into *Fachschulen*, though, thus far, medicine, concerned though it so largely is with students who expect to be physicians, has more successfully maintained its scientific character than have the medical schools of any other country. Philosophy — the faculty of arts and science — remains the fortress, as Humboldt intended. No other country, during the nineteenth century, assembled equally eminent groups of scientists and scholars, provided them with equal facilities, or paid them equal deference. On the whole, the faculty of philosophy has maintained its eminence, shaken a bit, though it has been, by the forces which I have mentioned. Two additional reservations need, however, to be made. The largest of the universities, finding the single faculty of philosophy unwieldy, have separated arts and science into two distinct groups — a loss to both and to the organic character of the university. Again, while language, literature, philosophy, mathematics, and the sciences have been objectively pursued, the social sciences were during the monarchical regime gravely hampered by one set of prejudices and may, under a social democracy, find themselves hindered by another. At one time, the historic approach indeed yielded significant results; but it has come to prove an obstacle to the realistic study which, despite its absurdities, has been developed in the United States and, without its absurdities, at the London School of Economics, Cambridge, and some of the provincial English universities. To the rise of social democracy, which, when the moment suddenly came, was to overturn all Germany and even make trouble for the universities, the German universities were singularly blind. They kept to history and abstractions, when fearless and disinterested scholars should have been studying the phenomena of industrial life and the social basis of law. Karl Marx was a phenomenon of the first importance; yet I have been credibly assured that the economic authority most highly regarded before the Revolution dismissed with a paragraph or so the philosophy that is now most influential in the *Reich*. That peculiar dangers attend the attempt to deal scientifically with politics, sociology, and law, I have freely admitted. The chaos of present-day American effort is sufficient proof of that. None the less, these fields contain phenomena, which, whatever the dangers attendant on their study, are more accessible than the Middle Ages. There must be a detached, scientific, and systematic method of observing and reflecting on the problems of politics, economics, and law as there is a detached, scientific, and systematic method of reflecting on the problems of disease. Professor Mendelssohn-Bartholdy's *Institut für Auswärtige Politik* (for foreign affairs), at once thoroughly objective and scholarly, is an admirable instance in point. One need not restrict one's self to the post-mortem; neither, on the other hand, need one, as so many educators and sociologists have done, abandon one's sense of humour, one's sense of values, or one's objectivity.

The beginning of a more realistic development in the social sciences is occasionally observable prior to the Revolution. The biographer of the late Dr. Stresemann calls attention to the fact that his doctor's thesis was entitled "The Development of the Bottled Beer Trade in Berlin." One can imagine what an American would have made of the topic; but Stresemann saw in it an evidence of the decline of the "independent middle class"; and it is from this point of view that his thesis was written.[16] His career is an excellent example of the legitimate way in which universities may play a part in public life. He received, first, a sound secon-

[16] "But before this he had published two scientific papers of some importance. The one, which appeared in the supplement of the Cologne *Allgemeine Zeitung*, dealt with questions of currency; the other in the *Zeitschrift für die gesamte Staatswissenschaft*, on 'Big stores, their origins, development and economic importance.' This is, as it were, the complement to that on the 'Bottled-Beer Trade.' In the one he describes how a class was destroyed in the general economic development; in the other he draws a picture of the rise of the huge general store and proceeds to the question of the economic and social significance of the great retail businesses. The underlying premise is the same in both papers. That on the stores may have been prompted by the demand of the individual trades for state protection in the form of special taxes on the general stores.

Stresemann denies that taxes may be imposed as a penalty on the efficient and progressive to help those who are too feeble to advance. He points to the development of industry, which crushed a multitude of independent tradesmen, but was ultimately the cause of a rise to new prosperity by the whole nation. He voices the conviction, which he never ceased to hold, that in economic and political matters one can never arrest a development, but can only guide it into the right channels." Rochus, Baron von Rheinbaben, *Stresemann: The Man and the Statesman*, pp. 30, 32.

dary education; then, at the university, a general education on the philosophical side without any " *ad hoc* " reference. Leaving the university, an educated man, he embarked in business. The War and the post-War situation created new problems, to deal with which no one had been trained or could have been trained. But the lack of *ad hoc* training was no obstacle: " Chance," as Pasteur said, " favours the prepared mind." And in the deepest sense, Stresemann had been prepared by training in method. It does not matter that 75% of German university students subsequently enter practical careers. Their education has enabled them to bring minds trained through teaching and research to bear on the problems they encounter. The uncritical even in Germany cry out, more or less, for *Fach* training; but, as I have shown, thus far, fortunately without much success. At the risk of tiresome iteration, I call attention again to the superiority of education over the *ad hoc* training by which education in America is being blocked.

To the four faculties, just discussed, no one attributes any peculiar sanctity. Theology could be dropped, if religious feeling were less intense. To the addition of other faculties there is no objection on the score of principle. Faculties of household arts, education, business, journalism, and pharmacy, could be at any time created, if the German universities and the education ministries were persuaded that such faculties belong within the framework of a university — on a par with faculties of philosophy, law and medicine. There is unanimous agreement that such is not the case. The one faculty regarding which a serious question exists is engineering. Should it have been incorporated as a fifth faculty? Would it have been better, had this procedure been followed? Lacking the historic and cultural interest of medicine, it resembles medicine in the combination of pure and applied science. Nevertheless, a different line was taken. "*Technische Hochschulen*" of university status — devoted, that is, to teaching and research — were either created anew or developed out of polytechnics. They are now on a par with universities, and teachers move freely to and fro. Originally the question of numbers was not serious; today, when they would add upwards of 22,000 students to already overcrowded universities, that question cannot be lightly passed over. As to the principles involved, I quote from a brief memorandum which was prepared for me:

"There were" — if I may slightly paraphrase the words — "fifty years ago two possibilities: the '*Technische Hochschule*' might have been incorporated in the universities as an additional faculty, or a separate institution on the same level as the university might have been created. Germany chose the latter; existing schools of technology were expanded into '*Technische Hochschulen*' which stood both legally and qualitatively on the same footing as the universities.

Was this sound procedure? Opinions differ. On the one hand, one could maintain that, had the technical faculties been incorporated in universities, either the academic spirit might have been damaged or the practical side of technical training might have suffered. Separation, on the same legal and qualitative basis, forced the technical schools to strive to reach the academic standard and thus provoked a wholesome and productive competition.

There are, however, weighty arguments on the other side. The solution chosen necessitated the creation of additional professorships in chemistry, physics, and mathematics, and increased the difficulty of avoiding instruction at a trade (*Fach*) level. This difficulty is the more acutely felt, as the opinion gains ground that the primary need of the engineer is a thorough and general training in science as such. In consequence, chairs of philosophy and even philology have been created in the '*Technische Hochschulen*.' In this direction, Saxony has gone further by setting up in the '*Technische Hochschule*' at Dresden a division devoted to the study of science from the humanistic point of view ('*Kulturwissenschaftliche Abteilung*'). The question naturally arises as to whether the 'humanization' of these faculties might not have been more readily accomplished, had they been placed within the framework of the university."

VI

But while additional faculties have not been created, additional chairs were created, until post-War poverty prevented — chairs of constitutional history, international law, economic geography, and education — as Spranger notes.[17] Since the War, chairs in orthodox subjects have been partially diverted to new subjects, for which the state was financially unable to provide; a few precious marks have been wasted on subjects that have no proper place in a university at all. There is, for example, no chair of genetics in Germany; but a professor of anatomy or biology may leave the routine work of the department to assistants and cultivate genetics, though he is still called professor of anatomy or biology; or he may reduce the lectures connected with his chair in order to lecture on a topic that is not represented in the faculty. Less happy is the creation at Hamburg of an associate professorship (*Extraordinarius*) for physical training [18] and equally dubious the *Institut für Betriebssociologie* at Charlottenburg. Indefensible is the associate professorship of journalism at Berlin. Its story is interest-

[17] E. Spranger, *Wandlungen im Wesen der Universität seit 100 Jahren.* (Leipzig, 1913), p. 16.

[18] The *Hamburger Universitäts Zeitung* (May 15, 1929) contains a vigorous protest by Ernst Möller against recognition by the university of " *Leibesübungen* " (physical exercise) as a legitimate subject of university lecturers. The vigour with which the introduction of " *Fächer* " is being opposed may, I believe, be relied on to keep them out of the universities.

ing. At Heidelberg an inconspicuous series of lectures on the history of the press — a topic legitimate enough, — had long been given. In America journalism had been lifted by Columbia and the state universities to the rank of a "profession," though every day it was becoming more and more a business. The stubborn and conservative universities, it was urged, alone prevented its recognition as a profession in Germany. The education ministries did not deceive themselves, but they bent before the storm, holding fast to the "central core," yielding as little as they could to embittered and chagrined business interest and popular clamour. So a *Lehrstuhl* of *Zeitungswissenschaft* (journalistic science) was set up at Berlin; shortly it procured for itself an *Institut* — a laboratory or library, where eight hundred newspapers are clipped and filed, to what ultimate end, who knows? Lectures were planned on the conventional model; likewise, practical courses. A philosophy was evolved "to suit the case." It begins with "*Praxis*," the analysis of which is "*Forschung*" (research); thence are elaborated "*Vorlesungen*" (lecture courses) and "*Kurse*" (courses) which train reporters, musical critics, literary critics, etc. The whole group expresses the "*Wesen*" (the inner nature or secret) of "*Journalismus*." *Journalismus* thus "makes a noise" like a *Wissenschaft;* but it will have as little effect on journalism in Germany as in America. A sociological phenomenon of immense interest and importance, journalism deserves to be studied as such within a modern university; but with that the interest and power of the university stop. Very truly Wilamowitz remarks:

"He who is constantly digging for treasure and is delighted if he finds earthworms will soon dig for earthworms. But thou

[333]

shalt not be discouraged if digging for treasure, thou findest earthworms: only throw them away." [19]

As irrelevant to university aims is the task imposed by some states of partly training trade (*Gewerbe*) teachers, who are required to attend the university for at least three semesters, taught apparently by assistants or *Privatdozenten* and examined not by university or teachers but by the *Gewerbeschulbehörde*. They are of course inferior intellectually and, if justice is done to them, as it ought to be, they would lower standards. Perhaps this is good for the trades; but it is very bad for the universities. The load falls mainly upon the younger men, whose income is increased; but the drain on time and energy is not negligible; and there is constant danger that in consequence of increased numbers and multiplicity of tasks the university may tend to fall apart into a group of vocational schools (*Fachschulen*). Indeed, not infrequently one hears it said in the research institutes that more and more the university will become a teaching institution, leaving research to be cultivated by institutes created for the purpose. I do not myself believe it; but increased numbers, increased teaching burdens, increased administrative responsibilities are all ominous. The peril is less serious than the corresponding peril in the United States; but every effort to make the university serve society or industry directly at a lowered intellectual level is deplorable. Do what one will, distraction increases in modern life. The university cannot protect itself by becoming cloistral. There remains, as its sole protection, inflexible adherence to its standards and ideals, and a constant struggle in the direction of simplification.

Certain other disfigurations one notes with regret,

[19] *Loc. cit.*, p. 104.

though they are without practical importance. Only journalism has obtained a chair; but stenography has crept into the *Verzeichniss* through *Lektoren* and physical training through " *Turn-und Sportlehrer.*" Of course, they do not count when it comes to degrees; they have not won and will never win the sort of academic recognition which has been accorded to them in America. Stenography is a useful skill, and it is better for the German student to fence and swim and box than to drink beer. But the academic type of announcement and arrangement is neither necessary nor appropriate; the university itself need not provide instruction in stenography, for that may be readily procured elsewhere; a gymnasium for physical exercise need not be decked out to resemble an institute or a laboratory. Flattering the self-importance of unimportant or subsidiary persons is a dangerous business, as America proves; it is less dangerous in Germany; but it derogates from the dignity of the university even in Germany. The university can play its part in the very centre of thought and action without cheapening itself.

It is interesting to contrast the attitude of the professor of journalism with that of the professor of *Literatur-* and *Theaterwissenschaft* at Kiel, Berlin, and elsewhere. Resembling each other outwardly, the journalists in the German as in the American university endeavour to train men for jobs. But the professor of *Theaterwissenschaft* is not trying to train either actors or playwrights. He is studying the theatre as a literary vehicle precisely as he might study the lyric. In his " *Institut* " he collects stage models or victrola records — but solely that he may exhibit things in the concrete as a professor of art might exhibit an engraving or a professor of architecture a model. He draws a sharp line between his own work and *Praxis*. He is not concerned to train people to write plays. They are either born to do it, or they learn it in the hurly-burly of the actual world. What one can do is to study the drama and even ways of producing drama precisely as one would study any other art form. This is obviously only an attempt to enlarge the grasp of literature so as to include serious forms of theatrical art, a very different thing from an attempt to train writers, critics of plays, authors of " movies " and " talkies," and journalists. It amounts in the end to an enlarged and enriched conception of literature.

VII

There is a general consensus of opinion, however, that the standard of university matriculation has been distinctly lowered through the too rapid extension of university opportunities to students whose previous preparation has been too varied to be uniform or solid. The pre-War professor addressed a body made up of graduates of three schools of approximately equal severity; a professor today addresses students who come from schools of gymnasial character and those from a variety of " *Aufbauschulen.*" The student body is therefore distinctly more miscellaneous in character than formerly; it is also much larger. Between 1907 and 1929, the number of universities increased by only two — Frankfurt, Cologne and Hamburg being added and Strasbourg dropped in 1919; the student body rose during the same period, however, from 45,656 to 90,743.[20] The number of minor teaching posts had of course also increased; but there was noth-

[20] *Deutsche Hochschulstatistik* (Berlin, 1929–30), p. viii. In the same period, the number of students at the *Technische Hochschulen* increased from 11,206, to 22,650, — practically the same proportion. *Ibid.*, p. ix.

ing like a corresponding or adequate increase in professorships. Between 1911 and 1929 there was a slight rise in the enrolment in the philosophical faculty, but a marked increase in medicine. Moreover, the students are worse off financially than before the War. Coming to the university with insufficient resources, large numbers are obliged to eke out a livelihood by doing odd jobs or to choose lines of study that are to be readily profitable. The increase in the *"Brotstudenten"* undoubtedly brings in some fine types of earnestness; it also brings in the practically-minded, whose presence tends to make the university a collection of *"Fachschulen."* Size itself tends in this direction. Lacking the absurdities that swell the enrolment of American universities, Berlin had in the winter semester 1929–30 14,126 students, Munich 8500, Leipzig 6387. As faculties increase in number, their members scatter through the great cities, seeing less and less of one another. A great scientist once remarked to me that a total stranger might attend a faculty meeting of the University of Berlin, rise, and make a speech without being ejected, because the professors are already so numerous, though not numerous enough for the student body, that they do not even know one another. He contended that, if, including all faculties and all subjects, more than 5,000 students are assembled in one university, the university is in danger of disintegration. For most students at the large universities the contact between members of the teaching staff and between teachers and students has been too much impaired.

Even the lowering of the standard of matriculation has not greatly affected the number of students who come from the working classes. It has been estimated that at this moment not exceeding three per cent of the university students come from the working classes, and the number was formerly even smaller. But former folly and injustice could not be cured and have not been cured by flinging the doors open to schools that are below the historic secondary schools in intellectual value. Sudden reversal of educational policy can only result in overcrowding the universities and the professions, in lowering the level of university instruction, and in forcing faculties to adopt devices, such as the creation of super-seminars, from which the insufficiently trained are excluded. A new issue has thus been created: in the nineteenth century, the German university protected quality at the expense of social distinction; that distinction has disappeared. But the importance of protecting quality has not disappeared. Will the Republic have the courage and intelligence to protect it? Germany is struggling towards democracy; but democracy is a social and political, not an intellectual possibility, beyond the fact that to the aristocracy of intellect every individual should be eligible on the basis of ability without regard to any other consideration whatsoever. To this position — that the university should be accessible on democratic terms, the Revolution brought Germany, a tremendous step in advance. Will some efficient means of excluding the mediocre and unfit be devised? It would, indeed, be a sorry day not only for Germany, but for the rest of the world if an aristocracy of intellect should become impossible in a German social and political democracy. The ministries are alive to the danger: they make no secret of their dismay, while confident at heart that they will eventually conquer.

VIII

Sound in principle and promising in practice are the steps taken mainly since the Revolution in the field of adult education and university extension. The inroads which popular teaching has made on American universities I discussed at great length because "service" has well-nigh destroyed the very conception of the university as an institution of learning. England has pursued a sane and conservative policy. It may, however, well turn out that the Germans have done best of all. At a time of vehement democratic uprising, the university has kept its head. The sound attitude has been admirably described by Spranger, whom I venture to paraphrase:

"I need not urge" — so runs his argument — "that a modern university professor should not be blind to the social conditions of modern life. But if this idea is loosely conceived, if holidays and free hours are devoted to giving popular courses, the university as an institution of learning is imperilled, for as such it must remain a selective, aristocratic institution. The university teacher must strive upward; the spread of knowlege among the people at large he has to leave to others. To this same category belong the temptations which come to investigators in the natural and intellectual sciences from the business world. There is danger that gradually scientific literature may be regarded as just so many commercial 'orders,' whose value will be determined by business considerations. The person who treads this path will soon sacrifice his scientific sense of values to a commercial or social sense of values. Indeed we live in an era characterized by a mania for 'instruction.' Every possible subject wants to win university recognition. Let us consider whether the university is best adapted to popular purposes and whether the public does not expect from disjointed lectures and courses results that cannot be thus obtained, because all the essential prerequisites are lacking." [21]

[21] *Loc. cit.*, pp. 20-21.

Prior to the War, the demand for adult education, growing with the increase in the number and influence of the Social Democrats, was unsatisfactorily met, partly by associations of workingmen, which offered one-sided and superficial instruction, partly by the universities, whose professors, out of touch with the workingman, talked over his head. The present movement, directed under the terms of the Weimar Constitution by the *Reich* itself, is concerned not only with the popularization of science, but with the invention of methods directed to cultural ends. Thus the workman himself contributes experience and problems. University extension and adult education are thus genuine; the *ad hoc* rubbish that flourishes in America is not only unknown to the university, but it is equally remote from the non-university movement. In the large cities evening *Hochschulen* have been organized, sometimes with the participation of professors, but never under their direction; home circles are also formed in which the less advanced are enabled to study together. Diplomas are never given; the work is done for its own sake, and, as at Coleg Harlech, distinctly *not* as a means of getting ahead.[22]

IX

The German universities are commonly referred to as *Hochschulen*. But the two terms are not synonymous. The term university is legally protected — it

[22] A considerable literature, discussing the problems of the subject, has already appeared. The reader, interested by reason of the false path followed by American universities, will be particularly helped by Paul Steinmetz's *Die deutsche Volkshochschulbewegung* (Karlsruhe, 1929); Franz Angermann's *Die freie Volksbildung* (Jena, 1928). Official publications can be obtained from the *Archiv für Volksbildung im Reichministerium des Innern*, Platz der Republik 6, Berlin.

is, indeed, embodied in the fundamental law of the land. But with an indifference that is American rather than German, the term *Hochschule*, by which the university is also designated, may also refer to a dancing school, (*Tanz Hochschule*), an establishment for physical training (*Hochschule für Leibesübungen*), or an academy for training in politics and international affairs (*Hochschule für Politik*).[23] A *Volks Hochschule*, which is really a contradiction in terms, was established in Berlin in 1879. Beginning with the current year evening *Gymnasien* have been established: inevitably, therefore, there has arisen a demand for an evening university, to be established in Berlin and to be limited to an enrolment of 100 gifted and determined persons. The suggestion is naturally based on American and to some extent on English examples, and frankly assumes that the German university has in the main ceased to be devoted to research. To be sure, the proposed evening university will be a "*Fach*" school. Nothing could be better calculated to pull the real university down and to break it into bits. If evening classes for practical purposes are feasible, there is no objection to them. But no limitation, whether in respect to size or in respect to location, will make a university of them. Nor will any limitation in respect to size or location long hold fast. American experience, if consulted, would warn other nations against lowering the idea of the university, on the ground that, when once lowering has begun, the idea itself will soon be lost. Let the service be rendered, but under a name that distinguishes it sharply. And if the university has

[23] A general account of the "*Hochschulen für besondere Fachgebiete*" is given by Lexis in Vol. IV, part 2, of *Die Unterrichtskurse im Deutschen Reich* (Berlin, 1904). Though out of date, the book is in the main still a reliable general guide.

already been injured, let it retrace its steps instead
of going further in the wrong direction.[24]

The rapid development of German trade under the
Empire led naturally to the establishment of schools
of business and colonial institutes in Berlin, Cologne
and Hamburg. Institutes of this kind meet a need —
a practical need, all the more urgent at a time when
the universities were teaching economics from an historical and abstract standpoint. But, quite aside from
this, they can perform tasks that simply do not belong to universities, as, once more, America has unintentionally demonstrated. The point was not clear
to the Germans at the outset: hence the present University of Cologne was developed out of the *Handelshochschule,* the present University of Hamburg out
of the Colonial Institute. But as the two universities
approximate the sound university type, the *Handelshochschule* at Cologne and the Colonial Institute at
Hamburg are more and more being discarded. One
still observes traces of both — for the universities have
just completed their first decade. But I was assured
confidently at Cologne, that, five years hence, the last
trace of the *Handelshochschule* will have vanished.[25]

The reason is plain. The two things start from a
different point and aim at different goals. The university faculties of economics, politics, and law have
no practical purposes to serve; they are conceived
from a scientific standpoint. There is peril — peril
that they may deal only with abstractions and theo-
ries. In my opinion, the sound attitude is to attack the
phenomena of industry, politics, law, or medicine in a
scientific spirit — nowise holding aloof from them, but

[24] *Die Berliner Abend-Universität — Ein Vorschlag von* Prof. Dr.
A. Silbermann *und Handelgerichtsrat* Oscar E. Haac (Berlin, 1920).

[25] At Munich the *Handelshochschule* is part of the *Technische Hochschule.*

endeavouring to analyse them, to classify them, and to see them in perspective. It is not the university's concern to train business men; it was not the university's business to train Stresemann to head a chocolate combination; it did far better by him when it educated him so that he could indeed head the chocolate-makers, but he could also in Germany's hour of need hold his own with foreign secretaries bred to the career.[26]

The *Handelshochschule* started, first, because the university faculties of law and economics shrank from too close contact with phenomena; second, because, through the evolution of modern business and the breakdown of apprenticeship, there was no institution offering specific business training both to students who were, and to students who were not, gymnasial graduates. On this basis, there is a sound reason for the continued existence of a separate *Handelshochschule* of high grade. The Berlin *Handelshochschule* has in mind a practical task which the university cannot discharge — the training of men and women for business careers, and it is, fortunately, as I think, responsible not to the Education Ministry, but to the Ministry of Trade. It offers a business diploma to " *Kaufleute* " (merchants) at the close of six semesters of study; the degree of Doctor of Commerce, an unwarranted use of the Doctorate, at the close of eight. Special students, lacking complete gymnasial training can also be admitted; and practical men lecture on their several callings. I see no objection to this; it is simply not university work and does not and should not contribute to overloading the universities.

[26] " As a young doctor of political economy, Stresemann had to familiarize himself in practice with quite novel conditions, when, in 1901, he took over his first industrial post as Manager of the Association of German Chocolate Manufacturers." Rochus (*loc. cit.*), p. 54.

To some extent of course, the *Handelshochschulen* overlap the university faculties of economics and law; but that is always happening. The chemist in the medical clinic overlaps the chemist in other clinics and in the department of chemistry. Indeed, only so is the web of knowledge woven tightly. But in each case, the point of view varies. The staff of the *Handelshochschule* is interested in the practice of business, selling, buying, accounting, trade. They are absorbed in doing things, getting things done, training persons to do them. That point of view marks them off from the university faculty without sterilizing either group. The Harvard Business School is essentially such an institution: it has its place — but not within a university. So the Berlin *Handelshochschule* seems to me to have a place.[27] Very properly it undertakes to train men and women for business and industry with a faculty made up of concrete-minded and thorough research workers, who care mainly for present-day needs and problems. This leaves to the university the main burden of developing in a scientific spirit economics, politics, philosophy, and law; and indeed, the further task of providing politics, finance, and industry with men of deep and broad university training. It is surely not without significance that the heads of great banks, industries, industrial combinations, and ministers of state are so frequently university "doctors," who might, in many cases, well have been university professors: Dr. Schacht, Dr. Stresemann, Dr. Marx, Dr. Luther, Dr. Wirth, Dr. Kastl, to mention a few that come readily to mind.

[27] Its whole spirit differs from that of the university faculty of medicine, for, even though 95% of the graduates in medicine become mere practitioners, the faculty is fundamentally interested in the problems of disease.

X

The relationship to the state awakens apprehensions in both England and America, in neither of which it would work satisfactorily. Yet from the standpoint of research and training, it has worked better in Germany than either English or American organization in their respective countries. If the university has not absolutely and entirely preserved its independence, as I have already pointed out, it has substantially succeeded in so doing.

We have already observed that in America, where both endowed and state-supported institutions exist, politics, personalities, and low standards may create a veritable chaos; and that in England, where two ancient institutions command the situation and large municipalities seek to develop universities on a coöperative basis, evils sometimes on the conservative, sometimes on the material, side creep in. Taking matters as they stood in 1914, the Germans with a state monopoly, in which the university is a legal partner on equal terms, did better than either: the universities were more highly developed, more nearly autonomous, far more highly respected and exerted a wider influence. Nevertheless, it must be clear that they were not without defects and that the present situation itself is not without danger. Under the old regime, as I have said, the university was a jewel in the imperial crown. It was never grossly subservient to the court; but in subtle ways it came under the influence of the court; it became gradually more and more conservative in its thinking, especially in the realm of economics and politics. The exclusion of the working classes is having its effects: for now that a Social Democrat may become a professor, there are few or none who have been completely trained: shut out, as boys from the *Gymnasien,* they could not enter the universities where they might have been educated for their present opportunities — assuredly a severe criticism of the former régime. In consequence, the universities in the more progressive states are widely regarded as unsympathetic. In the endeavour to correct leaning to the right, they have in occasional instances been rudely forced to lean to the left. Perhaps an occasional error in that direction will do no permanent harm, if it eventually impresses upon all parties the fact that the university has no concern with either right or left, no concern with political parties or policies at all: the university's objectivity and disinterestedness must be recognized by all alike. The recent resignation of the Prussian Minister of Education, Dr. Becker, who endeavoured "to stand above parties," is deplorable because it shows clearly that the ministry of education is a party prize. And yet, Dr. Becker, himself subsequently the victim of politics under the new order, while severely critical of the defects of the old, is still confident that the university will not lose sight of its essential function — teaching and research in an atmosphere of *Lehrfreiheit* and *Lernfreiheit* — and can still insist at the conclusion of a severe criticism, " at heart, the German university is sound." [28]

The explanation of the general security and independence of the university lies partly in the realm of ideas, partly in the manner of organization. The conception of the university as the home of *Wissenschaft* (both the natural and intellectual sciences) was launched with such tremendous emphasis that its hold on German imagination has not been seriously weak-

[28] C. H. Becker, *Gedanken zur Hochschulreform* (Leipzig, 1920), p. 17.

ened. Political problems, internal and external, have arisen; applied science has become of enormous importance; the business man and the industrialist have become perhaps the most prominent figures on the horizon. Yet "*Wissenschaft*" remains fundamental — fundamental to the solution of problems, fundamental to technical development, fundamental to the operations of the industrialist. And more and more, as knowledge increases in volume and life increases in complexity, an adequate provision for thought has also to be made. The changes that, on the surface, seem to threaten the university, thus result in increasing its importance — its importance indeed along the very lines of Humboldt's thinking — as an institution where men must be left free to learn and to teach.

Its organization was likewise in most directions favourable to freedom. The universities are, it is true, almost entirely dependent upon the state for funds. Departments cannot be developed unless the state provides the money; new chairs cannot be established without the sanction of the education ministry. The state regulates and participates in examinations; in large measure, it manages the budget — a great relief, as a matter of fact, even though in the absence of ideals and traditions, it might become a source of peril. Thus the power of the ministry is apparently great enough to make the university subservient. The safeguards are law, idea, and tradition: for the German university is protected in its autonomy and independence by all three. The German professor and administrator still discuss with force and learning the concept (*Wesen*) of the university: neither the nation nor the university is for a moment allowed to forget the historic and legal idea underlying the university, its achievements, and the national need for its development. The German has an almost religious reverence for the state; but so also for the university. The Republican Constitution, which changed so much, left the university untouched, despite its recognized conservatism: an amazing testimony to the respect in which the institution as such is held.[29]

XI

I have spoken of university standards — of the lowering of standards through the influx of a larger and more miscellaneous student body and through other causes. But it would be erroneous to infer that a uniform standard has ever obtained. On the whole, the spirit of a university is a more effective guarantee of high standard than any mechanical device, any kind of organization can possibly be. Yet though Germany was and is so nearly unanimous in its university creed, it has never been able to maintain a uniform standard. Within limits — narrower limits, by far, in my opinion than quite naturally prevail in America — the various faculties of a given university differ in respect of severity; again within a given faculty, individual professors vary; and neither faculty nor government can intervene to uphold standards if a university, a faculty, or a group of professors is relatively indifferent. Pride and tradition prevent a deplorable lapse; yet a student, found to be unsatisfactory at one place, has been known to be recommended to go elsewhere — "for there you can get a degree." The theses presented and accepted do not deal with the trivial or inane; they may be of little or no value, but they never deal

[29] The political upheavals which occur in American universities are beyond imagining in Germany. When one reads a German criticism of German universities, one must constantly bear in mind this fundamental difference.

with " our girls and what they tell us." It is, however, worth asking whether even in Germany the thesis should not be made optional — an exceptionally able, voluntary thesis earning for its author a mark of special distinction such as " *cum laude*," not otherwise obtainable. During the War, publication was not required; and the minimum thesis accepted could be of very inferior quality, indeed. In the medical faculty generally the thesis is today a merely formal requirement: it would probably be dropped, but for the income it brings into the faculty.[30] How can the ordinary overworked medical student be required to " produce " when he can with the utmost difficulty learn what is requisite? History, philology, and science make a better showing. In these subjects not infrequently, a professor assigns an advanced student some aspect of a large subject upon which he is himself engaged: the value of the thesis as such turns upon the question as to whether the student is virtually a technician or actually an investigator, working, of course, under adequate supervision. At Berlin, the doctorate in law has been held to a high level, the number of candidates annually approved being very small; the same cannot be said of all universities.

Standards may also be impaired in another way. The university trains scholars and scientists, of whom, of course, most expect to enter professional or business life. The doctorate is in theory the mark of the scholar; the *Staatsexamen* the mark of fitness for a *Beruf,* (calling). But the line between the *Staatsexamen,* which tests the individual's fitness to engage in a career, and the *Doktor Examen,* which tests his scholarship, has become more or less obscure. In the medi-

[30] The income does not go to professors, but into a fund drawn upon for general purposes.

cal faculty, a student who has passed the former passes the latter as a matter of course — an obvious departure from sound theory: for if the two are thus identical, one examination would suffice. That in practice the German professor is at times confused as between his duty to his subject and the requirements of the examinations cannot be gainsaid. At the outset of the 19th century, the subject was the thing; as the century advanced and the state needed trained men for its service, the *Staatsexamen* gained in relative importance. Even prior to the War, the doctorate, as the outward sign of primary interest in science and scholarship as such, had suffered; since the War, economic factors have still further emphasized the *Staatsexamen*. Spranger maintained in 1912 that research was tolerated and encouraged by the state because there was no getting along practically without it.[31] On the other hand, a decade later, Becker maintains the opposite thesis.[32]

XII

The changes that may be credited to the War are both imponderable and ponderable. Among the former must be reckoned, in the first instance, a reaction against the positivistic spirit that was the immediate result of technology and worldly success. The student body has been to some extent permeated by a new idealism. At the same time economic need has forced students and teachers to repair their losses and fend for the future as best they can. Up to the War, German

[31] *Loc. cit.*, p. 15.

[32] *Loc. cit.*: " *Der reine wissenschaftliche Geist der Forschung ist noch lebendig.*" (p. 17). And again: " *Die deutschen Professoren fühlen sich alle in erster Linie als Forscher* " (p. 18). There is no real inconsistency between the position of Wilamowitz (quoted p. 318) and that of Becker, *if the level of teaching is high enough.*

student life was delightful enough for those who were members of student organizations, but socially bleak for those who stood aloof. The relations of the professor with his favourite pupils, those who could ultimately be expected to form his " school," were indeed always admirable. But a large mass remained outside this charmed circle. Since the War the university has taken more notice of them. This fact is expressed in the so-called " youth movement," distinctly idealistic in character. Practically it takes various forms: 2,500 shelters have been erected in Germany for the use of students who in their vacations wander about the fatherland, imbued with a different outlook on life than was implied in duelling and fencing; the student and the common man have come more closely together; the influence of the woman student has, in this respect, made for good; student exchanges with foreign countries have induced wholesome and stimulating comparisons; student houses have encouraged a more humane and sociable type of contact; finally, the movement towards self-help, centred in Dresden, has assisted the deserving student of every social class to make his way in the university. On the other hand, poverty, too severe and too long continued, may lower and materialize the student's morale, may destroy idealism, may lead him to attach an exorbitant importance to money, so that the student who works his way may suffer intellectually. Again, new groups have been formed: *Studentenschaften* and societies (*Fachschaften*) that can present the students' viewpoint to the faculty. The influence of these organizations was all to the good as long as the organizations were merely local in character. Unfortunately, amalgamation was undertaken: and immediately politics entered in a highly conservative

and objectionable form.[33] The authorities thereupon
became hostile. Only Bavaria and Württemburg now
grant legal recognition to the "*Studentenschaft.*"
None the less, despite this disaster, the student body
is more alive as an entity than previously. Economic
conditions permitting, the more wholesome student
life of England and America — more wholesome, despite some of its attendant absurdities — may be expected to develop in Germany.

XIII

It is, I know, easy to over-estimate the importance
of instruments and organization, and an American is,
of all persons, the most prone to this error. We must,
therefore, endeavour to define the limits within which
instruments and organization make a difference. Obviously they make least difference to a genius. The
genius is independent of conditions; if a scholar, a
dark corner in an antiquated library answers his
needs; if a natural scientist, wire, a battery, a rude
bench, simple tools, a few test-tubes, and chemicals
may, in his hands, yield accurate results. But organized and equipped institutions may enable him to train
a succession. No genius completes the task on which
he engages. He opens up new vistas; who shall follow
them out to their fringes and implications? To these,
the workers on the second line, institutions are indispensable. The world gets its stimuli from the genius,
but it lives on talent. There is not genius enough to go

[33] There is a general belief that both the student body and the faculties
in Germany are overwhelmingly conservative. But the situation is not
really a simple one. The conservative student bodies are organized and
hence prominent; certainly since 1924, the more liberal professors have
striven to correct the conservative prejudices of the faculty. Hard financial
conditions have driven both students and professors towards the extreme
parties.

around; all the more important to create favouring conditions and facilities — be they libraries or laboratories, contacts, competition, or pressure. Well-organized institutions, if not over-organized, most readily provide these conditions. Thus institutions, wisely organized, protect science and learning against breaks and lapses; teachers have pupils, isolated workers may lack them, as, for example, did Mendel. The German geniuses — Kant, the brothers Grimm, Helmholtz, Ehrlich — would not have been defeated by lack of universities, though every one of them found his own work assisted, even if in some respects complicated, by his university connection. If, however, we drop a peg lower, drop from genius to talent, then, I think, the case for the institution is won — the case, I mean, for the institution which is created to do a particular thing or a congenial set of things. To be sure, students, examinations, conferences, politics, all take time and energy; but, on the other side, one must reckon the provision of varied facilities, the stimulating contact with workers in contiguous fields, the zeal of the better students, the ambitions and coöperation of assistants, themselves soon to occupy responsible posts; on the balance, I say, the institution wins. And there is nothing in the university that prevents the creation of other agencies to perform functions that the university does not efficiently perform; indeed the reverse is true: a sound university development carries a nation to the point where the capacity of the university is itself exhausted. Hence, it is precisely in Germany that the research institute and the academy have been most highly developed.

The academy is an ancient institution; the research institute was created during the Empire and is now maintained, largely by means of privately contributed means and a voluntary association known as the *Kaiser Wilhelm Gesellschaft*, with laboratories at Dahlem, near Berlin, and elsewhere. The organization of the universities has also been modified in a democratic direction. The faculty formerly meant the *Ordinarii*, against whom the *Extraordinarii* and the *Dozenten*, shut out from participation in affairs, had long cherished a grudge. The grievances have now been settled; representatives of the lower ranks now sit on the faculties;[34] other grades have been established — paid and unpaid, actual and honorary; the autocracy of the *Ordinarii* has distinctly weakened; coöperative committees representing all teaching grades assist in eliminating class feelings.[35] Progress has been made towards an equitable financial settlement. The pre-War *Ordinarius* received a substantial salary; and his lectures had to be paid for, even if not attended, because the student had to be " attested " by him before he could be admitted to the examinations. Not infrequently the *Ordinarii*, who, be it admitted, usually lecture admirably, keep to the lecture, when they would do far better to break up their classes into small groups for practical work in laboratories and clinics; they refuse to do so, mainly because the lecture system is easier and pays better. Thus pro-

[34] In Prussia, outside Berlin, all *Extraordinarii* are regular members of the faculty. In Berlin, on account of the already excessive size of the faculties, the *Extraordinarii* are merely represented.

[35] The differences between the various states are of minor importance. The main point is that the *Extraordinarii* and the *Privatdozenten* have at last been made to feel that in one way or another they participate in the government of the university, in the distribution of lectures, in examining, and in the judgment of dissertations. The *Extraordinarii* have, naturally, made more progress than the *Privatdozenten*, whose representation on the faculty is still small and who are mainly dependent for their income on fees, subventions, and assistantships. In this matter, again, the states differ, Prussia having, for example, progressed farther than Saxony,

fessorial posts in favoured branches are highly remunerative — sometimes too highly. But meanwhile the
income of the *Extraordinarius* has been relatively low,
his lectures have been much less generally paid for, and
the *Privatdozent* was entirely insecure. Feeling on this
subject ran high; it was even proposed that "fees" be
abolished in favour of salaries. The point has not yet
been satisfactorily settled, though progress has been
made. Unquestionably, the fee system with its promise
of a handsome income to a brilliant and successful
professor kept within the university men who might
have drifted out. The *Ordinarius* now receives, on the
average, a salary of 11,100 marks, the *Extraordinarius*
8,600 marks; the former may with length of service
increase to an average of 13,600 marks, the latter to
11,600 marks. Fees may run from nothing to almost
80,000 marks per annum. At present, out of 2,800
Prussian *Ordinarii*, 120 receive over 10,000 marks a
year in fees, and varying allowances are made for rent,
number of children, etc. The German professor may
thus be enormously better off than his American colleague — a clear reflection of the higher esteem in
which he is held, in a wise, even if impoverished country. But the fee system has its dark side; for it does
nothing worth mentioning for those whose students
are by reason of the nature of their subjects few — for
Sanskrit scholars and such, let us say. Fortunately, the
ministries, especially in larger states, have at their disposal certain fluid funds which to some extent are
utilized to equalize inequities. A professor of chemistry still receives much more than a professor of He-
brew, but the latter, if really eminent, is by no means
overlooked. On the whole, the professor now fares
well, though the difference in remuneration, due to
differences in " *Kolleg-Gelder* " (fees) is still too great.

When, during the inflation period, fees lost their value, the government guaranteed a salary on the level of other high officials; this salary the professor retains, plus his interest in fees, now once more substantial. Such importance does Germany attach to universities, notwithstanding the vagaries to which I have adverted. Indeed, in some cases assistants are so well paid that it is no simple matter to get rid of the less effective.

To one point I should call special attention. I noted that in England it is — outside the unpaid clinical faculty — not considered good form for a professor to make a profitable connection with industry. In Germany as in the United States, the professor in a field lying close to medicine or industry may draw the smaller part of his income from the university — a condition which the full-time departments in American medical schools have remedied, but which have not yet been attacked in Germany. The professor under such circumstances may come to look upon his university post as a thing of secondary importance; this has happened and with economic pressure is happening more often now than formerly.

In the dark days of the currency inflation, extraordinary efforts were needed to keep the universities afloat. With this in mind a *Notgemeinschaft* was created; money obtained from every possible source was utilized to eke out the uncertain income of promising men, to keep alive the various institutes, to procure and distribute the absolutely indispensable literature. Started as a temporary method of salvaging German learning, the *Notgemeinschaft* is now a kind of imperial research ministry. Its composition is apparently democratic enough; for it is controlled by a voting body made up of the members of all university faculties. But actual management inevitably falls into the hands of a small number of persons. At a time when the universities are themselves in sore straits, when buildings and equipment are obsolescent, it is questionable whether highly specific, even fanciful research problems ought to have first claim on such resources as the *Reich* can devote to university work — seven million marks for the current year.[36] To be sure, there are difficulties — perhaps unsurmountable difficulties — attendant upon the allotment of imperial subsidies to state universities. The *Notgemeinschaft* does something to remove the difficulties of the smaller and poorer states, something towards supplying their universities with books and apparatus that they could not themselves obtain. But on the other hand, no greater misfortune could befall the German university than a shrinkage of responsibility for research on the part of state and self-controlled universities. Althoff, of whom I have already often spoken, at one and the same time insisted on the importance of combining teaching and research in the universities, on the need of separate research institutes under special conditions and the wisdom of keeping universities and research institutes in close touch with one another. This easy and natural contact and interaction may conceivably be imperilled, if, in a country like Germany, a research council can select and organize research projects and subsidize publication; selection, coöperation, and organization are all necessary, but, given the zeal for investigation, they take place best, if they take place casually and informally. Meanwhile, it is but fair to say that even before the War private aid had been furnished to this or that savant. Industry and trade had

[36] A list of more or less far-fetched enterprises is given in the *Berliner Tageblatt*, Sept. 4, 1929.

contributed liberally to research, sometimes in the sheerest scientific spirit, sometimes for very practical reasons. Since the War, in so far as the financial situation has permitted, this coöperation has continued. Industry and industrial organizations and private individuals have contributed to the support of research institutes, to the support of university departments, and to the support of individual scholars and scientists. The stress of recent years has almost forced industry to demand a return; both industry and university will suffer if this demand becomes characteristic.

XIV

The most serious of the consequences of the War is its effect upon the *Privatdozentur*. I have said that for decades German *"Wissenschaft"* had been recruited from the voluntary and numerous body of *Privatdozenten,* devoted to teaching and the increase of knowledge, and living partly on fees, partly on their own resources, partly otherwise. The *Privatdozent* represented, to my thinking, the sheerest and purest form of the academic type; his choice of the career embodied an idealistic attitude toward life, an absorbing interest in knowledge and ideas. The *Privatdozentur* was thus a fortunate institution in which academic potentialities centred; it was the very heart of the university — a highly honourable introduction to a highly honoured career. Difficulties existed, to be sure, for nothing human is perfect. But despite poverty, hardship, excessive and premature productivity, the *Privatdozentur* ensured a competitive supply of recruits, inspired by the love of learning, for higher academic posts. When the War extinguished the savings of the middle class, it all but wiped out this nursery of German scholarship. The young *Privat-dozent* has now too frequently to obtain a salaried post. The Prussian Government is endeavouring to fill the gap by devoting upwards of one million marks annually to the support of *Dozenten* who have no active teaching duties; a smaller sum can be used by the ministry at discretion. Other states have pursued a similar policy — bestowing a modest salary without imposing upon the docent any definite function. Thus every possible effort is being made to keep this indispensable institution alive.

The universities are all suffering on the material side; for fifteen years they have done as little as possible in the way of capital expenditure for the renewal of laboratories, the extension of libraries, often even the support of research. Subjects like medicine, law, chemistry, and physics fare under such conditions better than philology, art, or philosophy. While nothing has been easy, it has in these recent years been increasingly difficult to finance the intellectual sciences — the "*Geisteswissenschaften*" — even though Germany dates the modernization of its universities from an adventure in those subjects. The impoverishment of the German universities — the wearing-out of their equipment, the peril to the *Privatdozentur* — is indeed a matter of world-wide concern.

Positivism, utilitarianism, and emphasis upon the economic aspect of socialism have provided in Germany as throughout the Western World hurdles enough to daunt the aspiring human spirit. It is to be hoped, not only in the interest of Germany, but in the interest of civilization, that poverty may not dry up at its source the idealism of the historic German student and the historic German docent.

XV

I am keenly aware, as I close this chapter, and with it, this book, that my picture of German universities is confused. It could not be otherwise: the universities and the nation at large are also confused. I have frankly recounted difficulties, follies, inconsistencies, absurdities, overcrowding, "*Schulmässigkeit*," lowering of level, concessions to party politics. The pre-War university was not perfect; the post-War university, pulled hither and yon by poverty, by new and untried leaders, by the clamour of a populace which was neglected by the Empire is bound to be even less so. None the less, I cannot but believe that, while aims have been to some extent muddled and obscured, lack of money is perhaps the most serious of the problems confronting the German university today. For the German ministers and the German faculties not only value education, but know what it is. And though, amidst economic distress, political turmoil, and social upheaval, the universities have suffered, the intellectual quality of the faculties and the permanent officials in the ministries is so high, the prestige of the universities so great, and their contribution to the nation's life so vital that, even if some problems can never be solved to the satisfaction of all, adjustments will be reached that will restore and perhaps even increase the efficiency of secondary and higher education. The struggle will, however, be neither brief nor easy. America, with almost boundless resources, neither regards higher education at its proper value, nor knows what it is: university presidents and university faculties are — with notable exceptions, of course — in the dark. They possess the means, as is attested by the beauty of the campus and the luxury of the dormitories. They have not learned to use them for sound ends, as is witnessed by the fact that they will not forego a lovely campus, a Roman stadium, and extravagant buildings in order to make teaching a decent and possible profession for men of brains and taste in sufficient numbers. England is rubbing its eyes and gradually discovering the difference between teaching youth and advancing science. That difference no one needs to expound to Germany. And for this reason, its aberrations and inadequacies, deplorable, absurd, or unsound, are more rare and less significant than the aberrations and inadequacies which we have encountered elsewhere.

INDEX